a Year of Tenacity

365 Daily Devotions

A Year of Tenacity: 365 Daily Devotions
© 2017 by Janet Sketchley

ISBN 978-0-9951970-4-6 (print)
ISBN 978-0-9951970-2-2 (epub)
ISBN 978-0-9951970-3-9 (mobi)

Permissions requests may be directed to the author via the contact page on her website: janetsketchley.ca/contact or via email at info@janetsketchley.ca.

Cover and photography by Janet Sketchley.

Published in Canada by Janet Sketchley.

365 DAILY DEVOTIONS

a Year of Tenacity

JANET SKETCHLEY

janetsketchley.ca

Foreword

The devotionals in *A Year of Tenacity* have been chosen and updated from almost nine years of weekly devotional posts on my blog, "Tenacity."

It's with pleasure, and a prayer for your blessing, that I invite you to journey with me for the next 365 days.

You'll notice each reading is numbered by day, not by date. I didn't want you to feel tied to a calendar year, or to struggle playing catch-up if you missed a few days. Because of that, and because observances like Easter don't fall on the same date each year, I've opted not to include seasonal reflections.

If you appreciate these short readings, look for my *Tenacity at Christmas* devotional, featuring 31 daily devotions for December.

May the Lord bless and keep you, and draw you ever nearer to His heart.

Janet Sketchley
Canada, 2017

PS: If you're particularly attentive to spelling, you'll notice that other than the King James Version, the Scripture quotations use US spelling, while my text is Canadian (a hybrid of UK and US). The Bible publishers are US-based, which defines their choice of spelling.

Our Good Shepherd

He will stand and shepherd his flock
in the strength of the LORD,
in the majesty of the name of the LORD his God.
And they will live securely, for then his greatness
will reach to the ends of the earth.
And he will be our peace...
Micah 5:4-5a, NIV

This seems to be one of those prophecies with different stages. Ultimately, Jesus will return. Every knee will bow, and every tongue acknowledge the sovereignty of God (Romans 14:11). The world will know Jesus is Lord.

But today, He rules in Christians' hearts and lives. He stands — a warrior who cannot be overcome — and shepherds us. He stands in strength, majesty and power. Despite our circumstances, our hearts can be secure — we can live securely — because He is shepherding us.

And He will be our peace.

Be my peace, Jesus, even in the storms. Nothing can separate me from You, and You'll never abandon me. Strengthen my faith to trust You.

God Sees

I cannot find God anywhere —
in front or back of me,
to my left or my right.
God is always at work,
though I never see him.
But he knows what I am doing,
and when he tests me,
I will be pure as gold.
Job 23:8-10, CEV

When he says this, Job is enduring unimaginable suffering. And his friends' pious half-truths aren't helping. He wishes he could find God and plead his case in person. His conscience is clean, and he knows he's not suffering as a punishment. Why won't God rescue him?

Sometimes things are so hard that we can't see God anywhere. But we don't need to panic. God sees us. Where we can only see the problems and pain, He sees how He plans to bring good from it.

When we don't understand, when all we have are questions and fears, we can choose to trust God. He knows. He loves us. And He will never abandon us.

Thank You, God, that You do see me and You are working even when I can't see it. Help me set my hope on You, and grant me the faith I need to persevere.

Wait in Hope

But as for me, I will look expectantly for the Lord *and*
with confidence in Him I will keep watch;
I will wait [with confident expectation] for the God of
my salvation.
My God will hear me.
Micah 7:7, AMP

Micah writes this at a time when people are so corrupt that he says you can't even trust your own friend or lover. Yet he looks ahead to the day God will forgive his people's sin and restore them.

His example sets a pattern for us:

Wait for God. Not impatiently, arms folded, toes tapping. Not passively, resigned, or wondering if He'll really show up. Wait in trust.

Hope in God. Not wish-hoping, like we hope it's good weather on the weekend. Expectantly anticipating, securely confident in Him. Actively putting our trust in Him, knowing He cannot fail.

Talk to God. Not complaining or blaming, although He understands if that's how we start. But finish with praise. He doesn't need to hear how wonderful He is, but we need to remind ourselves. When we're looking at how big God is, our problems come into a better perspective and we can trust Him to look after us. We can worship. Even while we're waiting.

Oh God, please give me confidence in You, so I can wait in hope and expectancy, trusting in Your character and Your goodness. Teach me to worship You in the waiting.

Be Still

He says, "Be still, and know that I am God;
I will be exalted among the nations,
I will be exalted in the earth."
The LORD Almighty is with us;
the God of Jacob is our fortress.
Psalm 46:10-11, NIV

This psalm opens with "God is our refuge and strength, an ever-present help in trouble" (verse 1). From there, the writer expands on both the greatness of God and the magnitude of the trouble.

Then he calls us to be still.

The context suggests this "Be still" is addressed to the clamouring nations, but it also applies to the frantic Israelites. One might paraphrase it as "Stop fighting the universe."

Be still... cease struggling... stop fighting. Sounds good, but once we're wound up we can't stop. We're like a toddler on overload who needs a loving parent to draw her into a big hug and whisper "shhh" against her hair.

Know that He is God. When we're still, we can see... experience... understand... learn that He is God.

How? By what He whispers to our hearts. By experiencing His presence. By seeing Him work in our circumstances. All this, and more.

Father, please calm my spirit. Still my soul until I can rest in You. Let me thrive in Your care.

Empowered

I am the vine; you are the branches. If you remain in
me and I in you, you will bear much fruit; apart from
me you can do nothing.
John 15:5, NIV

"I can't do this without You, LORD."

Many of us pray this way regularly, about hard tasks or scary
appointments, or just about hauling our exhausted selves out of bed to
face another day.

It's a fine prayer, and it's scriptural. Jesus' warning is clear: "Apart from
Me you can do nothing."

The key is where we put the emphasis. If we focus on the difficulty, "*I
can't* do this," it weighs us down. If we focus on Jesus, our hope and
strength, "I can't do this without *You*," it reminds us where our
confidence lies.

Acknowledging our weakness keeps us from getting into messes.
Focusing there could keep us from doing anything at all. Let our
weaknesses remind us that Jesus offers His strength. Our confidence is
in Him, and He is enough.

*God my Saviour and my Strength, I can't do life without You. Thank You
that You never intended me to try. Please help me grow in reliance on
You and in trust of who You are. Thank You that You truly are enough.*

Living by Faith

I have been crucified with Christ and I no longer live,
but Christ lives in me. The life I now live in the body,
I live by faith in the Son of God, who loved me and
gave himself for me.
Galatians 2:20, NIV

"I live by faith in the Son of God..." And Paul mentions two specific things: Jesus loved us, and He gave Himself for us. We're to live by faith in Jesus, live confident in Him.

Confident in His love. "We know and rely on the love God has for us" (1 John 4:16, NIV).

Confident in the power of His sacrifice. "If we confess our sins, He is faithful and just and will forgive us our sins and purify us from all unrighteousness" (1 John 1:9, NIV).

We're not alone, trying to live a good life in our own weakness. Jesus has paid our debt, cleansed and forgiven us, and restored us to relationship with God the Father.

We can live with confidence in Him today because He loves us. We can choose to live His way, with His help. And when we blow it, we can trust in His justice and not despair. He has already paid the price. He will clean and forgive us, and set us back on track with Him.

What a wonderful God!

Dear Jesus, what can I say but thank You for all You've done for me? Your love is more than I can comprehend. Help me grow in relationship with You, for my own benefit and so others will see Your transforming power.

Keep in Step

Since we live by the Spirit, let us keep in step with the
Spirit.
Galatians 5:25, NIV

Notice Paul doesn't just say "keep step" as in "walk beside," but "keep in step," which implies a pattern, maybe even choreography, as well as pacing.

Ordinarily we'd interpret verses about God directing our steps in terms of His leading. With dance in mind, perhaps this means more than leading us to our destination. It includes any side-steps along the way.

He's the Lord of the Dance, after all. And when couples dance, one leads and the other follows. At least when they dance well. Our challenge is to learn to follow the Leader.

What do you think of the image of the spiritual life as a dance with God? Let's "keep in step with Him."

Lord, please help me remember to listen to the music, to feel the rhythm... and to let You lead.

Defended

"And I myself will be a wall of fire around it," declares
the LORD, "and I will be its glory within."
Zechariah 2:5, NIV

God tells the prophet He will restore the city of Jerusalem. It won't need protective walls, because God will be its surrounding wall and its glory within. What a picture of the loving relationship He wants to develop with each believer: His protection around us, His Spirit within.

Self-defence is prudent: don't play in traffic, lock the doors at night, don't pick up hitch-hikers.

But defensiveness is different. It's not a healthy way to live. A difficult person phones, or we meet conflict in a store or at church. We feel the walls go up. We're in resistance mode. Defensive.

God is the one guarding our way. Instead of scrambling and scrapping for control of our circumstances, we can pray, "You are my wall, my barrier. You are my glory within. Help me see what You're doing and trust You. Help me cooperate with You."

Sometimes in fighting the circumstances, we find ourselves fighting God. Not smart. When we're secure in trusting Him, instead of wasting energy in panic or speculation, we can rely on His leading. And we can be quiet enough to hear Him.

Lord, thank You for Your promise to be my wall of fire and my glory within. Quiet me with Your presence, and help me take You at Your word.

Expectant

Tell him this is what the LORD Almighty says: "Here is the man whose name is the Branch... It is he who will build the temple of the LORD, and he will be clothed with majesty and will sit and rule on his throne. And he will be a priest on his throne. And there will be harmony between the two."
Zechariah 6:12a-13, NIV

The prophet is instructed to have a crown made for Joshua the priest, and to speak over him the words in today's Scripture. And the crown is to be kept in the temple "as a memorial" (verse 14).

A declaration and a memorial. The people are to act in the present, but as a sign of expectation of a future event. They expect to see God act, and this is their sign of hope, their demonstration of faith. They have confidence in God's plan.

Jesus is the fulfillment of the prophecy, the Branch who is building a temple of living stones, His followers.

We too can be confident that God will act. The hard part is, there's usually no guarantee how. Will He heal, or instead sustain grieving loved ones? Will He topple a corrupt regime, or strengthen the suffering? Provide a job, or give humility to visit the food bank?

I praise You, God, that You will display Your glory — Your character — for all to see. Don't let me miss it because I'm looking for an answer You choose not to give. I may not understand You, but help me to know I can always trust You.

Not Breaking Faith

"If you do not listen, and if you do not resolve to honor
my name," says the LORD Almighty, "I will send a
curse on you, and I will curse your blessings. Yes, I
have already cursed them, because you have not
resolved to honor me."
Malachi 2:2, NIV

The priests and people of Israel had returned from the Babylonian captivity, but they weren't honouring God. And the people had broken faith: with one another, with their spouses, with God.

Some of the negatives Malachi brought as accusations offer us positive reminders of how to live.

Daily, we need to set our hearts to honour God.

We need to be like the first Levite priests, who "revered [God] and stood in awe of [His] name" (Malachi 2:5b).

We need to diligently guard ourselves in our spirits, and not break faith (Malachi 2:16b).

God's name is His character. If we know Him, we can trust Him. If we say we're His but don't live like it, that gives others a poor reflection of who He is.

Father God, please grow in me a proper reverence for You, a love for You, and awe of You. Help me to set my heart to honour You. Help me guard myself in my spirit, that I not break faith with You or with those around me. On my own I can't do this, but I praise and thank You for Your grace, that the blood of Jesus has saved me and that Your Holy Spirit dwells in me. He can do what I can't.

Declaring God's Praises

> But you are a chosen people, a royal priesthood, a holy
> nation, God's special possession, that you may declare
> the praises of him who called you out of darkness into
> his wonderful light. Once you were not a people, but
> now you are the people of God; once you had not
> received mercy, but now you have received mercy.
> 1 Peter 2:9-10, NIV

As Christians, we are chosen, changed. Rescued, because God loves us. Having experienced God's mercy, we get to tell others how wonderful He is.

And our message isn't just "trust Jesus so you can go to Heaven when you die." It's "trust Him in the here and now. Experience the difference His presence makes."

Jesus paid to rescue us from the darkness that trapped each one. For some of us it may have been twilight-level darkness, for others the pitch black of a deep cave. Compared to God's clear light, any level of dimness restricted our vision and diminished our quality of life.

Now we've experienced redemption and we need to share the amazing opportunity with those who want to hear. Not a pushy "sister, are you saaaaved," but "tell me your story, and let me tell you mine."

When we see God at work in our lives, touching our days, we need to praise Him and we need to share it. It may cause someone who doesn't know Him yet to think about Him. It'll definitely encourage the heart of someone who already knows Him. We're on this journey together, so let's help one another along the road.

Father, please open my eyes to recognize what You've already done in my life and what You're doing each day. Grant me a grateful heart, and help me share You with others.

Let Go, Let God

When they hurled their insults at him, he did not
retaliate; when he suffered, he made no threats.
Instead, he entrusted himself to him who judges justly.
1 Peter 2:23, NIV

We may not be able to change our circumstances, but we can change our reactions to them.

The Apostle Peter tells us Jesus "entrusted Himself to Him who judges justly." The Message says He was "content to let God set things right." That implies He trusted God to be willing and able to do so.

And in 1 Peter, chapter 3, Peter tells us to live the same way.

Pain, tiredness, worry, whatever stresses us can provoke a strong emotional response. The same with anything we dislike or think should be done differently. We have control issues, definitely. But who actually rules the universe? Let's think: not us!

So when things go wrong in our day, our agenda's thrown off-course, someone chooses to do something at home or at church that's not what we'd prefer, if we're tired or in pain... we're to entrust ourselves to God who judges justly.

Not to lie down and play martyr. Or passively-aggressively sulk. To actively, positively... trust God. To commit our ways to Him.

Father, sometimes there's pain. Or tiredness, fears or struggles. But if I can't make it better, please protect me from making things worse. Give me Your peace. Help me know You're with me and that You have a plan. Help me trust You and live submitted to Your leading. Help me cooperate as You retrain my mind into healthier patterns.

God is on the Job

Friends, when life gets really difficult, don't jump to
the conclusion that God isn't on the job. Instead, be
glad that you are in the very thick of what Christ
experienced. This is a spiritual refining process, with
glory just around the corner.
1 Peter 4:12-13, MSG

Peter tells us to commit ourselves to our faithful Creator and continue to do good (1 Peter 4:19). And our doing good is to be with a willing heart (1 Peter 5:2).

Instead of fighting — our own circumstances, God, others or ourselves — Peter says, "Humble yourselves, therefore, under God's mighty hand, that he may lift you up in due time. Cast all your anxiety on him because he cares for you" (1 Peter 5:6,7 NIV).

Peter wrote to strengthen the persecuted believers, for their own sakes and so that the people around them would see Jesus in their behaviour and attitudes. We can apply what he says, the principles and the hope, to our daily stresses and relationships.

Father, help me remember daily to commit myself to You, to live trusting Your hand on my life. Help me recognize You in my day, help me serve You with a willing heart. And help me treat others with the love You desire. Thank You for taking care of me. Your grace is amazing.

Blessing

Summing up: Be agreeable, be sympathetic, be loving,
be compassionate, be humble. That goes for all of you,
no exceptions. No retaliation. No sharp-tongued
sarcasm. Instead, bless — that's your job, to bless.
You'll be a blessing and also get a blessing.
1 Peter 3:8-9, MSG

Our job is to bless. And we can only do this in the power of the Holy Spirit, as He enables us to follow Jesus' example and commit our lives to the God who judges justly (1 Peter 2:23).

He gives us no option for victim mentality or martyred airs — we're to live with confidence in God, with our hope securely in Him.

Peter says then people will wonder how we can carry on so well in life's stress. When they ask the reason for our hope, we can gently tell them how Jesus sustains us.

Father, please help me to fix my heart on You, be confident in You, and live to be a blessing. Thank You for the blessings You pour into my life.

Careful

Live carefree before God; He is most careful with you.
1 Peter 5:7, MSG

Carefree: not because we're careless, but because we know and trust God's character and have committed to Him all the things that would weigh on our hearts and minds.

Most careful: at first we may picture fine china being carefully wrapped and tucked securely in a box.

But elementary school children have to be "most careful" with their hatching chicks and emerging butterflies. "Helping" them, making their journey easier, will damage or kill them.

A chef is "most careful" in the measurements and quality of ingredients, but they get chopped and mixed and exposed to the right amount of heat for the proper time.

So as Peter says in chapter 4, we shouldn't be surprised at what happens in our lives.

Nor should we listen to the lie that God doesn't care. He is "most careful" with us. He knows our limits. After all, He made us.

He also knows *His* limits. Well, He knows He has no limits. There's nothing, however bad, that He can't heal if we'll trust Him. Nothing that can keep us from His love and care.

Father, thank You that You are indeed most careful with me. Thank You that You are fully trustworthy. Please help me learn to give You my cares and not to carry them myself.

Not Forgotten

I, Peter, am an apostle on assignment by Jesus, the
Messiah, writing to exiles scattered to the four winds.
Not one is missing, not one forgotten. God the Father
has his eye on each of you, and has determined by the
work of the Spirit to keep you obedient through the
sacrifice of Jesus. May everything good from God be
yours!
1 Peter 1:1-2, MSG

How many believers were scattered during the persecution? How many of us feel scattered or alone today?

Not one of us is missing or forgotten. There's no falling through the cracks with God. He has His eye on us, and He has plans for us, including plans to help us fulfill His plans.

He hasn't sent us out on assignment with only our wits and resources. Remember, He's given us the Holy Spirit as Counsellor, Comforter, Reminder of His Word.

No matter how we feel today, we are not alone. We're not lost or forgotten. God has a tender eye on each one of us.

He has plans and a purpose for us, and as we follow Jesus' example of being "content to let God set things right" (1 Peter 2:23, MSG) we can learn to rely on His Spirit's help in fulfilling our role of "priestly work... to tell others of... the difference He has made..." (1 Peter 2:5, MSG).

Father, I praise You for Your love, mercy and power to save. It's comforting to know You see us all, that not one is hidden or forgotten. And how could You forget us? You've engraved us on the palms of Your hands. What love — what an amazing God You are! Help me give my whole heart to You in trust, confidence and love.

Commanded to Love

We love because he first loved us. Whoever claims to
love God yet hates a brother or sister is a liar. For
whoever does not love their brother and sister, whom
they have seen, cannot love God, whom they have not
seen. And he has given us this command: Anyone who
loves God must also love their brother and sister.
1 John 4:19-21, NIV

We haven't seen God with our eyes, but we've seen His character in the ways He cares for us, in His Word, in creation around us. We love Him because He's already proved His love for us.

We've also seen our brothers' and sisters' characters in what they do. Some generate an automatic response of love. With others, our instinctive response may be avoidance, perhaps even dislike.

John's call to an active love toward God and toward one another is not a call to "feel love for," it's to "show love to," perhaps even to "serve."

That requires the perspective of Jesus, learning to see like He does. Learning to love the unlovable because He sees something in them — in us — that He loves.

Father, please forgive my hard-heartedness, and help me see people as You see them. Give me not only love and compassion, but wisdom too, because with the demanding ones, sometimes what they want isn't what You would give. Help me to depend on You and not trust my own instincts.

A Life of Praise

I will exalt you, my God the King;
I will praise your name for ever and ever.
Every day I will praise you
and extol your name for ever and ever.
Psalm 145:1-2, NIV

The active words in this psalm include "tell, speak, commend, meditate, proclaim, celebrate, sing, praise, extol." And it's all about God: His works, splendour, majesty, goodness, righteousness, graciousness, compassion, faithfulness, love, help, nearness, justice...

King David says he'll praise God every day and declare His praise for ever and ever. The Apostle John says if we tried to write down everything Jesus did on earth, the world couldn't hold all the books (John 21:25).

Could we live like this? Thanking Him for our daily food and enjoying times of solitude with Him are important, but there's more. What if we not only meditate on what He has done, but tell others — and hear them tell us what He's done in their lives? That encourages our faith and invites others to trust Him.

Father, I don't praise You enough. Please forgive me and change me. Please help me focus more on who You are and what You do, and help me share You with others. Open my eyes to see Your touch around me. Give me a delight in You that is natural and irrepressible and contagious. And bring glory to Your Name through the praise of Your people.

Rescue

Trust in the LORD with all thine heart; and lean not
unto thine own understanding. In all thy ways
acknowledge him, and he shall direct thy paths.
Proverbs 3:5-6, KJV

For we walk by faith, not by sight.
2 Corinthians 5:7, KJV

When we live confident in God, that's praise, because it's a testimony to His trustworthiness and power. That was how God wanted the people of Israel to live, in the Old Testament. And it's how the early Christians lived: openly dependent on God.

If He let them down, they'd fall. Of course, He didn't. But the point is, they were living examples, testimonies, God's "Exhibit A."

In our daily lives, we need to see what He does, and to praise Him with our words, both private and public, spoken and sung.

Public praise may not involve words.

If we live like we're secure in God's hand, that says something. We can tell people who ask ("always be ready to give the reason for the hope that is within you," says 1 Peter 3:15, NIV) and we can speak naturally about God, but it's the living by faith — calm and at peace — that's going to demonstrate God's power. It's living proof of God's goodness.

Father, please help me understand this and apply it even in the deepest levels. Help me walk by faith, trusting in You with all my heart, and help me not lean on my own understanding. Help me to acknowledge You in all my ways. Thank You that You will direct my path – please help me walk in it by faith, not by my limited sight. Because of Jesus, who rescued me. Amen.

God's Reign is Eternal

Your throne was established long ago;
you are from all eternity.
Psalm 93:2, NIV

Ever wonder what the psalmist was thinking when he wrote Psalm 93? In just five verses, he contrasts God's majesty and sovereignty with the full power of the sea, and he concludes that God's rule — and His holiness — will endure for endless days. Had he seen a miraculous deliverance? Or was he reaffirming his faith in the midst of an overwhelming situation?

The ocean in destructive mode is awesome and terrible. Think of a hurricane making landfall, a tidal wave, or a mid-sea storm devouring a boat. But the psalmist affirms that no matter how bad things get, nothing can shake God's throne: His authority, strength and rule. Whether we see Him or not, He hasn't disappeared.

Scripture often uses the sea as a metaphor for the nations who don't know God, and perhaps that's what the psalmist meant. Israel saw enough attacks from their enemies.

At our time in history, although there are Christ-followers all around the earth, the world seems made up of "the nations" who don't know God. Including Canada and the United States, which were founded on Judeo-Christian principles.

Godlessness is on the rise. Not "people of a different faith than ours," but a system of belief that tries to deny any deity or higher authority. A system that discards morality and holiness. Meditating on God's power can restore our perspective, whatever our situation — and it can give us hope.

Father, thank You that Your statutes stand firm. You are eternal, and so is Your rule over the earth. You are my Creator King. Please help me keep my eyes on You and my confidence in You, and not be terrified by the waves. You are God, You are at work, and someday the whole earth will see Your glory.

Glad in Our King

Let Israel rejoice in their Maker;
let the people of Zion be glad in their King.
Psalm 149:2, NIV

"Let the people... be glad in their King" — not just praise Him for who He is, but be glad in Him — be confident in Him, sure of His power, glad that He has rescued us and adopted us into His kingdom. Not repressed or fearful because of our circumstances or limitations, but vibrant and secure because of the character of our God.

Praise God that salvation is more than just going to Heaven when we die — it's also the joy we can have with Him on the journey.

Father, please forgive me for the times I take You for granted. Fill my heart, soul and mind with the light of who You are, and teach me to be truly glad in You.

My Way or God's Way

And this is my prayer: that your love may abound
more and more in knowledge and depth of insight, so
that you may be able to discern what is best and may
be pure and blameless for the day of Christ, filled with
the fruit of righteousness that comes through Jesus
Christ — to the glory and praise of God.
Philippians 1:9-11, NIV

Being "able to discern what is best" means we can choose God's way even in the small details. Our ways may be good or not so good, but His way is best. That's a fact of life. God, who is all-wise, will see what is best, while our clouded vision can't guarantee the same.

Instead of spinning in circles because we have more to do than time to do it, let's commit each day to God, asking Him to help us see where we should choose to spend our time, even in the little things.

Discerning what is best can include not only the best use of time and resources but the best response to a given situation. When a comment or situation triggers an automatic hurt or anger, can we stop and ask how Jesus would respond?

Sometimes He showed righteous anger, but He never pouted, sulked, or snapped back a cheap insult. His identity was secure in the Father, and He chose not to give in to those irritants that we can take so personally.

Father, please grow my love for You and dependence on You. Deepen my knowledge of Your ways... to Your glory and praise, and for my own peace of spirit.

Our Good Shepherd

The Lord is my shepherd, I lack nothing.
Psalm 23:1, NIV

This is a comfort psalm for many, with the green pastures, still waters, and restored souls.

We're aware of other key points: the paths God chooses to guide us in are for the sake of His glory, and sometimes those paths are through dark or enemy-infested places. Still, somehow we come away with a warm feeling and a sense of the message being for our personal wellbeing.

Verse 4 talks about His rod and staff comforting us. The rod fights off predators, the staff (or crook) pulls sheep out of the messes they get into.

The "comfort" here can mean the actual use of these tools, but knowing God's strength and desire to care for us is also part of the comfort. We don't have to wait until the situation requires Him to use them.

If our confidence is in Him, we don't need to fear or fret. With our eyes on Him, we see the psalm is really about Him anyway: He is the shepherd, He leads and provides, and it's for His glory. The goodness and mercy we receive radiate from Him.

And yet it's so typical of us to choose our own ways, to follow our own inclinations and interests. We try to follow God, but on our own terms. In the little things, and then the bigger ones, we put distance between us and the Shepherd.

Father, thank You for Your goodness, mercy and compassion. Please forgive me for trying to shepherd myself in different parts of my life. You know that never works out, and You are my Good Shepherd, ready and longing to draw me near again. Please help me hear Your voice. Help me see my need, and when You restore me, help me discover the delight of staying at Your side. Because of Jesus, Amen.

Shepherded

My sheep listen to my voice; I know them, and they
follow me. I give them eternal life, and they shall never
perish; no one will snatch them out of my hand.
John 10:27-28, NIV

There is security in being shepherded by Jesus. Eternal life gives us security for the future, but we have a day-to-day security as well: No one can snatch us out of His hand.

No one can snatch *Him* from *us* either. He's with us for the duration.

We know from Psalm 23 that the pastures won't always be green, nor the waters still, but He will always be with us. And if He leads us through a dark valley, He has a purpose and a plan.

Sometimes we see those valleys coming: the doctor's appointment or the bad news we have to break. Sometimes our easy path takes a sharp turn and we're blindsided.

Jesus is never caught off-guard. By His very nature, He cannot vanish in a puff of confusion. His rod and staff are with Him to comfort us, and He knows the best route through the valley.

The most beautiful discovery we make in those dark parts of the journey is this: God is still with us. Even when we've been caught off-guard, He already knew how He planned to bring us through.

Jesus, thank You that You are the good Shepherd. I can trust Your intentions, wisdom, strength and care, whatever happens. Please give me the faith and courage I need to stay by Your side instead of fleeing when I see danger.

Haughty Eyes

There are six things the LORD hates,
seven that are detestable to him:
haughty eyes,
a lying tongue,
hands that shed innocent blood,
a heart that devises wicked schemes,
feet that are quick to rush into evil,
a false witness who pours out lies
and a person who stirs up conflict in the community.
Proverbs 6:16-19, NIV

Most of these are self-explanatory, but what are haughty eyes? The Message translation calls them arrogant. Does the verse mean looking down on others? Critical or judgmental opinions of them based on appearance and behaviour? An elevated perspective of oneself?

Or perhaps it's about those times when we consider what we perceive, our take on the circumstances, as the truth? As more accurate or enlightened than anyone else's?

Most of us can be tempted by the first three attitudes, although we try our best not to live that way. The final two may surprise us, but they do fit. Relying on our own understanding, instead of trusting the Lord, comes so naturally. But the New Testament says we're to live according to faith, not by what we see (2 Corinthians 5:7).

Lord, please help me remember my sight is limited and even faulty. Help me remember to choose to trust Your way instead of going my own way. Because of Jesus, Amen.

Unity

Therefore if you have any encouragement from being
united with Christ, if any comfort from his love, if any
common sharing in the Spirit, if any tenderness and
compassion, then make my joy complete by being like-
minded, having the same love, being one in spirit and
of one mind.
Philippians 2:1-2, NIV

The way Paul starts here with "if you have any" implies he expects us to have a great deal of these things: encouragement from our relationship with Christ, comfort because He loves us, fellowship with the Holy Spirit.

These ought to be the things that keep us going each day. Relationship with God makes all the difference. We are a rescued people, and our lives need to show it. We're not the same any more.

Verse 2 is a natural progression from verse 1. Eyes and hearts filled with Jesus have to shape our relationships with other Christians. As we remember Who is our focus, He's going to grow us together in His love.

But we get used to Jesus' presence, and instead of relying on Him more and more, we tend to take Him for granted. And we start to look at one another with colder eyes, noticing flaws and irritants.

Father, please forgive me, and open my eyes and heart to joyful awareness of Your presence. Help me linger with You, walk with You in the days, and thrive in You. As You change my heart and the hearts of my brothers and sisters in faith, grant us unity to serve You in this world.

Holy Awe

When the people saw the thunder and lightning and
heard the trumpet and saw the mountain in smoke,
they trembled with fear. They stayed at a distance and
said to Moses, "Speak to us yourself and we will listen.
But do not have God speak to us or we will die."
Exodus 20:18-19, NIV

God had declared Mount Sinai off-limits to the people. Only Moses and Aaron were permitted to meet with God on the mountain to receive the ten commandments.

Thunder, lightning, black smoke covering the mountain... no wonder the people were terrified. They hadn't heard much about God's mercy or grace at this point, but didn't anyone feel a longing, a drawing toward this holy God who created and rescued them? A moth-to-flame compulsion?

It's sad that they stayed at a distance and begged Moses to stand between them and God. How would things have turned out if they'd said like Job, "Though he slay me, yet will I hope in him" (Job 13:15a, NIV). If they'd come as close as permitted, shaking with holy fear, unable to look away from the glory of God?

Yet we do the same thing. We ask our church leaders to teach us, instead of getting to know God ourselves. We ask a praying friend for a word from God rather than listening for Him in our own spirits. What are we afraid He'll do to us... or ask of us?

Or we ignore His majesty and buddy up to Him, enjoying His presence without letting it change us.

Father, teach me a proper respect for Your power and glory. Thank You that through Jesus I can come boldly and confidently before Your throne. Help me come myself instead of looking for intermediaries. And give me a holy awe of You. Let me never forget that although You've called me Your child, You are neither tame nor safe. I praise You that You are good.

Healing for the Soul

Praise the LORD, my soul;
all my inmost being, praise his holy name.
Praise the LORD, my soul,
and forget not all his benefits —
who forgives all your sins
and heals all your diseases,
who redeems your life from the pit
and crowns you with love and compassion,
who satisfies your desires with good things
so that your youth is renewed like the eagle's.
Psalm 103:1-5, NIV

The context here implies King David isn't listing God's benefits for *all believers* but for *all believing souls*. The distinction between soul and body changes how we see this passage.

Forgiveness of all the soul's sins — that's fairly straightforward. Some sins, such as inward rebellion, may even be specifically soul sins. Redemption language talks of our souls, once dead in sin, being made alive again.

Crowning a soul with love and compassion sounds like tender restoration. Renewal of youth sounds like rejuvenation of energy and wonder, maybe even of innocence. Reversal of the damage of sin.

Healing all diseases... what would be a disease of the soul, and how many might one soul have? Shame, self-deprecation, pride, fear...? God promises to heal them all, in the same breath as promising to forgive all sins. Past, present, and future. Shame and its companions are harder to get rid of at times than physical diseases. Praise God, He promises healing!

In this light, Father, please lead and show me how to pray in faith for the souls of those You lay on my heart. Help me walk in faith that You are healing my own soul and finishing what You have begun. Thank You so much for the forgiveness, healing and renewal You give.

Equipped

All Scripture is God-breathed and is useful for
teaching, rebuking, correcting and training in
righteousness, so that the servant of God may be
thoroughly equipped for every good work.
2 Timothy 3:16-17, NIV

Spending time in prayer and God's word, learning to love Him better, and growing in relationship with Him is essential, but that's only part of the goal. It's not just for our personal benefit.

He wants to equip us for good work. The Apostle Paul makes this even clearer when he says we must become "instruments for special purposes, made holy, useful to the Master and prepared to do any good work" (2 Timothy 2:21, NIV).

Christians are intended to show Jesus' love to the world. We have the Great Commission and the promise of His presence.

Loving Him, and expressing our love to Him, isn't complete if we're not looking around with His perspective, seeing what He sees, and acting as He wants to act through us.

If we want to know how to pray for people and events — if we want to know how God wants to use us in people's lives — we need to pay attention to what's going on. Ask Him about it, think about it, and not be so quick to drop it in pursuit of other tasks or diversions.

Father, thank You for loving me. Please help me pay attention as You show me how You want to love those around me.

Not Forgetting

Anyone who listens to the word but does not do what
it says is like someone who looks at his face in a mirror
and, after looking at himself, goes away and
immediately forgets what he looks like. But whoever
looks intently into the perfect law that gives freedom,
and continues in it — not forgetting what they have
heard, but doing it — they will be blessed in what they
do.
James 1:23-25, NIV

Young children need repeated coaching, because they're still developing cognitive and reasoning skills. Hence the age-old parental question, "How many times to I have to tell you that?"

As adults, we're often the same with spiritual lessons, forgetting what God says.

He *could* zap us in some mystical way to "get" the message, and sometimes people do learn in one take... often the hard way. But it seems His preferred method is to involve us in the learning. Any teacher will tell us that's a more effective way to ensure the message sticks.

Instead of passively reading the Bible and then carrying on as usual in our days, let's stay alert for the verses that really resonate with us. Maybe stick them on the fridge or steering wheel. Think about what they mean in our circumstances. Speak them aloud. After all, they're our defence against despair and defeat... and they're one resource God wants to use to grow us.

Father, I confess I tend to wait for You to change me, when You want to involve me in the change. You are the power in the equation. I can't change myself. But you want to develop my spiritual muscles so I'll grow up in my faith. Thank You for Your patient teaching. Please help me pay attention and practice what You teach.

Believing God

Abram believed the LORD, and he credited it to him as
righteousness.
Genesis 15:6, NIV

God told this childless old man that the longing of his heart — the aching wound he had carried so long — would be satisfied. And Abram believed him. Pure and simple. He accepted God's promise as truth, and trusted God to do as He said. There's peace in that.

For us today, his simple acceptance of God's word is key. Not the particular promise he received, but the general heart attitude of believing God. Not whether he understood the hows and whys, nor what was at stake, just that he heard God and believed him.

Sometimes we hear God speak a personal word to us. We may not understand, but we need to trust His character and believe Him. Every day, whether we hear Him or not, we have His character and promises revealed in the Bible. We can believe them.

It's the simplicity of Abram's belief that can inspire us. Let's not complicate things. Instead of fretting, can we quietly believe God? Accept His word? Today, let Him be the strong one, the leader. Trust Him and let Him have the wheel.

Help me, Father, to take my proper place trusting You, open to You, believing You. I'm sorry for the tangled complication I make of life — and of my own thoughts — and I ask You to lead me into a simplicity of spirit that rests in You — actively trusts You — believes You the way a flower believes the sun.

Perspective

But God demonstrates his own love for us in this:
While we were still sinners, Christ died for us.
Romans 5:8, NIV

We come to God, not to get hold of Him but so He may get hold of us, speak to us, lead and direct us, and do His work in and through us.

At first this seems like two sides of the same coin: we reach out to Him, He reaches out to us. Both are needed.

But who reached first? Who initiated the relationship? Scripture says it was God.

If we're focused on what we see, what we choose to do "for Him," that seems to place us higher. If the focus is on Him, asking what does He see, what does He want to do through us, then He is revealed in the position of power and authority.

It's not about us doing things for God, it's about Him: what does He want to do through us?

Father, I praise You for Your grace that makes me worthy to stand in Your presence, and for Your love which seeks me, finds me and changes me. Help me to seek first Your kingdom and righteousness, and to love You above all.

Speak to One Another

Be very careful, then, how you live — not as unwise
but as wise, making the most of every opportunity,
because the days are evil... speaking to one another
with psalms, hymns, and songs from the Spirit. Sing
and make music from your heart to the Lord, always
giving thanks to God the Father for everything, in the
name of our Lord Jesus Christ.
Ephesians 5:15-16, 19-20, NIV

The apostle Paul told us to be alert and intentional about how we live. He knew how easily we can miss opportunities or be distracted from the underlying battle, or even be distracted from God.

We need encouragement and motivation in living the Christian life, whether we're experiencing outright opposition or just the general wearing-down of daily stress, but with all our busyness, it seems like we rush into and out of church or Bible study groups and never have time to encourage one another.

When we take time to hear one another, we can share a word, a prayer, a song. Nobody wants a pat, trite answer, but a Spirit-inspired bit of encouragement from one Christian to another can really help.

Father, thank You for Scripture, and for the way You speak through fellow believers. Please help me encourage others with words from You. And help me keep silent when all I have is words from myself.

Joy in Trial

Consider it pure joy, my brothers and sisters, whenever
you face trials of many kinds, because you know that
the testing of your faith produces perseverance. Let
perseverance finish its work so that you may be mature
and complete, not lacking anything.
James 1:2-4, NIV

Notice that there's no period after "trials of many kinds" — there's a comma, an explanation.

James isn't saying "Consider it pure joy whenever you face trials." He calls us to consider it joy because behind the trial is a test of faith. And it isn't the pass/fail kind of test to disqualify us. It's the kind of test that proves our faith is real and strong. It's the kind of test that will strengthen and develop us.

So... we can consider it pure joy to see that God is using the circumstances of our current trials to prove the strength of the faith He has given us, and to develop perseverance within us. He's completing the work He began in us, and in that we can be joyful.

Father, You are so good to me. Thank You that nothing comes to Your children without being filtered through Your fingers. Thank You that what the enemy of my soul means for harm, You can work to good. Please strengthen my faith, help me trust You, grow me in perseverance. Because of Jesus. Amen.

Righteousness

My dear brothers and sisters, take note of this:
Everyone should be quick to listen, slow to speak and
slow to become angry, because human anger does not
produce the righteousness that God desires. Therefore,
get rid of all moral filth and the evil that is so prevalent
and humbly accept the word planted in you, which can
save you. Do not merely listen to the word, and so
deceive yourselves. Do what it says.
James 1:19-22, NIV

This is good advice on how to coexist, but James likely has more in mind than treating one another well.

Listening, speaking, becoming angry: they're all responses to people and situations. According to verse 20, our goal is to "produce the righteousness that God desires," and that's not something we can impose on those around us or on the world as a whole.

Instead, James asks us to look inward, to work diligently on cleaning up our own lives. To take out the trash, whether it needs an industrial-sized garbage bag or a dustpan, and to fill up with what's good.

We can't even do this on our own; we need to cooperate with and depend on the Holy Spirit. So why do we think we can force-clean someone else? But if we're not careful, we'll try.

Remember Jesus' words about taking the speck out of someone else's eye when there's a plank blocking our own sight (Matthew 7:1-5).

Father, You designed us to live in community and to grow up spiritually together. Sometimes You let me see areas where another needs to grow. Help me to pray instead of judging, and to depend on Your Spirit's clear leading about whether or not to speak. Please help me see the areas where You want to work in my own life, and help me cooperate with You in the cleanup. I can't thank You enough that You want to rescue me from the messes I've been in.

Where Our Help Lies

I lift up my eyes to the mountains —
where does my help come from?
My help comes from the LORD,
the Maker of heaven and earth.
Psalm 121:1-2, NIV

Our help lies with God. So do our purpose, direction, our only possibility of getting life right.

God is not a distant hope, a Divine sort of cavalry waiting in the hills to ride down and rescue us when we signal. He's here with each of us who have committed our lives to Him. He takes that commitment seriously — as seriously as His commitment to never leave us.

It's sad that so often we don't remember He's with us. In our best moments, we're aware of His quiet presence. In those moments we have peace, joy, assurance. We live each moment in Him, and it shows.

Father, help me in my weakness. Help me remember Your presence with me, and help me depend on You. Remind me that You are bigger and more powerful than the circumstances and challenges that threaten me today. On my own I am helpless, but I praise You that by Your grace, my hope... my help... is in You.

Fear... or Trust?

The LORD is my light and my salvation —
whom shall I fear?
The LORD is the stronghold of my life —
of whom shall I be afraid?
Psalm 27:1, NIV

Take fear out of the equation, and how much differently would we act? Most of us would be calmer, not so guarded. We could trust and not feel the need to protect our interests. We could be ourselves without being concerned about mockery. We could tell others about this wonderful Jesus who rescued us, and not worry about rejection.

As we learn to trust God, get to know His character, and prove His trustworthiness, the challenge is to let Him be our protector instead of protecting ourselves. Not that we'll abandon common sense and start walking in front of buses or into dark alleys, but will we drop the barriers we've learned to hide behind?

Will we concentrate more on others' unspoken needs and less on our own security? More on how God might be nudging us to get involved, and less on what it would cost?

Swindling, mockery and rejection happen, and we're to be "wise as serpents, and harmless as doves" (Matthew 10:16, KJV). Jesus wasn't blind to the dangers He faced, but He "entrusted Himself to Him who judges justly" (1 Peter 2:23, NIV) and did what the Father had for Him to do. We need to do the same.

Father, You are my strong tower, my shelter and refuge. Nothing and no one can snatch me from Your hand. Give me courage and grace to live with confidence in Your care, not shrinking back but trusting my heart and soul to You and following where You lead. Teach me to hear and obey Your voice, because of Jesus.

Submitting to God

Submit yourselves, then, to God. Resist the devil, and
he will flee from you. Come near to God, and he will
come near to you... Humble yourselves before the Lord,
and he will lift you up.
James 4:7-8, 10, NIV

Submission... our independent natures bristle at the word, and it conjures images of weakness, humiliation, subservience. Likely that's because of how the powerful have abused their status.

The NIV titles the bulk of James 4 "Submit Yourselves to God," and there's no connotation of abuse at all.

Jesus is the Good Shepherd. He laid down His life for us. We can trust His love.

The Prophet Jeremiah (Jeremiah 29:11) and the Apostle Paul (Romans 8:28) speak of God's plan to work all things out for good for those who love Him. We may not see how this will happen, but we can trust His intentions.

Our God is the one who spoke the universe into being, sent and stopped Noah's flood, and through Jesus calmed the storm, healed the sick, and raised the dead. We can trust His ability to look after us. (Yes, He sometimes allows His people to be martyred, but even there He has a purpose and we can be sure He carries their spirits safely into His healing presence.)

Sovereign Lord, help me start each day by submitting myself to You and committing to listen for Your leading and to obey in trust. You know the end from the beginning, and You are good. Remind me when I try to go my own way, and when I falter, help my unbelief. My spirit finds its rest and true purpose in You.

Praying in the Dark

Who among you fears the LORD
and obeys the word of his servant?
Let the one who walks in the dark,
who has no light,
trust in the name of the LORD
and rely on their God.
Isaiah 50:10, NIV

At times, circumstances weigh heavily. Prayers, alone and in groups, seem to dwell on a mountain of needs: sickness, death, emotional suffering. Sometimes people speak of having a hard time "seeing God's plan" in a heartbreaking need. Not that God caused the problem, but why isn't He intervening with the miracle we're praying to see?

Or consider Good Friday. Nobody could see God's plan when it included Jesus dying on the Cross.

But He had a plan. And it shook the universe.

If we know God's character, we know we can trust Him. Even when He's silent and everything is going all wrong.

So we can choose to keep bringing the sick and wounded to Him, bringing our lack of vision too.

Father, prayer isn't meant to dwell on the problems, but to dwell on You. Forgive me when I get it wrong. Thank You that I can bring these needs to You. Help me find my rest in who You are, in Your character and Your promises. When I can't see Your plan, let me see You — caring, moving, sustaining.

Praying into the Light

Give ear, O God, and hear;
open your eyes and see the desolation of the city that
bears your Name.
We do not make requests of you because we are
righteous,
but because of your great mercy.
Daniel 9:18, NIV

Sometimes the very magnitude of prayer requests can reach a point where prayer feels more like a barrier to fellowship with the Lord than a doorway into His presence. We ask and don't receive. We knock and hear no answer. The mountain's not going anywhere but up.

Still God invites us to bring our cares and needs to Him (1 Peter 5:7).

As we pray, may God grant us to yearn for Him, to see Him, to be still long enough to sense His presence. We may come because of external need, but let's stay until we're reminded that our souls' real need is Him.

Father, thank You that I can find my rest in You, that I can bring all things to You, my Rock and my Salvation. Turn my eyes and heart to Yourself, and by Your presence give me hope. Help me rejoice no matter what the circumstances, because You are mighty to save, and You are with me.

Confidence in God

Rejoice in the Lord always. I will say it again: Rejoice!
Let your gentleness be evident to all. The Lord is near.
Do not be anxious about anything, but in every
situation, by prayer and petition, with thanksgiving,
present your requests to God. And the peace of God,
which transcends all understanding, will guard your
hearts and your minds in Christ Jesus.
Philippians 4:4-7, NIV

This is all about confidence in God, trusting Him. The little word "but" highlights the contrast between two ways of life: on the one side, anxiety, on the other, the peace of God.

When we concentrate on Paul's instructions to rejoice in the Lord, trusting in His nearness, and to bring our needs to Him in prayer, petition, and thanksgiving for His goodness, our inner turmoil is less.

As the turmoil decreases, we find ourselves more thankful. God is so good, in so many ways. He does all things well.

Our God is good. We can depend on Him. He won't necessarily do what we think He should, or on our time, but He knows best and we can trust His heart.

With the Holy Spirit's help, we can practice confidence in God and experience His peace.

Father, thank You for being a God I can trust and worship with joy. There is no malice or instability in You, only righteous, holy goodness. You invite me to bring my cares to You, and You promise me so many good things if I'll come under Your authority where I belong. Help me grow in confidence in You, so that others will see the difference You make.

Thankfulness Killers

Finally, brothers and sisters, whatever is true, whatever
is noble, whatever is right, whatever is pure, whatever
is lovely, whatever is admirable — if anything is
excellent or praiseworthy — think about such things.
Philippians 4:8, NIV

It's important to discipline our thought life. We can't control what darts into our minds, but we can choose what we allow to stay. It's hard work, but most important things are.

The verse isn't saying to ignore the bad things in the world and live in some kind of la-la-la-happy-land, but Paul has just told us (Philippians 4:4-7) how to deal with the issues: we're to bring them to God.

Now he warns us not to take them back and stew on them. That only leads to anxiety, discontent, negativity... a whole host of thankfulness killers.

Instead, we're to concentrate on good things. Chief among those good things will be God and His work in and around us.

We need to be aware how many negative things flit through our minds, often to come out our mouths. Those negatives feed the very anxiety Paul warns us against.

A good daily prayer is "Set a guard over my mouth, LORD; keep watch over the door of my lips" (Psalm 141:3, NIV).

Father, what misery I'd be in apart from You! Thank You for rescuing me, and for giving me the Holy Spirit and Your Word. Please help me work with You so I can mature in faith and demonstrate the difference trusting You makes.

God's Light

For with you is the fountain of life;
in your light we see light.
Psalm 36:9, NIV

Without God's light, we'd be like the man in the first part of this psalm, not able to see God because all he sees is himself.

God's light helps us see others too. And it helps us pray for them, whether they see by His light or not.

It gives us compassion for those who are spiritually blind. Once they've let their eyes be darkened, how could they see even if they notice something's not right? They need His light.

We need His light, as His children, to see what He sees, so we can live and pray His way.

Father, thank You for quickening my soul to come into Your light, and please teach me to stay... walk... bask in Your light.

Repent and Believe

> After John was put in prison, Jesus went into Galilee,
> proclaiming the good news of God. "The time has
> come," he said. "The kingdom of God is near. Repent
> and believe the good news!"
> Mark 1:14-15, NIV

To repent is to intentionally turn from one way and walk in another. Feeling remorse yet staying the same doesn't count. You might say "repent" means "straighten up and fly right."

It's abandoning sin and embracing God.

"Sin" raises images of evil, and those are the things we know need repenting. But other types of sin are better defined as "missing the mark." Not bad, perhaps, but less than our best. Even things like giving in to discouragement and other weakening emotions.

"The Kingdom of God is near... repent... believe the good news."

God is near. Why is it so easy to forget, to think we have to handle everything on our own? (And then to fear messing it up?) There's such peace in knowing He is near.

Father, I choose to repent, to turn away from the sense of being alone. To believe the good news that You are near.

Missing the Inheritance

"My son," the father said, "you are always with me,
and everything I have is yours. But we had to celebrate
and be glad, because this brother of yours was dead and
is alive again; he was lost and is found."
Luke 15:31-32, NIV

This is the tail end of the Prodigal Son story. The stray son has come home repentant, and the father has thrown a party. Enter the older brother, wondering what the commotion is about. When he finds out, he's angry, because it's not fair. And it isn't. It's merciful, extravagant... love. It's a perfect picture of God's grace.

On the surface, it looks like the responsible son hasn't been treated well, despite his long obedience. Not even one measly goat for a pot-luck with his buddies! But did he ever *ask*?

Listen to him: "All these years I've been slaving for you and never disobeyed your orders" (Luke 15:29, NIV). Is that what the father truly wanted? Hard work, sure, but how about partnership? The family farm (and fortune) would be his someday, as firstborn, but he wasn't seeing his inheritance. Only his obligation.

Maybe we ought to give the black sheep son more credit. Sure, he made terrible choices, but at least he understood he had an inheritance.

Can you hear the great sadness in the father's response to his elder son's anger? Maybe it's not only sadness that his firstborn can't see the joy of restoration. Maybe it's also for a young man who's missed the joy of sonship and settled for a servant's role.

Father, I'm to hold You in holy awe because You are God. But You've also adopted me as Your child. Please open me to understand and receive the full benefits of intimacy with You. Forgive me for the times I've seen only responsibility when You longed for relationship. How great is the love You have lavished on us, that we may be called Your daughters and sons!

Time With the Father

Praise the LORD, my soul,
and forget not all his benefits.
Psalm 103:2, NIV

As Christians, we often don't realize what we have in God's Kingdom. Peter says we have everything we need for life and godliness (2 Peter 1:3, NIV), and sometimes we live like miserable creatures with little hope and less resources or joy.

That's a sad truth, and we do need to learn to appreciate and accept all that our Father lavishes on us when He adopts us as His own, but that's not the ultimate focus.

The best gift God gives us is relationship with Himself. If we can't delight in Him, we won't gain much from the other benefits of being His children. We probably won't even notice many of them.

God... the God of the universe, Creator, Sustainer, Rescuer... loves us and longs to spend time with us. And we come asking for endless lists of things, or complaining, or fretting. Or we're like the prodigal son's elder brother, too busy working *for* his father to spend time *with* him.

Father God, I'm so thankful You've made a way for us to be reconciled to You, to be Your children. Thank You for caring for me and inviting me to bring You my concerns and needs. Please forgive me for the times I stop there, or I don't leave my work long enough to talk with You. Please quiet my spirit and teach me the delight of abiding in You. Help me learn to recognize and rest in Your presence as I go about my day. Help me delight in You.

Praise God in the Now

I will sing to the LORD all my life;
I will sing praise to my God as long as I live.
May my meditation be pleasing to him,
as I rejoice in the LORD.
Psalm 104:33-34, NIV

We ask God to renew our hearts, and we trust that He's at work even when there's no visible evidence yet. Sometimes we wonder when we'll start to see some change. We're like the child who digs up a seed every day to see if it's sprouted yet.

These verses from Psalm 104 can change our focus: Let's forget what's seen or unseen, present or future. Instead, we can praise God in the now.

Sure, we'll praise Him when He's renewed our hearts. But why wait until then?

It's not just about praising God for what He's done. It's about praising Him for who He is: God, majestic and powerful, loving and compassionate, Creator and Restorer. What He *does* only shows glimpses of who He *is*.

There's plenty to praise Him for now, while we're waiting, and His praise is to be the song of our lives.

Father, help me be confident in who You are — Your character — not in what You do. Thank You for what You're doing in my heart. Whether that goes fast or slow, help me live each day in praise to You because You are good, and because You love me.

Satisfied by God's Goodness

Why spend money on what is not bread,
and your labor on what does not satisfy?
Listen, listen to me, and eat what is good,
and your soul will delight in the richest of fare.
Isaiah 55:2, NIV

Perhaps our culture's latent sense of dissatisfaction, this always reaching for something more, is a root of the vague fear that many of us carry. Or maybe that fear is what breeds the never-ending quest for "something more."

Maybe deep down we're afraid that God isn't really good, isn't really enough?

It's easy to say God is good. To affirm His love for us. But sometimes if we'd listen closely we'd hear our hearts telling a different story.

We make contingency plans on top of backup plans, we try to cover all the angles, as if we're facing the future alone. But the truth is, God will be with us when we get to the future. We won't have to face anything without Him.

The Psalmist says "The LORD is trustworthy in all his promises and faithful in all he does" (Psalm 145:13b, NIV).

Father, as Your child I believe You are good. I believe You love me and are mighty to save. Please trickle this head knowledge into my heart and help my unbelief. Help me develop a spirit of gratitude, and to be truly satisfied with Your goodness. You are enough.

Seeing... and Responding

Then [Jesus] turned toward the woman and said to
Simon, "Do you see this woman? I came into your
house. You did not give me any water for my feet, but
she wet my feet with her tears and wiped them with
her hair."
Luke 7:44, NIV

Simon the Pharisee certainly does see the woman, and he's offended that someone "of that sort" would invade his righteous household. But he doesn't *see* her at all: this woman drawn to Jesus, hoping, trusting, desperately needing a miracle.

How about us: do we see an individual's heart, or just skim over the surface? Do we *see*?

The Gospel of Luke also tells how Jesus interrupts a mission to heal a dying child. Someone in the crowd has sneaked a healing by touching His robe. As the desperate father is nearing wits' end, Jesus looks around and asks "Who touched Me?" (Luke 8:40-48).

He knows full well which of the many bumps and jostles made the difference, and He knows the woman's story: the 12 years' incurable bleeding, the physicians' helplessness, the woman's despair. Under the Jewish law, she would have been considered unclean for all this time, outcast, feeling defeated and unworthy.

Jesus could have let her slip away, healed and filled with wondrous hope. But He stops the whole progression and singles her out. Not to chastise her as she might fear, but to acknowledge her worth. He's not about to let her go whole in body but wounded in soul.

Who will we meet today who needs some kindness?

Lord, grant me to really see the people you bring my way. Give me Your compassion, and show me how to extend Your love.

Jesus is in My Boat

But the disciples forgot to pack a lunch. Except for a
single loaf of bread, there wasn't a crumb in the boat...
the disciples were finding fault with each other because
they had forgotten to bring bread. Jesus overheard and
said, "Why are you fussing because you forgot bread?
Don't you see the point of all this? Don't you get it at
all? Remember the five loaves I broke for the five
thousand?"
Mark 8:14, 16-19a, MSG

The disciples have a loaf of bread. Jesus has recently demonstrated that He can multiply a little food to feed a lot of people. Yet they're hung up on not having enough.

But Jesus is in the boat with them! If they stop to think, they'll realize He's all they need.

Many times we feel inadequate or uncertain about situations, afraid we'll mess up or won't do well. That fear can freeze us and become self-fulfilling. We feel alone.

These verses tell us something precious: Jesus is in our boat, and He will be all we need.

Whether it's energy, love, ideas: whatever is needed, no matter how small our loaf, we need to offer it to Jesus, and to remember what He can do.

Father, You promised to never leave me, and You've given the Holy Spirit to live in my heart. Forgive me for the times I panic and believe the enemy's lies. Thank You for using these verses to help me see I'm never alone. Help me remember and be confident in the truth that Jesus is in my boat, and that He is enough.

Peace in Trials

Many, LORD, are asking, "Who will bring us
prosperity?"
Let the light of your face shine on us...
In peace I will lie down and sleep,
for you alone, LORD,
make me dwell in safety.
Psalm 4:6, 8, NIV

Reading these verses today, we see that troubled times are hardly a new thing. Personally and globally, they come and go. Just as they did for King David and the people of Israel.

David found peace in the midst of fearful situations by trusting God. He couldn't change what was going on, but he anchored his faith in the One who could.

Fear steals our peace, and makes us feel helpless. Fear is not from God, but faith *is*.

The Apostle Paul says "For the Spirit God gave us does not make us timid, but gives us power, love and self-discipline" (2 Timothy 1:7, NIV). God has given us a spirit of confidence in Him. We need to remember and receive it, instead of believing the negatives.

Father, as I look around at the fighting, the economy, the sickness... help me remember I'm not alone. You've given me Your Spirit. Help me — teach me — to live with confidence in You. You are more powerful than anything the world or the evil one can dish out, and nothing can separate me from Your love.

Knowing God's Nearness Today

Because of the LORD's great love we are not consumed,
for his compassions never fail.
They are new every morning;
great is your faithfulness.
I say to myself, "The LORD is my portion;
therefore I will wait for him."
Lamentations 3:22-24, NIV

When we pray for others in need, do we ask the Father to reassure them that He'll be with them whatever the future brings, and that they'll know His nearness today?

We all long for some kind of reassurance for the future — specifically that things will be fine — but God asks us to focus on today. He wants us to live with Him in the moment instead of trying to see ahead.

Definitely, we need a solid faith that God knows what lies ahead and can deal with it, but we're not *in* the future. We're in the present. And as Jesus said, today has enough troubles of its own (Matthew 6:34).

Father, I'm so thankful that You know what tomorrow holds. Nothing will catch You off guard. Help me to trust the future to You and to live in the present, knowing You're with me. Open my eyes to what you want to do through me today, who You want to touch. Help me enjoy Your company on the journey.

Better than Offerings

The religion scholar said, "A wonderful answer,
Teacher! So lucid and accurate — that God is one and
there is no other. And loving him with all passion and
intelligence and energy, and loving others as well as
you love yourself. Why, that's better than all offerings
and sacrifices put together!"
Mark 12:32-33, MSG

It's so wonderful that God loves each of us — *loves* us — and that it's unconditional. Nothing we can do will make Him love us any more or any less.

But in response to that love, we want to please Him. To bless Him, maybe. That's where what we do makes a difference.

Once we get over the obstacle of thinking we have to earn God's love by our performance, sometimes we can fall into the danger of thinking that good works don't matter. After all, we're saved by grace, not works.

What we do, though, on the outside and in our hearts, does matter. Loving God, loving others, shows that our relationships with God matter. It lets us grow in our faith.

And it pleases the Father more than offerings or sacrifices. That's reason enough.

Father, there are no words to thank You for loving me. Please help my heart to truly grasp that Your love is deep, unchanging and unearned. Help me love You, and help me love those around me. Give me a desire to please You — not because it could make You love me more, but to bless Your heart.

All I Have to Give

Jesus sat down opposite the place where the offerings
were put and watched the crowd putting their money
into the temple treasury. Many rich people threw in
large amounts. But a poor widow came and put in two
very small copper coins, worth only a few cents.
Calling his disciples to him, Jesus said, "Truly I tell
you, this poor widow has put more into the treasury
than all the others. They all gave out of their wealth;
but she, out of her poverty, put in everything — all she
had to live on."
Mark 12:41-44, NIV

Don't you love how Jesus sees the heart and understands the whole story? Anyone else watching this lady drop in her two coins likely made two assumptions: first, two tiny coins have no value, and second, this is her spare change.

Not so. Jesus said she gave everything she had to live on. And He said it was of great value. That means the attitude behind it was pure. We don't know what she was thinking, but it obviously wasn't "let me throw away these worthless bits of metal and go home to die alone."

Somehow, she was trusting God to meet her needs, and she was loving Him enough to offer all she had. She knew it had no external value, but God could use it if she simply gave.

Some days we feel as if we have nothing to offer, at least nothing that looks to have any value. Even on our best and brightest days, do we really have much to offer the King of the Universe? Today and every day, let's be inspired by this poor widow who also had nothing to give.

Father God, nothing I can give would enrich or assist You in its own right, but Your grace invites me to offer myself with persistent, persevering, patient trust... and with a willing heart. Thank You for giving me value and purpose. Please take my offerings, feeble though they may be, and use them — use me — for Your kingdom.

When Our Best isn't Good Enough

Peter blurted out, "Even if everyone else is ashamed of
you when things fall to pieces, I won't be."

Jesus said, "Don't be so sure. Today, this very night in
fact, before the rooster crows twice, you will deny me
three times."

He blustered in protest, "Even if I have to die with
you, I will never deny you." All the others said the
same thing.
Mark 14:29-31, MSG

Jesus has been preparing His disciples for what's ahead, but it's too much for them to grasp. Except for one, their intentions are the best — but Jesus knows that won't be enough. He knows how each one will fail.

He knows the same thing about each of us, and we have this example to keep us from despairing when we mess up. Instead of condemning Peter — and us — Jesus takes on our unrighteousness so that we can find His righteousness in us.

There's nothing in any of us that's worth much, but Christ in us is our hope of glory (Colossians 1:27, NIV). He wants to grow us into His image, to direct and equip us to live worthy of His Name.

When we fail, He doesn't turn us away. He picks us up again and goes on working with us. It puts us one failure closer to finally choosing right.

The Apostle Paul would say that doesn't mean we should be slack and keep going our own ways (Romans 6:1-3). But if we're doing our best and it's not enough, we can rejoice that God isn't finished with us yet.

Father God, You are holy and I worship You. Because You love me so much, I want to please You by living a righteous life. Thank You so much for the Holy Spirit who helps me, and for Your patience and mercy to forgive me and to continue the work You've started in my life.

Choosing God's Way

Going a little ahead, he fell to the ground and prayed
for a way out: "Papa, Father, you can — can't you? —
get me out of this. Take this cup away from me. But
please, not what I want — what do *you* want?"
Mark 14:36, MSG

How many of our choices are based on what we want, or how we feel? When the right choice goes against our preferences, is there a bit of internal grumbling?

And that's just the little choices. In this passage, Jesus is wrestling with a huge one. Yes, He's already chosen, but He's down to the hardest moment and desperate for another way.

When He puts it back to the Father's will, it's not a case of "Your preference over Mine" as if they were choosing a restaurant. Nor is it a grudging "I guess we have to do it Your way."

It's a conscious trusting in the plan they made together, a decision to follow through because He agrees with the ultimate goal despite the cost to reach it.

When God asks us to do life His way, it's not some megalomaniac desire for personal satisfaction. It's about fulfilling His plan to rescue us and restore us to full life in relationship to Him. It's about fulfilling His purposes in us, those things we said yes to when He called us to do them. And He will provide the means if we're doing our part by choosing His way.

Father, help me choose Your way in the big and the small things, not to put myself down, not even because You out-rank me, but because I trust You to fulfill Your purposes in and through me — to Your glory, and for the good of those who love You. Forgive my selfish desire to put myself first and chase immediate gratification. Help me concentrate on You, in whom all fullness dwells.

God's Purpose for Me

I cry out to God Most High,
to God who will fulfill his purpose for me.
Psalm 57:2, NLT

God may have some "greater purpose" or particular calling for our individual lives, but what about the "ordinary" purposes that take up most of our days?

Spouse, parent, child, employee, volunteer, neighbour, church member... Each role has various responsibilities that we can see as chores or obligations if we view them as keeping us from what we really want to do.

Our whole perspective changes when we remember that God has a purpose for us in each of these roles. Instead of being mundane stuff that interferes with our "greater purpose," they may well *be* our greater purpose. Who knows what He might do through our fully-surrendered hearts and schedules?

These aren't things we *have* to do. They're things we *get* to do, with hearts of worship looking to our God who loves us.

Father, please give me Your perspective on life. Help me start each day and enter each role with a prayer for grace and an attitude of loving gratitude to You. Remind me that You want to work out Your purpose for me.

Healed and Free

"He himself bore our sins" in his body on the cross, so
that we might die to sins and live for righteousness;
"by his wounds you have been healed." For "you were
like sheep going astray," but now you have returned to
the Shepherd and Overseer of your souls.
1 Peter 2:24-25, NIV

Peter's words echo Isaiah 53, and they speak of a spiritual healing: from sin into righteousness, from our transgressions and iniquities and sorrows into peace.

Physical healing is important, but spiritual hurts go even deeper — and they are clearly promised to be healed.

The Apostle Paul tells us to count ourselves dead to sin and alive to God (Romans 6:11), and he doesn't mean to ignore our failings and pretend they don't exist. He calls us to walk in the truth of God's Word and not give in to the old ways.

We're to take Jesus' promises as true and trust Him to be at work in us. To believe that His power is greater than our pain. To cooperate with Him as He changes us into what He designed us to be.

Father, there are so many things You want to heal and change in each of us, including me. You are the Shepherd and Overseer of my soul. The Message says You have named us and keep us for good (1 Peter 2:25). Help me love, trust and obey You.

Conscious of God's Care

Slaves, obey your earthly masters in everything; and do
it, not only when their eye is on you and to curry their
favor, but with sincerity of heart and reverence for the
Lord.
Colossians 3:22, NIV

It's important to do right for the right reason: pleasing God — instead of the wrong reason: appeasing people.

We're not little children with authority figures looming in judgment. If someone does chastise, rightly or wrongly, that doesn't need to crush us. Jesus is the Shepherd and Overseer of our souls (1 Peter 2:25, NIV) and we don't need to fear other people.

Today's verse in Colossians leads us to 1 Peter, which expands on what to do if we're suffering undeservedly: Jesus "entrusted Himself to Him who judges justly" (1 Peter 2:23, NIV), and "it is commendable if someone bears up under the pain of unjust suffering because they are conscious of God" (1 Peter 2:19, NIV).

Among other things, this addresses the fear of harshness, which can crush us if we let it. Instead, we're to be conscious of God, who's with us and who loves us, and we're to entrust ourselves to His care.

Our hope and confidence are in Jesus. He says we have value, and He loves us. He accepts each one of us and is growing us into His image.

Father, when we're alone I know You're near, but the fear of others' responses can take my eyes off of You. Please forgive me, and teach me to walk in the truth of the healing Jesus gives. Help me stay conscious of You, trusting myself to Your care and protection no matter where You lead.

Scattered Strangers

To God's elect, exiles scattered throughout the
provinces... who have been chosen according to the
foreknowledge of God the Father, through the
sanctifying work of the Spirit, to be obedient to Jesus
Christ and sprinkled with his blood: Grace and peace
be yours in abundance.
1 Peter 1:1-2, NIV

So begins the Apostle Peter's first letter to the early Christians. He uses the word "scattered," and the text doesn't say if they'd been intentionally scattered by persecution as some were, or if Peter is just talking about how the believers are few and far between.

Whatever the reason, telling them there are other Christ-followers spread through the area reminds them they're part of a larger group. They're not as alone as they may feel.

Perhaps that's why he calls them "God's elect" too. It's not a snooty term for "better than the others." It reminds them they've been chosen by God and belong to Him. He loves them.

Living in obedience to Jesus Christ can make us feel like we don't belong. In a sense, we don't. We're changing, and while we pray those around us will recognize that God has also chosen them, for now we're the oddballs, the aliens. But that's okay.

Our hearts need acceptance, but the world around us is not the place to expect to find it. Peter reminds us we've found acceptance in Jesus. We do belong.

Father, thank You for choosing me, for knowing and loving me before I came to You. Thank You that Jesus came, God in the flesh, to heal the broken. Everyone is broken somehow, Lord, and you're not willing that any should perish. Help each one recognize that You've chosen them too. Help them come into Your healing embrace.

What He Says

For you know that it was not with perishable things
such as silver or gold that you were redeemed from the
empty way of life handed down to you from your
ancestors, but with the precious blood of Christ, a lamb
without blemish or defect.
1 Peter 1:18-19, NIV

Some days have more to do than hours to do it in, and if we're not careful, they can weigh us down from the moment we wake. But the same practice should apply here as if we were going into any other type of stressful or scary situation.

We need to trust God. We need to pray for wisdom to discern what He sees as important for the day, rather than assuming our entire list is the day's agenda. And we need to remember what He says.

He says He'll never leave us, in Matthew 28:20.

He says nothing can separate us from His love in Christ Jesus, in Romans 8:38-39.

He says all we need to do is ask for wisdom, because He wants to give it, in James 1:5.

He says to trust Him and not rely on our own understanding, in Proverbs 3:5-6.

He says our times are in His hands, in Psalm 32:14-15.

Remembering what He says, we then need to choose to believe Him and to watch for and follow His lead.

Father God, thank you for redeeming me from the empty way of life handed down for generations. Thank You that circumstances and hurry-panic don't own me anymore. Jesus, my Shepherd and the Overseer of my soul, has rescued me. Thank You that I'm in His care now, under His leading and authority. I choose to walk in that today, Christ being my helper.

Time for a Cleanup

Create in me a pure heart, O God,
and renew a steadfast spirit within me.
Do not cast me from your presence
or take your Holy Spirit from me.
Restore to me the joy of your salvation
and grant me a willing spirit, to sustain me.
Psalm 51:10-12, NIV

King David wrote this psalm after sleeping with another man's wife and then trying to cover things up by having the man killed: pretty drastic misbehaviour. Not surprisingly, it inhibited his relationship with God.

Sometimes Christians fall like David did. It shouldn't happen, but it does. And our God is gracious to restore us rather than throwing us out. The Bible promises that if we sincerely confess our sins, He will forgive them (1 John 1:9). And He'll help us face the fallout of our actions.

Other times Christians avoid the "big" temptations but get numbed or dulled by the distractions of every day. Pressures, annoyances, bills, telemarketers, the common cold... you name it, there are enough things to take our minds off God if we're not diligent to keep Him in first place.

Have we let our focus drift from the God who loves us? Is He first in our hearts, or has that place been taken over by our own feelings and opinions?

Father, please create in me a clean heart, washed from unwillingness, resentment and hostility. Renew a right, righteous, healthy and steadfast spirit within me. Draw me deeper into Your presence, take down any walls I've built, forgive any ways I've quenched Your Spirit, and be pleased to dwell in me. Restore the joy of my salvation that I didn't see was missing. And grant me a willing spirit, to sustain me. Because of Jesus, in whom I put my trust.

Consciousness of God

Your life is a journey you must travel with a deep
consciousness of God. It cost God plenty to get you out
of that dead-end, empty-headed life you grew up in. He
paid with Christ's sacred blood, you know... It's
because of this sacrificed Messiah, whom God then
raised from the dead and glorified, that you trust God,
that you know you have a future in God.
1 Peter 1:18, 19, 21, MSG

Is there such a thing as spiritual attention deficit disorder? "SADD" sounds kind of applicable.

It's so easy in the quiet of prayer to bask in God's presence, but as soon as we get around other people or performing routine tasks, we can forget to keep our spirits tuned to His.

We need to live each part of each day in relationship with Him, conscious of and relying on Him, serving and worshipping Him. Neither working in our own strength nor begrudging some duties because they keep us from the "important" stuff. Not leaning on our own understanding, trusting our own perspective.

It's up to God where He assigns us, after all. Whatever there is to do, we're to be God's children serving Him in that role at that time. Being with him there instead of wanting to be somewhere else.

Father, You know how easily distracted I am. Please open my heart and my spirit to a deeper awareness of You. Help me rely on You and rest in Your love. Help me be conscious of You and live in Your care wherever You place me. Thank You for giving me faith to trust You, and thank You for giving me a future in You.

In the Light

Jesus told us that God is light and doesn't have any
darkness in him. Now we are telling you.

If we say that we share in life with God and keep on
living in the dark, we are lying and are not living by
the truth. But if we live in the light, as God does, we
share in life with each other. And the blood of his Son
Jesus washes all our sins away.
1 John 1:5-7, CEV

Have you ever noticed the way sunlight strikes trees early and late in the day, slanting to emphasize details of branches and trunks we don't notice at midday? It helps us see more clearly, and it warms the trees.

Today's verses use the image of living, or walking, in God's pure light. It's not a one-time deal, it's a new way of behaviour that takes practice.

We expose ourselves to His light through the Bible, prayer, listening to the Holy Spirit's promptings and in all the ways we interact with His believers.

God's light will reveal thoughts, attitudes or actions that we need to change. And it will warm and strengthen us. Unlike the sun, it won't damage us if we stay too long or don't protect ourselves.

Father, help me stay in Your light. Warm me and help me grow. As You show me things in my life that don't belong, help me work with Your Spirit to remove them. Help me take wrong thoughts and attitudes captive and help me continually replace them with those which will honour You. Help me behave in ways worthy of the gospel.

Love Each Other Deeply

Above all, love each other deeply, because love covers
over a multitude of sins.
1 Peter 4:8, NIV

The Apostle Peter places a lot of emphasis in this letter on how Christians should conduct ourselves in relationships and in hardships. He's already told us to "love one another deeply, from the heart [or from a pure heart]" (1 Peter 1:22b, NIV).

Now he reminds us again to love deeply, and says it covers a multitude of sins. He's been urging us to live well in relationship, and I think this is the "how."

Most translations of 1 Peter 4:8 speak of love covering sins. The Message expresses it as "love makes up for practically anything." The Amplified Bible says love "overlooks unkindness and unselfishly seeks the best for others."

Peter's not saying love will turn a blind eye, excuse or enable wicked or destructive behaviour, but consider this:

People are irritating (rumour has it, this includes you and me!). If we choose to ignore the thing(s) that grate us in another person, choose to focus on that person's value and to love him or her, that helps us obey Peter's teaching and live like Jesus.

Also, by choosing to love rather than to be critical, we're dealing with or negating sin in our own lives. Jesus had lots to say about being critical and judgmental.

Father, You know true, Christ-like love doesn't come naturally... or easily. Thank You for Your Holy Spirit, who longs to produce it in me. Please help me learn to rest more in Him and not hinder His fruit in me. Help me to love others, because You love them. Thank You for loving me too.

Administering God's Grace

Each of you should use whatever gift you have received
to serve others, as faithful stewards of God's grace in
its various forms.
1 Peter 4:10, NIV

The specific examples Peter uses in this chapter are hospitality, words and service. We're given gifts for the good of others, not to keep to ourselves.

This verse applies to more than those attributes we commonly think of as "spiritual gifts." The Message renders 1 Peter 4:10 as "Be generous with the different things God gave you, passing them around so all get in on it."

We've received so much of God's grace... let's think about how we can administer, or share, it: when we smile at the checkout clerk, when we make our kids' lunches, when we stop to listen to an elderly person's question, or hold the door for a shopper with parcels. Even when we're patient with the customer service rep after waiting on hold "forever."

We've received His love, forgiveness, acceptance... His joy and Himself. Let's share it by the way we treat others.

Father, thank You for the privilege of administering some of Your grace. Help me remember to see my service in this special way and to serve willingly, in love and gratitude and in Your strength, for Your glory.

Waiting for God

This truth gives them confidence that they have
eternal life, which God — who does not lie — promised
them before the world began. And now at just the right
time he has revealed this message, which we announce
to everyone. It is by the command of God our Savior
that I have been entrusted with this work for him.
Titus 1:2-3, NLT

God made a promise in the beginning, and waited for the time to be right to fulfill it. As we move through each calendar year, we celebrate the birth of the Saviour, as well as His sacrificial death and triumphant resurrection. Someday we'll celebrate His return.

God's timing is perfect, although we can't usually see that until after the fact. He has demonstrated it with His biggest promise, and so we can trust Him with His smaller ones.

Is there something you're waiting for? Something He's promised, be it a specific event or a word from Scripture like the assurance that He works all things to good for those who love Him? (Romans 8:28).

Father God, thank You for Your faithfulness and Your integrity. What You promise will be fulfilled. Please forgive and sustain me when I falter in the waiting. Help me keep my eyes on You and my confidence in You. Help me wait in patient trust, and help me worship You in the waiting.

Why We Do What We Do

You, however, must teach what is appropriate to sound
doctrine... so that no one will malign the word of God...
so that those who oppose you may be ashamed because
they have nothing bad to say about us... so that in
every way they will make the teaching about God our
Savior attractive.
Titus 2:1, 5b, 8b, 10b, NIV

In the book of Titus, the Apostle Paul places great emphasis on teaching Christians to live in a godly manner and to do good. He's writing to a new church, its people recent converts from paganism and immoral lifestyles, and that may explain why they need so much teaching on how to behave as children of God.

Today we still need this teaching — not only on how to behave, but *why*. Paul never forgets that the outward behaviour has a purpose: "so that in every way they will make the teaching about God our Savior attractive" (Titus 2:10).

Who wants to follow a Way that makes its people rigid, repressed or ranting? Hopeful people, on the other hand, those who can stay strong even in hard times and who radiate an inner joy... now they have something others might want.

Jesus came to show us what God is really like, and to reconcile us to Him. He charged His disciples (and us down through the centuries) to carry on His work. He kept close to the Father and served in love. We need to do the same.

Father, thank You for saving me, and for changing and equipping me to live in ways that please You. I could never do that on my own. Help me remember why I'm to do good and to live right, that my behaviour isn't the ultimate end. Help me be a living demonstration of Your love, because I love You.

Included in Christ

And you also were included in Christ when you heard
the message of truth, the gospel of your salvation.
When you believed, you were marked in him with a
seal, the promised Holy Spirit, who is a deposit
guaranteeing our inheritance until the redemption of
those who are God's possession — to the praise of his
glory.
Ephesians 1:13-14, NIV

Too many times we live life on edge, with a low-level anxiety that we'll
be disqualified or rejected. We're trying so hard, but what if something
we say or do — or don't do — puts up a barrier with our loved ones or
with those we respect?

Sometimes we don't even know this theme is playing in our mental
soundtracks until we wonder why we're tense. It's something we can
learn to recognize and to let God change in our lives, and this is the sort
of Scripture passage that can help.

Look at what the Apostle Paul says in these verses: we are included in
Christ — we belong — it's guaranteed by God's own Holy Spirit. Jesus
knew both our best and our worst when He rescued us, and His promise
is forever. Nothing can separate us from His love (Romans 8:38-39).

*Father, forgive me when I get hung up on pleasing people and I give
their opinions too much power over my life. Thank You for saving me...
for choosing us and loving me. Thank You for including me in Christ.
Please help me remember this truth, to the praise of Your glory.*

Good Works

For it is by grace you have been saved, through faith —
and this is not from yourselves, it is the gift of God —
not by works, so that no one can boast. For we are
God's handiwork, created in Christ Jesus to do good
works, which God prepared in advance for us to do.
Ephesians 2:8-10, NIV

Good works aren't the cause of salvation, they're the effect of it. Christians know that, although sometimes we catch ourselves trying to "earn" our way.

God has prepared the good works for us. They'll flow out of our obedience to Him; we don't have to go hunting for them. After all, if we initiated our own good works, that might be grounds for boasting.

The good works, like everything else, are not about us. They're about God, "to show the incomparable riches of his grace, expressed in his kindness to us in Christ Jesus" (Eph. 2:7b, NIV).

They're not all big things, or dramatic. Remember what Jesus said about giving a cup of cold water in His name (Matthew 10:42). They might be as simple as preparing nutritious meals for our families and keeping the laundry up to date. They include our daily interactions with those around us.

One way to fit better into God's plans is to learn to ask Him, "What did you give me to give today?"

Precious Father, it amazes me that You would love me like this — and save me when I was helpless and very unlovely. Thank You it's all a gift from You, and not something I have to earn. Thank You for giving me a part to play in Your work, and Father, today please help me recognize what You've given me to give — and to whom. Help me serve in Your strength, because it's about You. In Jesus' name, amen.

Approaching God

In him [Christ Jesus our Lord] and through faith in
him we may approach God with freedom and
confidence.
Ephesians 3:12, NIV

God on His throne is a frequent image in the Bible, and it's echoed in this passage from Ephesians.

Approaching God... Remember the story of Esther and King Xerxes? To approach the king in his throne room was to risk death — if your uninvited presence didn't please him, if he didn't hold out his sceptre in welcome, that was your fate by law (Esther 4:11).

Esther was beautiful, but now picture this: You — me — any of us — without Jesus, standing in the doorway to the Father's throne room, filthy and matted with sin and failure, broken and bruised by self and by others... Not an attractive sight for a God who is perfectly holy and is offended by the mess that clings to us. Would He hold out a welcoming sceptre? Because of His holy and just nature, He couldn't.

But we come to Him in faith, because Jesus made a way. Jesus washed and healed us, and put clean clothes on us. When we stand in the throne room doorway, God the Father sees us as righteous, and He welcomes us with delight.

Holy, majestic and righteous God, there aren't words to thank You for Your grace and mercy given through Your Son Jesus Christ. Please fill my spirit with awe and wonder, and help me to love and worship You. Help me radiate the joy of Your presence.

God's Power in Us

Now to him who is able to do immeasurably more than all we ask or imagine, according to his power that is at work within us, to him be glory in the church and in Christ Jesus throughout all generations, for ever and ever! Amen.
Ephesians 3:20-21, NIV

This is a commissioning, a reminder of God's power and our goal of living to His glory. Paul isn't writing about God's power restraining or unleashing forces of nature or holding the universe together. He's talking about God's power *at work in us*.

Earlier Paul prays that God will "strengthen you with power through his Spirit in your inner being" (Ephesians 3:16, NIV).

How often do we stop to consider that God's power is at work in us? That when He wants to work through us it's by His power, not our own?

Do we really believe it? Too often, we don't. Our minds may know the words, but we also know how little energy or ability we have — and we get frustrated by the demands on our time.

Paul also says, "I can do all things through Christ who strengthens me" (Philippians 4:13, NKJV). We need to understand his words to not only to mean Christ giving us a boost as we climb, but that He is the power source that supplies energy, ability and vision.

Father, when I limit myself to my own ability with Your "help," I miss chances to show how glorious and powerful You are. I place more trust in my own understanding than in Your strength. Please forgive me, and help me truly believe and trust Your power working in me to accomplish what You direct me to do. Help me not to view my tasks as drains or burdens, but as areas where You want to work through me. You are the Potter; help me be a vessel You can fill and pour out of.

Grumbling in the Camp?

But you are the ones chosen by God, chosen for the
high calling of priestly work, chosen to be a holy
people, God's instruments to do his work and speak out
for him, to tell others of the night-and-day difference
he made for you — from nothing to something, from
rejected to accepted.
1 Peter 2:9-10, MSG

God called Abram and built his descendants into the nation of Israel: a holy people, chosen by God, with one tribe called to priestly work and all twelve to be living illustrations of the difference God makes.

When Moses led the Israelites in the desert, God was visibly with them, in the cloud by day and the fire by night. He spoke to them through Moses. They knew He was with them, and they feared His power. But what did they do, over and over?

They complained. They grumbled. It's enough to make us shake our heads in wonder. God was with them. He brought them out of slavery and protected them from Pharaoh's army. He parted the Red Sea and provided their daily manna. Couldn't they trust Him to look after them?

Hold on... As we investigate our own hearts to see what's gumming up the works, as we listen to how we talk with our friends, is that a... *grumbling* spirit? Oh, dear. We have head knowledge that God loves us, but often we don't act on it in belief. We let circumstances (and people) irritate and disturb.

But God is good. And He loves us.

Father, thank You. Please keep reminding me of the truth and quieting my spirit to receive it. You are good. You love me. Help me rest in this knowledge and grow in gratitude and trust. Let it be an antidote to grumbling, striving and discontent. Help me demonstrate by my life that You are trustworthy and good.

Day 74

Listen to Jesus

> While he [Peter] was speaking, a cloud appeared and
> covered them, and they were afraid as they entered the
> cloud. A voice came from the cloud, saying, "This is
> my Son, whom I have chosen; listen to him."
> Luke 9:34-35, NIV

"Listen to Him."

Because Peter had been babbling, it's easy to read this with the emphasis on *listen*, but what if we put the emphasis on *Him*? In an encouraging tone?

"Listen to *Him* — to Jesus. You can trust Him." As if the Father's saying, "Out of all the competing voices, focus on His and He will lead you safely through."

Yes, we need to be quiet so we don't miss what He says, but isn't it wonderful to be assured that Jesus, our Good Shepherd, knows the way and is fully trustworthy? That quiets a lot of the tension inside.

Father, thank You for Jesus. Thank You for saving me and for not leaving me helpless and alone. Help me to trust in You with all my heart and not to rely on my own perspective. Teach me to acknowledge You in everything and to trust You with my path.

Convinced

For I am convinced that neither death nor life, neither
angels nor demons, neither the present nor the future,
nor any powers, neither height nor depth, nor anything
else in all creation, will be able to separate us from the
love of God that is in Christ Jesus our Lord.
Romans 8:38-39, NIV

God will never leave us, nor forsake us. He promised. Songs like Matt Redman's "You Never Let Go" and David Crowder's "Never Let Go" help us internalize and respond to this amazing truth.

But sometimes, don't you catch yourself wondering? Circumstances and the enemy of our souls whisper otherwise, and sometimes we listen: "not me... not this time... not after what I did..."

Our heads know the truth, but our hearts are prone to believe the lie.

But we can believe this: The price for our salvation was too high for God to ever let us go. Jesus went to the Cross for us and defeated death. He's not going to give up on us after that, no matter how troublesome we are.

Father, You knew what You were getting in the transaction, how stubborn and slow of heart I am, and You still loved me enough to pay a horrific price to rescue me. You've promised never to let go of me, and yet at times I doubt that. Forgive me, and help me to trust You and to stand amazed and secure in the shadow of the Cross.

Attitude Check

"To obey is better than sacrifice,
and to heed is better than the fat of rams.
For rebellion is like the sin of divination,
and arrogance like the evil of idolatry.
Because you have rejected the word of the LORD,
he has rejected you as king."
1 Samuel 15:22b-23, NIV

Obey. Heed. Rebellion. Arrogance. It all comes back to attitude, doesn't it? God asks for a trusting, obedient heart, for a person who will love, listen, and live under His authority.

God rejected King Saul because his heart wasn't in the right place. When King David committed a series of sins that we might judge as worse than Saul's, he pleaded for God to renew their relationship. His prayer for "a willing spirit" (Psalm 51:12) is key.

David's heart needed God. Yes, he needed forgiveness, but he also needed to be close to God. It seems Saul didn't see this deeper need.

What will enable us to make the ongoing choice to heed and obey God? To trust His character enough to do it His way rather than our way? A willing spirit.

Father, I can't thank You enough for saving me — and for Your promise never to leave me. I confess it's easier to walk by sight than by faith, to follow my own understanding rather than trusting You. In Your mercy, please keep working to change me. Because of Your Son, forgive me. Restore to me the joy of Your salvation, and grant me a willing spirit, so that I can follow You.

Escape Route

No temptation has overtaken you except what is
common to mankind. And God is faithful; he will not
let you be tempted beyond what you can bear. But
when you are tempted, he will also provide a way out
so that you can endure it.
1 Corinthians 10:13, NIV

This isn't just about outward "sins of commission," those temptations to steal, lie, cheat, whatever. It applies to temptations of attitude and self-focus too.

We tend to believe the lie that what happens inside us just "is," and while we may pray for release, we think it's up to God to change us. But as He retrains our minds, we have a part to play. We have to cooperate, or to use Paul's words, we have to bear what we can and to stand.

And we have to be patient with ourselves, like God is, when we mess up. We need to get up and go another round... or another twenty... until the fight is won.

God promises to make a way out. When temptation whispers, does your spirit also echo a Scripture verse or part of a song? Something to help keep focused? When we choose the good thoughts, the bad fade away. How often do we not recognize these as escape routes?

Father, thank You for the promise of a way out. You know my weakness, and You are faithful to help me. I believe You want to strengthen me as I learn to rely on You. Help me do that. Help me recognize the mental temptations that come, and help me see — and take — the way out.

Everything We Have

*... those of you who do not give up everything you have
cannot be my disciples.*
Luke 14:33b, NIV

"Give up" doesn't necessarily mean "give away" in the sense of giving away of all our cash and possessions. For material things, it's a call to hold them loosely, instead of clutching and saying "Mine!" To share, and above all to put God first. Not to make them idols.

Jesus isn't only talking about *things*, either. His meaning includes our *time*.

Time is something many of us guard jealously. A lot of it's already spoken for, but what discretionary time there is, especially once we've made plans for it, is not to be messed with.

God has the right to interrupt us, to redirect, or redeploy us. We need discernment to know whether any given thing is a distraction to ignore or a redirection from God to heed.

When redirected, the challenge is to surrender and serve Him willingly in the new place instead of begrudging the change in our plans.

Father, Jesus is not only Saviour but Lord. I know Your way is best, but sometimes it's so hard to let go. Please give me a willing heart, and help me follow and obey. Help me truly give up control of everything I have — including my time — because it's all Yours, and You are good.

We Can't Do it On Our Own

We always thank God for all of you and continually
mention you in our prayers. We remember before our
God and Father your work produced by faith, your
labor prompted by love, and your endurance inspired
by hope in our Lord Jesus Christ.
1 Thessalonians 1:2-3, NIV

This is faith making a difference, and it's something each Christian needs to have in his or her own life. As Paul goes on to say, it's not something we do in our own strength: we need to receive the gospel "with power, with the Holy Spirit and deep conviction" (1 Thessalonians 1:5a, NIV).

It's God in us who makes the difference.

Although individuals need to have a personal and vibrant relationship with God, Paul is speaking here to a group of believers operating as a whole — functioning as the body of Christ.

Could Paul write these words to churches today? Certainly to some, but not to all. Praise God for those congregations where His power and love are on display. And rather than judging or criticizing those where not much activity is visible to our eyes (which are not all-seeing!) let's pray for growth and empowerment.

Father, I pray for Your global church and its individual congregations, that Your gospel would truly come with power, with the Holy Spirit and with deep conviction. Revive us where needed, forgive where needed, and teach us how to live in unity. Grant us faith in You, to produce good works; love for You and for others, to prompt our service; and hope in Jesus, to inspire our endurance.

Hungry for God

*...your faith in God has become known everywhere...
They tell how you turned to God from idols to serve
the living and true God, and to wait for his Son from
heaven, whom he raised from the dead — Jesus, who
rescues us from the coming wrath.*
1 Thessalonians 1:8b, 9b, 10, NIV

Paul said that the Thessalonians received the gospel with power, the Holy Spirit, and deep conviction (1 Thessalonians 1:5). In verse six, he adds more to this: "you welcomed the message in the midst of severe suffering with the joy given by the Holy Spirit" (NIV).

Their work, endurance, love, and hope after turning to God have become known not just locally, but "everywhere." When God gets hold of people, news travels.

These are people who had been hungry for God. They hadn't known who He is or how to find Him, and their idol worship was all the culture offered. If they'd been satisfied with it, they wouldn't have jumped ship.

God knew the people were searching for Him, and He sent Paul, Silas and Timothy. Remember how clearly He directed Paul into the region of Macedonia? (Acts 16:8-10).

He knows the people in our lives who are searching for Him now. This passage reminds us not to judge or make assumptions based on someone's behaviour. Yes, maybe they're purposely defying Him. But more likely, they're getting by the best they can and reaching for Him in ways only His Spirit can see.

Father, my own perceptions can blind me to what You're doing. Please help me see what You see in the people around me. You love each one, and You know when someone needs a touch or a word. Help me share the hope and the joy that only You can give. Thank You for the freedom Jesus bought for us.

A Quiet Life

...make it your ambition to lead a quiet life: You should
mind your own business and work with your hands,
just as we told you, so that your daily life may win the
respect of outsiders and so that you will not be
dependent on anybody.
1 Thessalonians 4:11-12, NIV

This "quiet life" doesn't mean "silent" so much as "at peace, not striving."

When life, even just our inner thought life, is crazy-busy, we can't hear Him unless He shouts. When we rattle off prayer requests at machine-gun speed, same problem.

There's a reason Psalm 46:10 says, "Be still, and know that I am God" (NIV).

Yes, God can get our attention dramatically if need be, but that seems more like Divine intervention than an ongoing personal relationship. Scripture repeatedly calls us to be still, to abide with God, to shelter in His presence.

Father, please quiet my spirit to know that You are God and that You are here. Help me live in quiet trust in You, for my own sake and so that the people around me will see how You make a difference. Thank You for your mercies, new every morning.

Happy Ending to a Long Story

God is just: He will pay back trouble to those who
trouble you and give relief to you who are troubled, and
to us as well. This will happen when the Lord Jesus is
revealed from heaven in blazing fire with his powerful
angels.
2 Thessalonians 1:6-7, NIV

Don't you love happy endings? They can make even the most difficult story worthwhile. Sometimes it's a hard slog to get there, but at last things work out.

Around the world, people are suffering. Christians aren't the only ones, but they're doing their share. In North America, Christians have it easy: we're mostly treated as irrelevant or repressive.

In Paul's day, the believers in Thessalonica were suffering persecution because of their faith. Today's verses were to give them hope, but also to give them perspective: help is on the way, just hang on until He gets here.

It looks like they expected Jesus to return any day and wrap things up. Good thing they didn't know we'd still be waiting in the 21st century. But He is coming, when the Author and Finisher of our faith declares that the time is right.

We don't understand everything in the Bible, but reading the end of the Book tells us this: there's a happy ending for God's people. Revelation chapters 21-22 are beloved passages. After all the hardship, suffering and false turns, we'll reach the end — and what a glorious end it will be!

Father, thank You for Your Holy Spirit — God with us, who strengthens and keeps us in the hard times. Help me fix my eyes and heart on You and live by faith. Thank You that I have Your promises, including Your promise that in the end I'll be with You.

He Is Able

I know whom I have believed, and am convinced that
he is able to guard what I have entrusted to him until
that day.
2 Timothy 1:12b, NIV

"*I* know... *I* have believed... *I* am convinced..."

We need a personal confidence in God. It grounds us in Him and it's the basis for enabling us to encourage others, so we won't be threatened either by their needs or by our inadequacies.

This verse offers more than the initial assurance that God will keep our souls at the end.

It promises that He is ready and able to look after us in the here and now. Whatever comes.

Father, You are so good to me. You show Your care in so many ways. Help me to believe You and to stay confident in Your care whatever the day brings. I won't necessarily like what comes, but You can use it. And it's not about me, it's about You. Help me live in love and confidence in You so others will see the difference You make.

Weak is Okay... When Your God is Strong

But he said to me, "My grace is sufficient for you, for
my power is made perfect in weakness." Therefore I
will boast all the more gladly about my weaknesses, so
that Christ's power may rest on me.
2 Corinthians 12:9, NIV

Sometimes we feel unsettled. We need comfort, reassurance. An anchor.

What if, instead of regretting our weakness, we chose to be glad that it points us to our Strength?

We can learn to rest in God, draw what's needed for each moment as it comes, and be glad of the reminder to do this. Forgetting only leads to launching out alone, which tends to mean missing the mark.

We don't *have* to be strong in ourselves. God never asks that. He asks us to recognize our need and His bounty, and to love to run to Him.

Father, I'm so thankful that in my weakness Your strength shines, and that together we'll navigate today by Your plan. It will be enough. Today I will be neither introvert nor extrovert, but Christovert.

Love Letter

Reflect on what I am saying, for the Lord will give you
insight into all this.
2 Timothy 2:7, NIV

Paul is writing to Timothy, a young pastor with a difficult charge, and perhaps the only man Paul can trust with this particular group of people.

Timothy is gifted, but he's prone to be timid. Paul has been encouraging him to be strong in Christ Jesus, not to try handling things in his own strength, to teach boldly.

This letter carries a sense of urgency, as if Paul's trying to cram in every bit of advice Timothy could possibly need.

It's like Paul knows he's running out of time.

He doesn't want to die without passing on everything he has to this young man whom he loves like a son. So he sends this brief but full letter, written with love.

He knows it's more than Timothy can take in with a single reading. That's why he instructs him to reflect on it and to trust the Lord to help him understand.

Isn't that what God has done for us, with the entire Bible? And isn't it good that He doesn't expect us to process it all on our own?

Father, thank You for loving me with an intensity greater than Paul's love for Timothy. Thank You for that urgency in Your desire to communicate with me. Please give me ears to hear, eyes to see, and a heart to receive, to trust, and to love. Help me reflect on what You say, and make me receptive to the Holy Spirit's teaching. Thank You for not leaving me to find my way alone.

He Is Who He Is

...if we are faithless,
he remains faithful,
for he cannot disown himself.
2 Timothy 1:13, NIV

And this is why we can trust Him: we can trust His character. God can't be other than who He is.

Look at the foolishness, immorality, and capriciousness of the Greek and Roman gods. The only reason people worshipped them was fear. Not the good kind, the healthy respect and awareness of sovereignty that God asks of us, but the superstitious, need-to-appease kind.

God's character — and our understanding of it — is central to our ability to live with confident faith in Him.

He is who He is. As the old hymn, "Great is Thy Faithfulness," declares, "there is no shadow of turning in Him." Not even a hint of uncertainty. No reason to doubt.

At times He relents, like when the people of Nineveh changed their ways (Jonah 3:10). That's good: it means He allows second chances. But He never goes back on His word. And He's faithful to all His promises.

Holy and sovereign God, You are worthy of my worship, my trust, and my love. And You love me. You've proven that through Your Son. Teach me and help me to live by faith in You, so that I can grow into all You've designed me to be.

Grace for Today

You then, my son, be strong in the grace that is in
Christ Jesus.
2 Timothy 2:1, NIV

Often when we speak of God's grace it's in terms of forgiveness, salvation, eternity with Him after we die. And it is. But it's also strength for today and for all of the tomorrows until we reach the end. It's God — His presence with us.

Grace is something given by a person who "has" to a person who "has not," with no strings attached.

There's no obligation to give, just a valid need that will otherwise go unmet. The giver acts out of goodness, compassion, or a similar motivation. The recipient can't *earn* it but desperately *needs* it.

The recipient has no claim on the giver. The recipient is unworthy, but with the gift comes worth. We are worthy because God conferred worthiness on us along with the gift of His grace.

We are not entitled. But we're valued — validated — by God.

Father, on my own I'm nothing, and what little I have, I've damaged. But You love me. And You choose to rescue and mend me, and to dwell in me. Amazing grace indeed!

What Will Jesus Say?

In the presence of God and of Christ Jesus, who will
judge the living and the dead, and in view of his
appearing and his kingdom, I give you this charge:
Preach the word; be prepared in season and out of
season; correct, rebuke and encourage — with great
patience and careful instruction.
2 Timothy 4:1-2, NIV

Reading these verses, the focus is usually on Paul's charge to Timothy. Today, let's consider the word "judge."

First, there's a sense of reassurance: it's Jesus as Judge. We can trust Him. 1 John 1:9 and other verses promise His verdict for those who've accepted His salvation will read, "paid in full."

Thinking a little deeper, we realize it won't stop there. Will we hear, "Well done, good and faithful servant" (Matthew 25:21, NIV), or have we been wasting our time, coasting, doing our own thing? We need to be sure God is directing. To spend time with Him daily. To trust and obey.

We can't let the fear that we might mess up make us not *step* up when there's an opportunity. Nor can we believe the lie that pictures a stern God shaking a finger. We need to trust His grace and forge ahead, in love, not out of dread or obligation.

Father God, thank You for reminding me I am accountable to You. Sometimes I forget I have limited time and opportunities, and I waste them. Thank You for Your grace that forgives and empowers. Grow in me a willing, trusting, obedient heart. Help me be a good, faithful child of the King.

Finishing Well

I have fought the good fight, I have finished the race, I
have kept the faith.
2 Timothy 4:6, NIV

These things Paul tells us at the end of his life are the things that mattered most to him. They are his marks of success, and the things he was afraid he'd fail in. His daily, yearly, lifetime goals. The goals he's trying to pass on to Timothy.

He's not being smug here. He's satisfied, and perhaps relieved. Failure would have devastated him, but failure is a constant danger.

Being human, he may have slipped a bit, but he stayed the course. And he'd say it was because "I can do all this through him who gives me strength" (Philippians 4:13, NIV).

He did it by relying on Jesus' strength, and by keeping his focus. What's our focus on any given day? To serve God, or just to deal with the tasks at hand? His opportunities, or our duties?

Father God, remind me whose I am and help me focus on Kingdom priorities. Let my life count for You.

Expectant Prayer

On the third day a wedding took place at Cana in
Galilee. Jesus' mother was there, and Jesus and his
disciples had also been invited to the wedding. When
the wine was gone, Jesus' mother said to him, "They
have no more wine."
John 2:1-3, NIV

Mary doesn't ask Jesus in so many words to do something about the problem, nor does she suggest how He solve the problem. She just brings Him the need. Her words imply her trust that not only can He meet it, He will.

These verses remind us that simply bringing Jesus the need, in quiet trust that He will want to meet it, is a valid form of prayer.

Whether the Spirit leads us with specifics in prayer, or we bring requests like Mary did here, or whatever the form(s) of prayer we use, let's be reminded to come in an attitude of expectant trust: He cares, He's interested in our needs, and He has the power to meet them.

Loving God, thank You that You want me to pray: to praise and enjoy You, to confess, to bring needs. Sometimes You show me specific requests to make. Sometimes, like Mary, I can only speak my concern. Help me to always come in an attitude of expectant trust. Thank You that You care, that You're interested in my needs, and that You have the power to meet them.

Hanging Out With Jesus

After this [turning water to wine at the wedding in
Cana] he went down to Capernaum with his mother
and brothers and his disciples. There they stayed for a
few days.
John 2:12, NIV

What would it be like, spending a few days hanging out with Jesus? He's not crossing words with His adversaries, He's not offering signs to people who need convincing, He's not teaching the multitudes.

He's probably teaching His disciples, but likely in relaxed conversation. There are probably laughter and jokes. Casual conversation and quiet times.

Whether He's talking one on one, sitting in companionable silence, speaking in a group, each one present feels they're valued by Jesus. When He makes eye contact, that's clear. When He listens it's clear, even if what He says next challenges them to see the familiar in a new way.

What would it be like to hang out with Jesus between the public events?

That's most of our daily life, "between public events."

And He's here. His Spirit lives in us. What might we discover if we tuned in and remembered He's with us?

Father, there are no words to thank You for drawing me to Yourself, for saving me and adopting me into relationship with You. For valuing me and seeking me out. I praise Your goodness, mercy, and love that have placed Your Spirit in me as a deposit, keeping Your promise to never leave me. Open me to His leading, so I can be shaped into who You've designed me to be.

Seeing and Believing

"Go," Jesus replied, "your son will live."

The man took Jesus at his word and departed... Then
the father realized that this [his son's healing] was the
exact time at which Jesus had said to him, "Your son
will live." So he and his whole household believed.
John 4:50, 53, NIV

Jesus originally told him, "Unless you people see miraculous signs and wonders... you will never believe" (John 4:48, NIV). Why would He say this here? After all, the man wasn't demanding a sign, like Jesus' opponents so often did. He was pleading for his son's life.

This man came because he wanted something.

But it wasn't until he received that miracle that he was open to receive the full package of who Jesus is. To move from believing what He could *do* to believing who He truly *is*.

To see what the miracle actually meant. It testified that this itinerant rabbi could command the power of God.

How many times do we come to Him for what He can do for us — for what we want Him to do — instead of for Who He is?

Father, You invite me to come boldly, and to bring my prayers, petitions and praises. But too many times they're the only reason I come. You didn't reconcile me to Yourself just to listen to my prayer list. You drew me back into fellowship with You. Relationship. Sometimes the needs are huge. But my need of You is central. If you were to never answer another prayer, I'd still need to be in Your presence.

How to Pass the Test

When Jesus looked up and saw a great crowd coming
toward him, he said to Philip, "Where shall we buy
bread for these people to eat?" He asked this only to
test him, for he already had in mind what he was going
to do.
John 6:5-6, NIV

God's tests reveal to us what we've already learned, or how successfully we apply it, or they show us we still have some learning to do.

Imagine Philip looking around and seeing the impossibility of feeding a crowd of 5,000 men plus women and children. He heard Jesus' question and felt responsible to provide a solution.

To pass the test would have been to turn to Jesus for the solution.

The disciples had already experienced Jesus' miraculous signs, and this new challenge was an opportunity to extrapolate their faith from what they'd seen into new territory.

It would be nice to think that at least Andrew passed the test by telling the group about the boy with the loaves and fish, but he finished his sentence with "but how far will they go among so many?" (John 6:9, NIV).

How many times do we do the same thing?

Father, by Your grace I've seen You work in my heart and circumstances. I've heard the testimonies of other believers. When life throws the next question at me, please help me pass the test. Help me remember You already have in mind what You plan to do. Help me trust You.

Where Else Could We Go?

From this time many of his disciples turned back and
no longer followed him.

"You do not want to leave too, do you?" Jesus asked
the Twelve.

Simon Peter answered him, "Lord, to whom shall we
go? You have the words of eternal life. We have come
to believe and to know that you are the Holy One of
God."
John 6:66-69, NIV

Jesus has been teaching, proving His authority with miraculous signs, and has attracted a large group of followers and hangers-on. Now, perhaps partly to weed out the crowd, His words aren't so easy to understand. They're even a bit disquieting. Many of His listeners leave.

If we've followed Jesus very far, we've probably hit a wall of some kind: circumstances; a relationship; even, like these disciples, something He said. Maybe it doesn't make sense. Maybe we just plain don't want to do it.

Given the choice, sometimes we'd like to walk away. But where? Peter was right. Where could we go? Who else is there?

There's only God: Father, Son, Holy Spirit. Wise beyond our knowing. And He has proven Himself trustworthy many times over.

Father, Your thoughts and ways are past my comprehension, but this I know: You are faithful and true, and You love me. In that I will rest. You understand my weakness. Help me rely on Your strength.

Light for a Lifetime

When Jesus spoke again to the people, he said, "I am
the light of the world. Whoever follows me will never
walk in darkness, but will have the light of life."
John 8:12, NIV

The way may get dark, and it probably will, but this promise tells us that if we're walking with Jesus, trusting and obeying Him, we won't become "darkened in our understanding" (Ephesians 4:18, NIV) and we won't bang into things or stray off-course.

The promise is more than its future implications: "will never... will have." Let's hear it in its three-fold sense.

As we've followed Jesus, we have been kept from walking in darkness and we have received the light of life.

In this moment, we are not walking in darkness, and we have the light of life.

And yes, as we continue with Him, we will never walk in darkness and we will continue to have the light of life.

Let that reassure us today. This isn't something we have to wait for, or persevere for. It's here and now, surrounding us, and we only need to rest in Jesus and keep walking with Him. It's practicing the presence of Christ, following Him moment by moment.

Father, I pray in confidence, because of who You are and because of the promises You've made. Make me mindful of Your presence throughout the day, not just when I stop to read Your Word or to pray. Let me appreciate Your company on this journey, let me remember to follow closely so I'll stay in the light and reflect it to those around me.

Belonging at Last

Jesus said to them, "If God were your Father, you
would love me, for I have come here from God. I have
not come on my own; God sent me... Whoever belongs
to God hears what God says. The reason you do not
hear is that you do not belong to God."
John 8:42, 47, NIV

This group of Jewish listeners think Jesus is saying they aren't legitimate children in the line of Abraham — but He takes it farther than that. He calls them children of the devil.

Not that they're particularly evil or nasty, but that they can't receive the truth and are naturally inclined to sinful behaviour. In short, they're human. Children of the Fall, tainted by Adam's and Eve's disobedience. Just like us.

But these are people who had believed Jesus' words (at least until this point). This conflict springs from His offer to set them free (John 8:31-32). "Who, us? We're not slaves! The nerve of You!"

He isn't blaming them for not being able to hear. He understands the problem and that's why He came to solve it.

He's offering spiritual rebirth, the chance to actually *hear* God again. To *belong* in relationship with Him. To be adopted into His family.

We can have that. What could be worth more?

We can know we belong. To Him, with Him, because of Him. He gives meaning to our lives.

Creator God, because of Jesus I can call You Father. Because of Your Spirit in mine, I'm connected with You. You know what a deep need this meets, because You designed me this way. In Jesus You have accepted me. You've welcomed me. I am at home in You. I belong.

Soul Rest

Come to me, all you who are weary and burdened, and
I will give you rest. Take my yoke upon you and learn
from me, for I am gentle and humble in heart, and you
will find rest for your souls. For my yoke is easy and
my burden is light.
Matthew 11:28-30, NIV

The rural language of yokes isn't as clear to city-dwellers in 21st-century North America, but it's said that farmers will pair a new ox with an experienced one to help the new one learn how to pull (and probably how to interpret and obey the farmer's guidance).

Usually when we think of learning from Jesus we think of His teachings, although He was a living model of following the Father. (Paul wrote about following Jesus' example too, in Philippians 2.)

Today let's consider the example, the attitude, that He wants us to learn. Yes, there's the doing, but it's too easy to overlook or neglect the *how*.

Jesus demonstrated a life that's gentle and humble in heart. He didn't try to control or dominate. Although by His nature as God He has that right, He modelled submission to, obedience to, and trust in God the Father.

Rest for our souls indeed! Trying to be mentally in control, pushing to do it our own way, is not just unsatisfying and unproductive, it's soul-draining.

Father, let me learn from the Son, and be led by the Spirit, to live the way You intended, and to come into Your rest.

Rebuild the House

"You expected much, but see, it turned out to be little.
What you brought home, I blew away. Why?" declares
the LORD Almighty. "Because of my house, which
remains a ruin, while each of you is busy with your
own house."
Haggai 1:9, NIV

The Israelites returning from exile had started to rebuild the temple, but how could what they put together out of rubble compare with the remembered glory of Solomon's temple?

Building homes didn't seem as impossible, and it was a legitimate need too. So that's what they did.

Christians today don't have a temple to rebuild, but we're each temples of the Holy Spirit (1 Corinthians 6:19). And we're not to neglect meeting together as congregations of faith (Hebrews 10:25).

We're also busy with our own "houses": work, household duties, busy schedules... nobody has much time for church events.

It's hard enough to fit in time for Sunday worship. The last thing we need is another church group or committee meeting. And people can burn out or weaken their families by being too busy in the church.

But this idea of building... rebuilding... If we are the body — the church — then maybe the building isn't about formal meetings or events. Maybe it's about relationships. Some of that can happen in structured settings, but it can also happen one-on-one as we take the initiative.

Father, some things from my own "house" will need to move aside to make time for Yours. But doing things Your way is always better than pushing for mine. Please help me to seize the opportunities You give to connect with my spiritual brothers and sisters — so You may take pleasure in us and be honoured.

A Pure Heart

Create in me a pure heart, O God,
and renew a steadfast spirit within me.
Psalm 51:10, NIV

To step out from behind our walls of self-protection and live authentically with others...

To trust God to be our Protector and to let His life give itself through us...

We need a pure heart and a steadfast spirit.

Purifying the heart, renewing the steadfast spirit, comes by removing the fallen wall's rubble so that we can step out through it.

Sometimes purification needs strong cleansers. Or fire. It needs an expert and delicate touch — only God, who broke the wall, can do it.

What feeds a pure heart? Dependence on God and delight in Him. Time alone with Him, with heart, mind and spirit tuned to His.

Father, thank You more than words can say for rescuing me from a life — and a death — separated from You. You have saved me... You are saving me... You will save me. In the saving, make my heart pure. Make my spirit steadfast. Help me learn to depend on You and to live authentically in Your world.

Pain and Joy

Now a man named Lazarus was sick... When he heard
this, Jesus said, "This sickness will not end in death.
No, it is for God's glory so that God's Son may be
glorified through it." Now Jesus loved Martha and her
sister and Lazarus. So when he heard that Lazarus was
sick, he stayed where he was two more days...
John 11:1a, 4-6 NIV

Jesus didn't even have to go see Lazarus to heal him; He could have just said the word. Instead He waited until Lazarus was dead before starting out.

He loved this family. Their home seems to be one of the few genuinely safe places where He could visit without loaded questions and malice.

Loving them, knowing their faith and character and that they could pass this test, He let Lazarus the provider die. Because there was something bigger at stake. This was for the glory of God the Father and God the Son.

As much as this was clearly about God, it wasn't for God's benefit. He wasn't on an ego trip. It was for the people, the believers. Jesus told His disciples in verse 15, "...for your sake I am glad I was not there, so that you may believe" (NIV).

Jesus wept and was deeply moved by the sisters' grief. Probably more so because He knew He could have prevented it. The people needed to know Him better, and joy was on its way. But that didn't negate the pain.

Sustaining and compassionate God, help me remember in my tears that You feel my pain. Help me rely on You in faith, trusting although I don't understand. Reveal Yourself to me, not for Your benefit but for mine, so that I can trust You more.

Expectations and Complaints

Then Moses led Israel from the Red Sea... For three
days they traveled in the desert without finding water.
When they came to Marah, they could not drink its
water because it was bitter... So the people grumbled
against Moses, saying, "What are we to drink?"
Exodus 15: 22-24, NIV

The Israelites were jubilant at what God had done: deliverance from Egyptian slavery, parting the Red Sea to rescue them (and neatly eliminating their enemies). They believed He could fulfill the rest of His promise and bring them into the promised land.

After a string of miracles and evidences of His great power, it's understandable that they'd expect Him to melt all remaining opposition and obstacles in their way.

Then right away they have three waterless days in the desert, only to find water they can't drink. No wonder they complain!

Moses, on the other hand, is used to setbacks, from his dealings with Pharaoh. He cries out to God (Exodus 15:25).

The people know God can help, but they don't ask. They expect, and then protest when He doesn't operate the way they want.

Don't we do the same?

Father God, mighty to save and wise to teach, You could give me smooth paths. But I seem to learn better when I experience Your help in the rough places. Help me to trust Your leading and to listen, obey, and learn to do life Your way. Help me to be grateful for Your presence.

A Gift from the Heart

Do not let your hearts be troubled. You believe in God;
believe also in me... If you love me, keep my
commands.
John 14:1, 15, NIV

A true offering to God is one that comes from the heart: Believing in God, trusting Him, just because of who He is. Because of what we know of His character. Because we know He's trustworthy. Even when we don't see the whys and hows. Even when it hurts.

Our love and trust will result in obedience if it's real. If we act on it. If we don't put it into practice, it stays theory and we're never truly *sure* about God.

Adventure novels often have a hero/heroine who's a strong leader, one the other characters will follow in the bleakest circumstances in blind (but fully warranted) trust. One who operates on the "need to know" principle because stopping to explain takes too long and because the followers don't have the knowledge base to be able to understand. One who brings them through incredible odds to victory.

God is like that, except better. He's real, and nothing surprises Him. And He never makes mistakes.

Reading the novels, when we see characters mistrusting the leader or trying their own ways, we know they're wrong and we keep hoping they'll wise up before it's too late. Before they either ruin everything or get themselves killed.

In real life, it's sometimes easier to be the doubter than the faithful follower — even when God is the leader.

Father, I'm glad You know my weaknesses. I'm gladder still that You love me anyway, and that You're working all things out to the end You've planned from the beginning. You are the only wise, all-powerful God. The only one who can bring victory in the messes we make. Help me love, trust, and obey You, in the big and in the small. Sometimes the small is the hardest part.

God With Us

The virgin will conceive and give birth to a son, and
they will call him Immanuel (which means "God with
us").
Matthew 1:23, NIV

Have you ever looked at God's detailed instructions in the Old Testament — to be followed to the letter — for preparing and consecrating the Tabernacle and its contents and the priests and their garments?

Chapters upon chapters in Exodus and Leviticus deal with the construction and consecration of the Tabernacle and the procedures for offering acceptable sacrifices. It was a serious business to make a space where God could dwell among humans and not destroy them.

This is just a glimpse of how holy God is, how different from us. Obedience meant the Israelites could see His glory, could be near Him.

The majestic God of Hosts is dangerous. Fearsome. Not to be trifled with. Yet, He loves us and wants to be with us.

When we forget His power, and focus on the privilege of our access to Him through Jesus, we can forget how strong He is, and end up worrying about our circumstances.

Father, I praise You for making a way that we can come freely to You because of the blood of Jesus. Forgive me when I forget Your strength. Help me know and rely on Your presence with me, You who are mighty to save.

A Heart Set on Pilgrimage

Blessed are those whose strength is in you,
whose hearts are set on pilgrimage.
As they pass through the Valley of Baka,
they make it a place of springs;
the autumn rains also cover it with pools.
Psalm 84:5-6, NIV

Psalm 84 is a homesick heart's cry to be near to God in His house — the Israelites' Tabernacle, or maybe the Temple itself. It's one of those psalms many of us know well.

"Pilgrimage." From the context, the psalmist is probably writing of a literal journey.

For us reading it today, it can resonate in a different way. Christians, with the Holy Spirit dwelling in us, are told that our bodies are the temple of God (1 Corinthians 6:19). We're not on pilgrimage *to* God's Temple, but we're on pilgrimage *with* God through our days.

Yes, "this world is not our home, we're just passing through," but we're to pass through attentively. Compassionately. Like Jesus did.

We're not to ignore our surroundings or our neighbours' pain, but to spread His blessings to others. On our own, we can't do much, but God's strength in and through us can make a difference in the lives around us.

Father, grant me a heart set on pilgrimage with You, knowing I'm bound for Heaven but charged with spreading Your light while I'm here. Help me find my strength in You, and let me leave each day a little better than I found it. Because of Jesus.

Loving God, Loving Others

Whoever claims to love God yet hates a brother or
sister is a liar. For whoever does not love their brother
and sister, whom they have seen, cannot love God,
whom they have not seen.
1 John 4:20, NIV

It often feels much easier to love God, who is perfect, and worthy of love, than to love imperfect people who may not seem lovable. Even the brother or sister we've seen, worked with, and discovered the foibles of is harder to love than the one we've only met online and seen the positive side of their nature. Likely others feel the same about us.

But when we find ourselves arguing with Scripture, we know there's a problem. Maybe what we've been calling love for God, that response of our spirit to His, is *worship*, not love. *Adoration*, even.

When the Bible talks about love, it's usually as an action rather than a feeling. We're commanded to love our Christian brothers and sisters. That's not a call to manufacture or pretend warm feelings toward one another. It's a call to active love.

That brings a second question: if loving our brother and sister, whose needs we have seen, is the act of caring for them, what does it look like to love God? In the next chapter, John says we love God by keeping His commands.

We need to do this in His strength and by the power of His Spirit in us. With willing, thankful and surrendered hearts, as an offering of worship. There's no room for legalism here.

Father, give me Your heart toward others, Christians and non. Empower me by Your Spirit to actively and practically show love to them, and by so doing to love You as well.

Sustained

The Son is the radiance of God's glory and the exact
representation of his being, sustaining all things by his
powerful word.
Hebrews 1:3a, NIV

"Sustaining all things by His powerful word."

Our world seems a little out of control. Natural disasters are more frequent and widespread, society's morals keep sliding, sickness and anxiety thrive.

Today's verse is from the beginning of Hebrews, and later in the same chapter we read about the heavens and the earth perishing (Hebrews 1:10-12). The writer ends that passage by reaffirming that God does not change.

God the Father won't grow weak or fail. Jesus the Son will sustain all things. The Holy Spirit will never leave us.

We can take comfort in that. The world may be a scary place, and material things will wear out, break and decay, but we can trust the God who made the universe to sustain what matters to Him... and that includes us.

Mighty God, I can depend on You to sustain me. Give me the grace and faith I need to keep my confidence firmly fixed in You, who alone are worthy. Because of who You are, I can rest in hope.

Not Anxious

Do not be anxious about anything, but in every
situation, by prayer and petition, with thanksgiving,
present your requests to God.
Philippians 4:6, NIV

When we're concerned, our prayers can sound something like this: "See the problem, God? Please help."

We may thank Him for His power and love, and for being with us. We thank Him for the plans He's already made, that whatever the situation is has not caught Him by surprise. But we keep an eye on the problem.

There's a bit more to the "with thanksgiving" part of today's verse. We need to thank Him *with expectation* that He will act. Not to decide *how* He'll act, because that's His call. But after committing the issue to Him, we need to stop looking at it and trust Him.

We have a definite choice to make. Will we go through the day reminding Him of our need, or will we look expectantly for His reply?

There's a difference. The first way still has the tension, the uncertainty. The second has a confidence that God will do what He planned, even though we don't see it yet.

It may take us quite a lot of practice to move from one to the other, but our God is patient, and He loves to teach us.

Father God, Your plans for me are good, and You love me. I don't always like what happens to me, nor do You. But You are my Creator and Sustainer, and Your patient grace teaches me to trust You. Give me the confidence to pray with thanksgiving and with expectation that You have heard... and that You will act. Thank You for Your grace.

Spiritual Self-Control

But the Holy Spirit produces this kind of fruit in our
lives: love, joy, peace, patience, kindness, goodness,
faithfulness, gentleness, and self-control. There is no
law against these things!
Galatians 5:22-23, NLT

Self-control. Maybe because the King James Version calls it "temperance," it's easy to think of this fruit of the Spirit as "refraining from excess and from bad behaviour."

What if this passage about the fruit of the Spirit uses self-control not so much for the outer actions (as important as that is) but to describe bringing our spirits into line with the Holy Spirit, placing them under His direction?

Not in a repressive way, but a loving submission, a trusting surrender, a placing of self under God's authority and direction. A making room for His Spirit to shape, develop and refine us.

Lord, help me hear and recognize Your voice. Help me not follow my default pattern of hardening my heart by choosing my way over Yours. Help me to control and quiet my inner self so that Your Spirit within me has room to rise and to develop His fruit in me. To Your glory, and for my own spiritual wellbeing.

The Job is a Gift

The LORD said to Aaron, "... I myself have selected
your fellow Levites from among the Israelites as a gift
to you, dedicated to the LORD to do the work at the
tent of meeting. But only you and your sons may serve
as priests in connection with everything at the altar
and inside the curtain. I am giving you the service of
the priesthood as a gift."
Numbers 18:1a, 6-7a, NIV

From our perspective, the person in a key ministry position or crucial role is someone important — they're special. Our star-struck culture inclines us to admire him or her because of the position, not because of character or deeds.

Today's verse reminds us of God's view: the high-profile role is a gift *to* the person, *for* God's greater plan to bless the people who that individual will serve. The support roles are also gifts, and just as significant. There's no room for "He likes you more than He likes me," or the other way around.

With the "great" roles comes great responsibility, and it's better to pray "Lord, use me where You will," than to set the sights of personal ambition on a high-profile position. Are we here to please ourselves, or to give honour to our Creator?

He puts some of us in the lead roles, and more of us in the supporting ones. But in God's overall view, each part matters. Our responsibility is to be consecrated, ready, and obedient to His call.

Father, thank You for those You empower for leadership roles, and for those You empower for behind-the-scenes roles. Thank You that no job is too big for the person You choose or too small for a person to need Your strength and leading. Help me remember it's not about me — it's for Your glory. Give me ears to hear and a heart to obey. Let me neither envy another's service nor begrudge my own.

Daily Faith

All these people [Abel, Enoch, Noah, Abraham, Sarah,
Isaac, Jacob] were still living by faith when they died.
They did not receive the things promised; they only
saw them and welcomed them from a distance,
admitting that they were foreigners and strangers on
earth.
Hebrews 11:13, NIV

These and other heroes of the faith listed in Hebrews 11 were commended for being sure of what they hoped for and certain of what they did not see. Their faith was not in themselves or in their hopes and dreams. They put their faith in God, because they considered the Promise Maker faithful.

So what about us? Most of us are in that safe, ordinary range between the two extremes: we're not going to be big names in the history books for either our victories or our defeats. But that doesn't mean where we are is any less important to God.

We're still called to please Him by our faith. We can believe He made the universe, we can offer the sorts of sacrifices He really wants (mercy, justice, walking humbly with Him).

Instead of getting distracted by the here and now, we can live today mindful of God's promises. He said He'd always be with us in our todays, and He also said we'd be with Him for eternity.

Creator God, You keep Your promises and nothing can change that. Forgive me for getting distracted by the present. Help me to enjoy the present and serve You well in it. But help me keep my eyes on You — and on eternity with You. That makes my time here more purposeful, because I'll be acting in faith in Your promise.

Loving God

Love the Lord your God with all your heart and with
all your soul and with all your mind and with all your
strength.
Mark 12:30, NIV

Jesus said this is the most important commandment. Love isn't just a feeling. It's an act of will, a choice. And it's what God wants most from us: love in action.

We know that outward-only love, the going-through-the-motions action without any heart behind it, isn't what God wants. Nor is it what our family and friends want. It's legalism, hypocrisy. Fake.

Gratitude, appreciation, respect, honour, obedience... these can be earned. Even required, by people and by God.

True love is a response to who God is, not to what He does. We can't give it without knowing Him. But we need to throw our whole selves into it, heart, soul, mind, and strength.

Father God, please draw my heart to love You for who You are, to worship You with all that's in me. Don't let me settle for anything less than a growing relationship with You. You loved me first. Teach me to reflect it back to You in abundance, with all my heart, soul, mind and strength, knowing it all comes from You.

Not We Ourselves

Know that the LORD is God.
It is he who made us, and we are his;
we are his people, the sheep of his pasture.
Psalm 100:3, NIV

When life gets busy and responsibilities crowd, do you feel pressure to keep pace, to meet every demand on your own? Sometimes when the pressure's on, we feel like there's not enough of us to go around. We forget there's enough of *God*.

Somehow today's one verse from a short psalm puts it all back in perspective. We are not the real authority. Everything does *not* rest on us, no matter how it feels.

Renewed perspective gives us a quietness and a confidence. We can trust in God, because He is good. His love endures forever. The NIV declares this phrase 41 times.

Father, forgive me for getting distracted and relying on myself. You are God, and greatly to be praised. Help me trust You not to overload me with more than You want to accomplish through me. Help me stick with what You give and not try to do my own thing — or to cram my own interests in there with what You say is enough. You're the Shepherd, I'm the sheep. And You are the Good Shepherd. Keep me close to Your side.

Pray Before Giving

Go and tell my servant David, 'This is what the LORD
says: Are you the one to build me a house to dwell in? I
have not dwelt in a house from the day I brought the
Israelites up out of Egypt to this day. I have been
moving from place to place with a tent as my dwelling.
2 Samuel 7:5-6, NIV

King David's desire to build a temple for God came from a good heart. He wanted to honour God, not to live in an elaborate palace while God's dwelling was a tent.

David loved God, and God had given him so much. Perhaps David saw a chance to do something for Him as a gift he could give in return. Good heart, good idea, wrong timing.

We get love-born impulses too, to do things for God or for others. These verses remind us we need to pray before acting.

God may want us to bless Him with our hearts' attitudes but to not act — or to not act *yet*. In His plan, timing matters. Sometimes the very things we long to do for others are the things that would undermine what God is doing in their hearts.

Father God, I want to give back to You out of the love You've given me. Impress on my heart how best to please You — and how to show love to those around me. Help me to always come first to You for wisdom. Make me sensitive to Your prompting to act or to not act. Keep me in the centre of Your will.

God's Work

> "My food," said Jesus, "is to do the will of him who
> sent me and to finish his work."
> John 4:34, NIV

Sometimes we can think of doing God's work only in terms of recognized, organized ministry. We dismiss our regular lives. But the type of work Jesus talks about in today's verse can happen anywhere: on the job (sacred or secular), at home, in a chance encounter at the grocery checkout.

Our days come pre-filled for the most part: work, home, appointments, whatever. If that's where God has us, then that's where He wants us to work with Him, however mundane the task. Or however inconvenient the interruption He allows.

There's something about the routine and the everyday that dulls our attention. Meal preparation and household chores, even conversation around the family table, can feel like the same-old-same-old.

But shouldn't each thing we do for our loved ones — for our employer — be truly done for God? Isn't each conversation a chance to show His interest in the other person?

In that case, it's all God's work if we can only see it. God's work, an offering to Him. Even if it's peeling potatoes or scrubbing toilets. Or taking a coffee break with a friend.

Father God, who sent Jesus into the world to do Your will and who has sent me to do the same, take me out of myself and make me mindful of You and Your ways. Help me live for You, and teach me to be on the lookout for Your leading in my daily life. Feed me with the satisfaction of serving You.

Miracles and Kindnesses

When our ancestors were in Egypt,
they gave no thought to your miracles;
they did not remember your many kindnesses,
and they rebelled by the sea, the Red Sea.
Yet he saved them for his name's sake,
to make his mighty power known.
Psalm 106:7-8, NIV

We need to remember and be mindful of the majesty of God, of His vastness and His glory. His miracles.

Yes, He gives us tender, personal gifts. His kindnesses. Things like a blooming flower or a bit of music that seem tailored to bless just one spirit. They root us in awareness of His love for us, and that's a good thing.

The danger of intimacy is when our thoughts try to bring God down to our level. He's so close, so real. But we need to look at His larger-scale acts and works too.

It's about balance. We need both intimacy with God and holy awe of His majesty. It's all to keep us praising. Worshipping. Living in obedience and trust.

God who formed the universe, who numbers the stars in the sky and the hairs on my head, You are majestic in holiness, far beyond my comprehension. Yet You love me and woo me into a personal relationship. Help me to know and rely on Your love, and help me develop a confidence in You and a holy awe of You. Help me know You as both King and Abba — Daddy — Papa.

God is Still at Work

Great are the works of the LORD;
they are pondered by all who delight in them.
Psalm 111:2, NIV

God's acts and wonders are recorded and remembered in the Bible, but in North America today we often live with a sense of "that was then, this is now."

Is it because the Bible is the "official" written testimony? That doesn't mean God stopped working when John wrote the final "Amen" to end the book of Revelation. God hasn't changed, as Christians in other parts of the world know.

One antidote to this thought process is to open up with our Christian friends to share what God has been doing in our lives, what He's been teaching us, where He may be leading us.

That kind of conversation encourages our faith, and it reminds us to keep a sharper eye out for God at work in the little as well as the big. And don't you think God enjoys hearing that we've noticed — and appreciate — His care?

Father, help me remember You are at work whether I see or hear or not. Help me look, help me recognize what You're doing and return thanks. Give Your people boldness to declare Your work. And forgive us for beginning to believe that if we don't see it, it's not happening. How self-absorbed is that?

To Know God Hears

I love the LORD, for he heard my voice;
he heard my cry for mercy.
Because he turned his ear to me,
I will call on him as long as I live.
Psalm 116:1-2, NIV

Psalm 116 is more than intellectual acceptance of the deity of God. It overflows with love and gratitude.

Three times in these first two verses, the writer says he called out. But what really thrills him is that God heard. And acted.

It's the psalmist's experience of God's answer that compels his loving worship. If this is a David psalm, it's not the beginning of a personal relationship with God. If it's someone else, maybe this is the moment when he moves from faith by hearing to faith by experience.

People need to hear the truth about who God is and what Jesus has done to offer them rescue. But it's the personal encounter when they risk calling out to God that makes it real.

We each move from "I have heard" to "Now I know."

I love you, Lord, for You hear each voice, You hear each cry for mercy. When Your children cry out, reassure them that You hear, and sustain them with Your love and peace. Please draw those who don't know You to cry out as well. Show them that You hear — and that Your answer is distinctly personal and life changing.

The Goodness of the Lord

I remain confident of this:
I will see the goodness of the LORD
in the land of the living.
Wait for the LORD;
be strong and take heart
and wait for the LORD.
Psalm 27:13-14, NIV

Sometimes we need help believing there can be good days ahead.

Holding onto the Lord's promises can give us strength to hope that we will yet see His goodness this side of Heaven.

Notice, though, that this promise doesn't say anything about what this goodness will look like. Doesn't say the pain will go away, health or wealth be restored, wars and natural disasters cease.

What it says is that we will see the goodness of the Lord. *See* the goodness of the Lord.

When circumstances don't change, or while we're waiting for the change, don't we need to recognize — to *see* — the goodness of the Lord present with us? Don't we need His goodness to get us through? That's grace.

Father God, Giver of all good gifts, open my eyes and my spirit to see Your goodness here with me, in the land of the living. I still pray in trust that You will deliver me from my hard places and heal my hurts, but in the here and the now, help me praise You. Praise You with no strings attached: not if You work things out a certain way, but because of who You are.

Expecting God's Mercy

Turn to me and have mercy on me,
as you always do to those who love your name.
Psalm 119:132, NIV

"As You always do." Do you hear the absolute trust and confidence in God's character and in His commitment to care?

We may not have a clue what God will do, or how or when, but we can know that He will always keep His word. For those of us who love Him, part of our responsibility is to actively trust Him, and to keep alert to recognize His mercy when it comes.

It isn't easy for people who like to see, touch, and forecast our world. People who are used to instant fixes. But that's how God works, and it trains our spirits to trust Him.

Sovereign and loving God, thank You for Your Word that teaches who You are and what You've said. Help me in my moments of unbelief, increase my faith, and open my spiritual eyes and ears to notice Your touch on my life and circumstances. Help me to give You praise, and to live in this "gracious uncertainty" that is certain of You — for my own sake and for a demonstration of Your goodness to the people around me.

For the Sake of the House of the Lord

Pray for the peace of Jerusalem:
"May those who love you be secure.
May there be peace within your walls
and security within your citadels."
For the sake of my family and friends,
I will say, "Peace be within you."
For the sake of the house of the LORD our God,
I will seek your prosperity.
Psalm 122:6-9, NIV

This is one of the songs of ascents the people would sing as they journeyed to Jerusalem for the prescribed feasts.

They were coming to worship, and this lets us see their prayer of blessing from a different perspective: it's not patriotism, they're blessing the Holy City because of the Temple at its heart.

What about our own churches? We pray for individuals when we know of a need, and we may pray for the congregation as a whole, for vision or attitude. We pray for our church leaders and events.

But this passage challenges us to pray after the pattern of Psalm 122 for our congregation today, for those who love our segment of the Body of Christ. For unity, for peace, "for the sake of the house of the LORD our God."

Lord of Heaven and Earth, thank You for making a way for all people to come to You in worship. You're building us into a living temple, and I need to have that same care for the Body of Christ that the Israelites had for the physical Temple. Help us intercede for one another. Grant Your congregations peace, security, prosperity... according to Your definition, and for Your glory.

Unless the LORD

Unless the LORD builds the house,
the builders labour in vain.
Unless the LORD watches over the city,
the guards stand watch in vain.
In vain you rise early
and stay up late,
toiling for food to eat—
for he grants sleep to those he loves.
Psalm 127:1-2, NIV

We need God — in each day, in each part of it — at a foundational level. Or there's no point in what we're doing.

We need to seek Him first in the day and in each endeavour.

Too often we find ourselves running around, self-directed and self-powered because we've forgotten to let God be God, in first place in our lives. We've complicated it. And added stress.

In vain.

Father God, Creator and Sustainer, forgive me for the times I run ahead of You. Quiet my spirit to seek You first. Remind me I'm never too busy not to pray. Root me deep in Your love. Show me where You're working, and how I can best work with You.

Dependence on God

Though the LORD is great, he cares for the humble, but
he keeps his distance from the proud.
Psalm 138:6, NLT

This is reminiscent of the psalm where the writer would rather be a gatekeeper in the Lord's house than to dwell (presumably in luxury) in the tents of the wicked (Psalm 84:10).

Why do we get so caught up in wanting it both ways? We long for closeness with God, but at the same time we want to be powerful enough to handle things on our own.

We're *not* God, we can't do it all, and in the grand scheme of things we're pretty insignificant. But He loves us. And He cares for us. And He works His strength through us for far greater impact than if we relied on our own abilities.

Dependence on Him doesn't diminish us. It completes us and lets us live in close relationship with the One who embraces us as His sons and daughters.

Father God, help me quiet myself in Your care. Help me remember to live in confidence in You instead of wanting to put confidence in myself. Help me delight in what You're doing.

God Has Plans for Us

The LORD will work out his plans for my life —
for your faithful love, O LORD, endures forever.
Psalm 138:8a, NLT

Don't you love David's quiet assurance in this psalm?

There's danger all around, but he's calm in his confidence that God has plans for his life and that God will fulfill those plans despite circumstances which give evidence to the contrary.

If David wrote this before becoming king, he's likely thinking about those plans for his life. If it's afterwards, he knows God has further plans for him even if he doesn't know the details.

God has plans and purposes for each of us, too, sometimes large-scale leadership roles, but also smaller ones in the everyday.

And we don't need advance notice of what they are, although we try to insist on it. It's enough that He knows, and that we be ready and recognize them when it's time.

Father God, help me be content with the step I'm on. Help me trust You to make the next step clear when I need to take it. Forgive me for those times I've strained to see ahead and felt entitled to know what's next. You know. Let that be enough.

Scattered Thoughts

We demolish arguments and every pretension that sets
itself up against the knowledge of God, and we take
captive every thought to make it obedient to Christ.
2 Corinthians 10:5b, NIV

Paul is calling Christians to live God's way, and not to judge by human standards but by God's. He's talking about spiritual warfare and tearing down everything that "sets itself up against the knowledge of God" (2 Corinthians 10:5, NIV).

The idea of taking every thought captive suggests not allowing ourselves to dwell on negatives and other temptations, but to think about good and positive things and to choose gratitude.

But what if there's more?

Take captive every thought... Sometimes when we're tired, this means pulling our thoughts together and gathering enough mental energy to carry on in His strength. Far more frequently than that, it means not letting our thoughts skitter away in all directions. Some of them rabbit-trail, others try to get into the future ahead of us.

"Take captive" is a good picture of what's needed: thoughts can bolt like a herd of wild horses, and it takes a firm hand to lasso them and get them back into the corral.

Father, I want to live in the present, grounded and aware, seeking You first, but I can't do this on my own. Help me bring every thought and focus in line with You. Help me take one thing at a time, walking with You, open to hear anything You might say.

Who's Bringing the Water?

[Moses] and Aaron gathered the assembly together in
front of the rock and Moses said to them, "Listen, you
rebels, must we bring you water out of this rock?"
Numbers 20:10, NIV

When God called him to lead the Israelites to freedom, Moses was a man deeply aware of his own inadequacy for the task. God gave him power to do miraculous signs, and promised to be with him, but he still resisted.

Fast-forward to the Desert of Zin. Moses has relied on God's power every step of the way. He has stood between God and the people when God was angry with them, but this time it's Moses who's angry.

One frustration-laden outburst, one *whack* of staff against stone, and Moses forfeits his own entrance into the Promised Land.

God said it was "Because you did not trust in me enough to honor me as holy in the sight of the Israelites" (Numbers 20:12, NIV).

It looks like such a little slip to us, but God has the full picture and is the righteous judge. One thing that stands out is "must we" bring the water? It's God who supplied the power and the water, but Moses is taking on the responsibility, the burden, and the credit, for the miracle.

How does this apply to our lives? When there's a need or a demand, the natural human instinct is to meet it in our own strength and from our own resources. God wants us to look to Him first, and to respond out of His equipping... His strength, His wisdom, His resources. Not our own.

Creator and Sustainer God, You never meant me to rely on myself, but I do. You said to trust in You with all my heart, and not to rely on my own understanding. Forgive me for taking on more than You intended, and teach me to seek You first in everything. Help me trust You enough to honour You as holy in the sight of those around me. Help me rely on Your provision instead of trying to manufacture enough resources on my own.

Pleasing God First

Whatever you do, work at it with all your heart, as
working for the Lord, not for human masters, since you
know that you will receive an inheritance from the
Lord as a reward. It is the Lord Christ you are serving.
Colossians 3:23-24, NIV

Why are we doing what we do, or not doing what we don't? For God's glory and praise, or to please ourselves or others?

If we raise our hands in worship at church... is it to please Him? Or to defy those who stay still? If we keep our hands down, is it sensitivity to a less-demonstrative neighbour... or fear of what someone might say?

That's a silly example, maybe, but the little choices can matter as much as the big ones, because God sees the heart.

What are we thinking about while slicing strawberries for jam? Grumbly thoughts about how such tiny berries make the job take longer, or thankful ones about fresh strawberries and how sweet the small ones are?

When we're tired at the end of the day, does it please God if we slip into a mental pity party? Or does He still want us praising Him?

Father God, You know me better than I know myself. You see my heart and deepest thoughts. Help me to seek Your approval first — to want to please You most. Help me take every thought captive and to examine it to see if it's pleasing to You. I can't help what thoughts come in, but in the strength of Your Spirit I can evict those that aren't welcome to stay.

Following the Leader

In your unfailing love you will lead
the people you have redeemed.
In your strength you will guide them
to your holy dwelling.
Exodus 15:13, NIV

God rescued the people, and the word "redeemed" here reminds us that His work with Israel in the Old Testament was often a prophetic picture of His work to rescue and redeem us all through Jesus.

Today's verse declares that the God who had shown Himself mighty to save was able to lead His people into the land He had promised. They didn't make it easy for Him, and He had to keep reminding them to obey Him.

He led them *out*, but because of disobedience, that generation lost the chance to be led *in* to the Promised Land.

Believers in Christ face the same danger. He's rescued us from bondage to sin's destructive ways. Let's not miss the abundance He's provided for us.

We need to trust and honour Jesus as Lord as well as Saviour. All the way into the deepening relationship that He promises, and that we won't fully experience in this life. But let's get as close as we can.

Our God and Shepherd, Strong Deliverer and Redeemer, thank You for saving me and promising me abundant life. Help me rely on Your unfailing love and live in trusting obedience to Your guidance.

God is Present

*When Jacob awoke from his sleep, he thought, "Surely
the* LORD *is in this place, and I was not aware of it."*
Genesis 28:16, NIV

This is the Jacob who stole his brother's birthright and was now fleeing for his life under the guise of visiting extended family to seek a wife. Not exactly abiding in God's presence at this point in his life, was he?

On the road, "He had a dream in which he saw a stairway resting on the earth, with its top reaching to heaven, and the angels of God were ascending and descending on it" (Genesis 28:12, NIV). And he saw God, who spoke to him.

God had been with Jacob all along, and Jacob hadn't known it. Or lived like it. But when he recognized God, he worshipped.

It's so easy to worship God in church and daily devotions, but then to go into daily life as if He's not present. It's so easy to forget, or to get distracted. If we're not vigilant, intentional, and reminding ourselves to rely on God, we can act as if we're on our own.

Promise-Keeping God, You said You'd never leave nor forsake me, and yet I sometimes live like you've set me loose. Forgive me for being so easily distracted by life, and remind me of Your nearness. Help me learn to live daily in Your presence, confident in You and following Your leading.

Confident that God is at Work

Do not be afraid or discouraged because of this vast
army. For the battle is not yours, but God's... You will
not have to fight this battle. Take up your positions;
stand firm and see the deliverance the LORD will give...
2 Chronicles 20:15b, 17a, NIV

The attacking armies were overwhelming. King Jehoshaphat cried out to God for help and received one of God's more dramatic answers. Then Jehoshaphat led the army out with praise, trusting God to keep His promise.

We don't often know when a crisis is approaching, and even then God rarely tells us what He's going to do and how it'll turn out. But we can know He's always with us, at work and in control.

What if we went into each day, each situation, with praise going ahead of us? Expecting to see God working, even when we don't know how or where?

God promised to never leave nor forsake us. We can go forward in confident praise and trust that He's working. Whether we see Him or not doesn't change the fact of His active presence.

In the looking, we'll be more likely to see Him at work and to respond with gratitude.

God who saves and shepherds me, help me rely on Your grace and power. Whether I see trouble approaching or think I'm safe, help me remember that You are with me. Help me trust Your plan. Train my spirit to step out in praise and to recognize and give thanks for Your touch.

Praying in Trust

The whole Israelite community set out from the Desert
of Sin, travelling from place to place as the LORD
commanded. They camped at Rephidim, but there was
no water for the people to drink. So they quarrelled
with Moses and said, "Give us water to drink."

Moses replied, "Why do you quarrel with me? Why do
you put the LORD to the test?"
Exodus 17:2, NIV

The Israelites knew, better than we often do, that if God is present He can help. And they weren't subject to our common fear that we've already asked too much and used up His gifts for us.

Perhaps they feared abandonment. "If trouble hits, does that mean He left us?"

They knew they had nothing in themselves to convince Him to stay. They didn't think about His character that keeps Him faithful to His commitments, or remind themselves of His covenant that they would be His people and He would be their God.

We often need to be reminded of the same thing. As we persist in prayer, the proper attitude is not to nag for answers but to pray continually in thanksgiving and confidence, and keep alert to recognize the answers... especially if they come in small stages.

Father God, help me remember that You're leading me. Help me trust Your character and Your promises and rely on You. Whatever my needs, I have Jesus. All I have to do is ask for help and be alert to recognize the answer. I understand it may well not come in the form I'd like, but I pray with confidence in Your perfect wisdom and timing.

Reminded of God's Holiness

Mount Sinai was covered with smoke, because the
LORD descended on it in fire. The smoke billowed up
from it like smoke from a furnace, and the whole
mountain trembled violently. As the sound of the
trumpet grew louder and louder, Moses spoke and the
voice of God answered him.
Exodus 19:18-19, NIV

Many Old Testament passages emphasize God's holiness and power, the splendour of His majesty that makes Him unapproachable except by His chosen few like Moses.

Since New Testament days, believers can come to Him in boldness and confidence.

God didn't mellow over the years or decide to have an open-door policy. From the very beginning, He wanted a close relationship with us. Our sin broke that fellowship.

When we read passages like this one from Exodus, it's a good reminder of how holy and terrible our God really is. A good reminder to cultivate a reverent fear of Him even while we've been granted safe access through Jesus Christ.

A good reminder to live in obedient trust before Him in the Spirit's strength, and a good reminder that He who is for us is greater than whatever is against us.

Holy and majestic God, who dwells in inapproachable light, I could never be clean or pure enough on my own to approach You. Thank You for Your grace poured out through Your Son to redeem me and to clothe me in His righteousness. Thank You for the wonder of restored relationship with You. Help me not to take it for granted, and let the open door to Your throne room not lull me into forgetting the holiness that dwells within.

Personal Holiness

You are to be holy to me because I, the LORD, am holy,
and I have set you apart from the nations to be my
own.
Leviticus 20:26, NIV

God chose the people of Israel as a living example or sign to the rest of the world of what relationship with Him would look like. They didn't do very well over the long haul because they weren't very faithful.

Sometimes our churches don't do much better, even though Christians have the Holy Spirit within us instead of depending on hearing Him speak through the occasional prophet.

We're meant as a sign, and we forget that. We get so caught up in our needs and desires that we miss the bigger picture.

Personal holiness is important. Legalism and rigidity aren't appropriate (certainly not attractive displays of the joy of belonging to the Lord) but we need to live in obedient trust in God. We need to "learn the unforced rhythms of grace" (Matthew 11:28, MSG).

We need to be good. Not because we must, but because in Jesus Christ — and only in Him — we can. And living in confident trust in Him even in the hard times shows others the truth about God. It can show us too.

Holy and perfect God, thank You for the privilege of belonging to You, and for the grace that washes me clean. I could never earn the right to be Your child, but You give it freely. Help me to be holy, by Your grace, as You are holy.

A Sign Between Us

Say to the Israelites, "You must observe my Sabbaths.
This will be a sign between me and you for the
generations to come, so you may know that I am the
LORD, who makes you holy."
Exodus 31:13, NIV

For a people liberated from slavery, being commanded to observe a weekly day of rest would be a definite switch.

The Old Testament is filled with visual aids: markers and activities that remind the people who God is and what He has done for them. Exodus 31:13-18 twice calls the Sabbath "a sign between us."

Ignoring the taint that legalism has given the Sabbath, we see some benefits to this gift from God: Work without a break is not healthy, identifying ourselves by our work isn't healthy either, and allowing work to take first place — making it an idol — is dangerously unhealthy.

Also, abstaining from work lets us be still and know that God is God, and it lets us seek Him

Perhaps this is where the Sabbath (for Christians, Sunday or whatever day our work schedules allow us to observe) is a sign between us and God. It's a spiritual marker that celebrates our freedom from slavery to the world's ways and praises the God who rescued us.

And it reminds us that our God is good.

Holy and Almighty God, who chose Israel to show Your glory to the world, thank You for Jesus' blood that makes a way for all people to belong to You. Thank You for the gift of Sabbath rest and its benefits. In the bigger picture, it's still about revealing Your glory to all who can see: You rescue. Your way is best. You are a good Master.

The Source of Our Worth

The seventy-two returned with joy and said, "Lord,
even the demons submit to us in your name."

[Jesus] replied… "I have given you authority…
However, do not rejoice that the spirits submit to you,
but rejoice that your names are written in heaven."
Luke 10:17-20, NIV

No wonder the disciples are pumped: their mission succeeded beyond their wildest dreams. That's a good thing. And Jesus isn't rebuking their excitement. He's giving them perspective.

We know how much harm comes from basing our worth on how well or poorly we perform. And we know what a widespread problem it is even among Christians.

From that angle, this verse provides an antidote to use when we don't meet our own (or others') achievement standards.

Step one: seek God's direction first, not our own or someone else's arbitrary standard. Step two: rely on God's strength. Step three: celebrate success, acknowledge and learn from failure. Ask God's opinion. Step four: know our value isn't performance-based but redemption-based.

Mighty and righteous Creator God, all my righteousness is only filthy rags compared to Your perfection. None of us can earn Your love or approval. Thank You for Your grace that redeemed me and made me acceptable — adopted — valued. Help me truly believe this, at the deepest level. Help me find my worth in You.

Gratitude

Now the people complained about their hardships in
the hearing of the LORD, and when he heard them his
anger was aroused. Then fire from the LORD burned
among them and consumed some of the outskirts of the
camp... The rabble with them began to crave other
food, and again the Israelites started wailing and said,
"If only we had meat to eat!"
Numbers 11:1, 4, NIV

The people complained... the Israelites started wailing...

Despite their trouble, look at all the good things in their lives: God
provided manna to eat. He had rescued them from slavery, and was
leading them to the promised land.

He made a covenant with them, named them as His own people, and
promised to protect them. He gave them priests to make atonement for
their sins. He consented to "dwell" among them in the Tabernacle, and
He spoke to them through His servant, Moses.

They were led by the Ark of the Covenant and the cloud of God

That's a lot of good! What if they'd concentrated on the blessings
instead of their hardships? What if they'd trusted God to do what He
said?

What about us? The Bible says we're welcome to bring Him our pain,
because He is our refuge. But He doesn't want us spreading dissension
and discontent among our brothers and sisters.

*Mighty and rescuing God, holy and faithful, forgive me for the times I
concentrate on the negatives and complain. Open my eyes to the gifts
You give. Help me not to take them for granted, and not to prefer my
own ways. Create in me a grateful heart to worship and to wonder at all
that You're doing in our world.*

Are We Irritating to God?

The LORD said to Moses, "Put back Aaron's staff in
front of the ark of the covenant law, to be kept as a sign
to the rebellious. This will put an end to their
grumbling against me, so that they will not die." Moses
did just as the LORD commanded him.

The Israelites said to Moses, "We will die! We are lost,
we are all lost! Anyone who even comes near the
tabernacle of the LORD will die. Are we all going to
die?"
Numbers 17:10-14, NIV

Do you ever think about how irritating it is for God to put up with us?
Yes, He loves us. He wants to rescue us from the mess we've dug
ourselves into, but so many times we just don't get it.

The Israelites didn't get it, either. God brought them out of Egypt to bring
them into the promised land, but all they did was grumble and complain
and wish they were back under Pharaoh's thumb.

The context of today's passage is that some of the people had accused
Moses and Aaron of elevating themselves as better than the rest.

God settled it in dramatic fashion, destroying the usurpers and giving
the people an enduring sign of approved leadership, so they would quit
complaining and would not die. And what did they immediately do? They
yelled, "We're all gonna die!" And they exaggerated: "We can't even go
near the tabernacle now!"

What if they'd trusted and obeyed? What if we trusted and obeyed,
instead of misunderstanding and overreacting?

*Holy and patient God, how simple life would be if I'd just let You
shepherd me, instead of trying to be in charge of my own life. But like
sheep, sometimes I wander away. Teach me to seek You first, to trust
You. To stop ascribing frightening motives to You and instead
remember You are the only trustworthy one. Help me believe You
instead of trusting my own fallible understanding.*

The Lord Will Fulfill His Purpose for Me

The LORD will fulfill his purpose for me;
your love, O LORD, endures forever—
do not abandon the works of your hands.
Psalm 138:8, NIV 1984*

Not everyone has a large and visible calling-type of purpose, but we're each called to the "long obedience in the same direction," to the faithfulness and openness to God that lets us touch many people's lives in small ways.

And it's *His purpose*, not *our plans*. This takes the pressure off. Instead of trying to keep track of everything and move it forward, we need to be looking to see what He's going to do in any situation. What He might want to do through us.

We're under authority. We're neither the strategist nor the victim of circumstances. We are vessels the Potter has made, to fill and pour out as He sees best. And on the other side of this life we'll look back from His perspective and see that He has done all things well.

"The Lord will fulfill His purpose for me..."

Simple. Straightforward. We can hold onto that today.

Father, help me keep perspective and balance. Help me not get too self-absorbed or take too much responsibility for my own usefulness. Help me trust and obey You.

* The 2011 NIV says "The LORD will vindicate me..."

Handle With Care

Do your best to present yourself to God as one
approved, a worker who does not need to be ashamed
and who correctly handles the word of truth.
2 Timothy 2:15, NIV

What does it mean to correctly handle the word of truth?

If we prayerfully study the Bible, mindful of context and culture, looking for what God really says instead of for ways to justify our own opinions, we're learning to handle it correctly. We can learn to live by its precepts and to trust God's character.

But there's more: To correctly handle the word of truth, we have to *believe it*. Not just believe intellectually that it's the inspired, inerrant Word of God, but believe the promises God whispers to our hearts and spirits.

Believe *God* instead of believing the lies that try to snare us.

If we're feeling scared, are we going to believe the fear and its many whispered lies about inadequacy and failure, or believe the truth? God is with us. In Christ we can do all things. And if we fail, He can do something with the pieces and He will still love us.

If we're feeling down, will we believe what that insinuates about our worth, or will we receive the truth that God delights in each one of us?

Promise-keeping God, thank You for Your written Word. Help me recognize Your truth, and help me to use that truth in defence against the lies of the enemy, the culture around me, and my own feelings and misunderstandings. Help me believe You, not just in my mind, but in my heart and spirit. Help me act on the truth You give, so that others can see the difference You make.

To Praise the Lord

It is good to praise the LORD
and make music to your name, O Most High,
proclaiming your love in the morning
and your faithfulness at night.
Psalm 92:1-2, NIV

Some of the reasons it's good to praise the Lord: It's right and fitting, and He deserves it, it makes us stop and notice what He's done and who He is, and those who don't know Him may hear and learn.

It restores our perspective on our troubles, encourages our faith, and encourage others' faith too. It restores our hope and causes us to flourish, to stay fresh and green, and to bear fruit.

The header for this psalm says it's "For the Sabbath day." As Christians, we're invited to live in the Lord's rest day by day, moment by moment, but there's still something special about taking a Sabbath break.

It's a chance to stop, breathe, and renew. To spend some time with God and remember who — and how big — He is. To regain perspective.

Holy and magnificent God, it does me good to get my eyes off myself and onto Your glory, and the more I look at You the more I see to praise. How great is our God, and how blessed we are to be Your redeemed people! Please open my eyes to see You more clearly, and soften my heart to adore You.

Fear and Lies

You grumbled in your tents and said, "The LORD hates
us; so he brought us out of Egypt to deliver us into the
hands of the Amorites to destroy us."
Deuteronomy 1:27, NIV

It seems we have a propensity for believing lies over the truth.

Here, Moses is referring to the people's reaction to the spies' report of
the Promised Land, when instead of entering the land they ended up
wandering in the desert for 40 years (see Deuteronomy 1).

You can hear the fear in the Israelites' words. And there were indeed
giants in those hills. But instead of bringing their fear to God,
remembering that He's bigger, relying on His promises, they went the
other way with it and accused Him of hating them.

We may be more subtle, but don't we do the same? We'll feel anxious
or put upon, maybe discouraged or even resentful, and believe the
feeling instead of investigating its origin to root out the lie. We fall,
instead of standing on the truth.

Holy and sovereign God in whom is no lie or shadow, if not for Your
grace, patience and love, I'd be doomed. Teach me to recognize the
enemy's lies and to rely on Your word and Your character. Thank You
for setting me free; now help me learn to live in that freedom and in
confidence in You.

Feelings and Emotions

He was despised and rejected by mankind,
a man of suffering, and familiar with pain.
Like one from whom people hide their faces
he was despised, and we held him in low esteem.
Isaiah 53:3, NIV

Trusting God instead of ourselves means not believing false feelings: the vague unease, dissatisfaction or sadness that can have us living "in the dumps" instead of in the confidence in our heritage in Christ.

Then there are true feelings. Things like grief, fear, loneliness. Anger. Happiness — why does that one not come around as much as the others? If angry, we're still responsible to refrain from delivering a sinful response. Grieving, we still need to treat others in love.

Jesus experienced emotions. There's nothing wrong with them, and they're a key ingredient in what makes us human. It's not healthy to suppress or deny them, but we still can't let them rule us. Recognizing them can help us rely on God's sustaining grace in our daily lives.

In the words of author/speaker Grace Fox, if we feel fear about something God calls us to do, we need to obey anyway — to "do it afraid." Or do it sad, or whatever. And He *is* calling us to do things.

God our Maker, You know my weakness and You promise to give wisdom when I ask. Teach me to discern between deceptive feelings and genuine emotions. Teach me to rely on Your truth and to reject the lies. And help me rightly handle my emotions so I'll be able to trust Your care, neither denying what I feel nor being ruled by it.

When God Says No

At that time I pleaded with the LORD: "...Let me go
over and see the good land beyond the Jordan — that
fine hill country and Lebanon."

But because of you the LORD was angry with me and
would not listen to me. "That is enough," the LORD
said. "Do not speak to me anymore about this matter."
Deuteronomy 3:23, 25-26, NIV

This is part of Moses' final address to the Israelites, and he's referring to the incident where he lost his temper with disastrous results (see Numbers 20).

Moses blames the people, who surely tried his patience, but he was the one who acted in a way that didn't honour God. He tells them he asked God to relent and let him into the Promised Land. But God said no. Not just "no," but "Don't ask Me again." Period.

There are other times in the Bible where God gives the people what they want when they insist on it, even though it's not in their best interests. Psalm 106:15 says in the King James Version, "And he gave them their request; but sent leanness into their soul."

It comes down to trust: God is good, and He knows best. And He has the right to make choices — from His greater wisdom — that we may not like.

We're called to persist in prayer until we get an answer — not until we get the answer we want. Silence may be a sign to keep praying. "No" is an answer.

Mighty and holy God, You are all-wise and You love us. Help me to pray with praise that You listen and answer. And help me to hear Your answers, be they yes or no. Grant me faith to trust Your goodness, and obedience to not push for my own way when You reveal that it's different than Yours.

Careful to Remember

Be careful that you do not forget the LORD your God,
failing to observe his commands, his laws and his
decrees that I am giving you this day. Otherwise, when
you eat and are satisfied... then your heart will become
proud and you will forget the LORD your God, who
brought you out of Egypt, out of the land of slavery.
Deuteronomy 8:11-12a, 14, NIV

After everything Israel saw God do to rescue them from Egypt and bring them to the Promised Land, someone from a different planet might ask how they could be in danger of forgetting Him.

As humans, we know better. We still do the same thing.

We start off well, depending on God and walking closely with Him. Especially when times are hard and we see our need.

But it's so easy over time to rely more and more on our own strength and understanding. We slip into trusting what we do instead of trusting the God who made us. We start fighting our own battles with the universe. We forget to pray and to do our battles in His name and strength.

Father God, my Saviour and Deliverer, forgive my forgetfulness and draw my spirit nearer to Your Spirit. Grow me in dependence on You, teach me to walk closely with You and to be careful to stay near Your side. Help me remember how You brought me out of sin's slavery into Your grace. Help me to love, honour and worship You and live in Your light.

Enticed Away?

Be careful, or you will be enticed to turn away and
worship other gods and bow down to them.
Deuteronomy 11:16, NIV

This is part of Moses' warning to the people of Israel as they're getting ready to enter the Promised Land. Idol worship is rampant among the nations they're to evict, and they need to stay set apart for God.

There's much to entice *us* away too: possessions, problems, pleasures... With multi-tasking and constant communication and noise, our thoughts scatter like seeds in the wind.

We forget.

Being careful takes intentional effort. Moses had some suggestions for the people that will help us too: We need to talk about God, with our family and friends. Not to preach, in this context, but to teach our children and to encourage and remind our believing peers.

Visual reminders help. We may not tie them to our foreheads or write them on our door posts as Moses said, but art, jewellery, and symbols are all good reminders as long as we remember to think about what they represent.

We need to keep God as part of each day, all day long and wherever we are. One way is to consciously notice the beauty of creation around us and to remember to thank God for His gifts.

Sovereign Lord, You have called me to be one of the people belonging to You. I want to be faithful. You know how easily distracted I am. I need help! Please teach me to be careful not to be enticed away. And when my focus slips, please draw me quickly back. There is no one like You, God, none other worthy of worship and adoration.

Love, Listen, Hold... Live

Now choose life, so that you and your children may
live and that you may love the LORD your God, listen
to his voice, and hold fast to him. For the LORD is your
life...
Deuteronomy 30:19b-20a, NIV

Moses is winding up his recitation of God's faithfulness to the Israelites in their journey. Their choices will shape their future. He's previewed the blessings and warned of the curses. He leaves them with a motto for life.

"Love the LORD Your God": it's a heart and spirit response. It has active implications — don't just feel it, do it.

Listen to His voice. Be diligent to hear, be diligent to obey.

Hold fast to Him. Cling to Him. Rely on Him as an anchor and fortress.

Why?

We always need a reason why, even if it's just that God says so and we choose to trust Him. Moses answers the question: "The LORD is your life" (Deuteronomy 30:20, NIV).

Holy and eternal God, You are my life. I'm not whole when I'm not close to You. Help me love You, help me listen to You, help me cling to You, so I can live. Thank You for such grace that gives me this gift!

Our God is With Us

Who among you fears the LORD
and obeys the word of his servant?
Let the one who walks in the dark,
who has no light,
trust in the name of the LORD
and rely on their God.
Isaiah 50:10, NIV

Our first desire in hard times is for escape, and if we can't have it right away, we at least need to know there's the proverbial light at the end of the tunnel. Even Jesus focused on the joy ahead of Him when His road went through the Cross (Hebrews 12:2).

Sometimes we can't even see that light ahead, either because the path looks so long or because the tunnel bends. What do we hold onto then?

God. His character, His promises, His presence with us even if we feel all alone.

We hope and pray things will get better. We thank God for what He's doing that we can't see. And sometimes we just have to keep on keeping on, acting in faith that God is still good and in control.

Sovereign and loving God, I praise You for Your care and for the many times You make my path easier. Thank You for sending Jesus as my Redeemer, so that no matter what life brings, I can walk through it with You and be assured of a place with You when it ends. Give me the faith I need to trust in You in the dark and in the light, and the courage to live boldly as Your child.

Intentional Holiness

Everyone who competes in the games goes into strict
training. They do it to get a crown that will not last,
but we do it to get a crown that will last forever.
1 Corinthians 9:25, NIV

How seriously the Apostle Paul takes spiritual growth and development, compared with how casually it's often treated these days.

Even when we know it's important and we try our best, it's easy to *wish* ourselves more spiritually mature and then forget to actually practise the spiritual disciplines that will help us grow.

A quick search of BibleGateway.com turned up six variations on the command to "be holy because God is holy." We know it's not so we can earn His love, nor for legalistic purposes. It's spiritual training, where outward acts deepen inner devotion.

Part of the call to holiness is so barriers won't grow between us and God after Jesus took them all down. The repeated act of recognizing and confessing our sins of commission or omission keeps the barriers broken down and sensitizes our spirits to God's way.

Perhaps the main reason, though, is so our devotion to God will show others how incredibly worthy we know Him to be: worthy of our obedience, worship and love. After all, if we don't seem very captivated by Him, what will attract them to consider Him?

Living and holy God, You've saved me and called me to be a person set apart for Yourself, and You've promised to grow me into Your Son's image. Help me take this seriously, with the right motivation, and teach me to live a holy life that worships You. Thank You for the privilege of being restored to relationship with You.

Trusting God's Love

Immense in mercy and with an incredible love, he
embraced us... Now God has us where he wants us,
with all the time in this world and the next to shower
grace and kindness upon us in Christ Jesus. Saving is
all his idea, and all his work. All we do is trust him
enough to let him do it.
Ephesians 2:4, 5a, 7, 8, MSG

What amazing love is this, that "where God wants us" is close to Him, in restored relationship! And that in patience and grace He will take the time to train us, heal us, and shape us into the potential He's set within us.

He saved us, He is saving us, He will save us.

The "all we do is trust Him enough to let Him do it" is that simple, and that hard. Choosing to trust God's love, and that He's shaping us even through the things we don't like, is a hard obedience. It's "a long obedience in the same direction."

God who is Peace, the perfect peace of completeness when I'm in relationship with You, thank You for a love beyond what I can imagine. Thank You for rescue and for renewal. Help me, deep in my spirit, to know and rely on Your love and to trust You enough to let You work in me.

Built into God's Home

God is building a home. He's using us all —
irrespective of how we got here — in what he is
building. He used the apostles and prophets for the
foundation. Now he's using you, fitting you in brick by
brick, stone by stone, with Christ Jesus as the
cornerstone that holds all the parts together. We see it
taking shape day after day — a holy temple built by
God, all of us built into it, a temple in which God is
quite at home.
Ephesians 2:20-22, MSG

Don't you love the way The Message puts this? God building a home, fitting each brick and stone, each of us built into it.

The individual bricks and stones may be a variety of sizes, shapes, colours and textures, but each one has a place, and we need to cooperate with God as He fits us into our spot.

As the builder, God applies the mortar to join us together, but first He cleans us. You wouldn't stick a dirty brick into a wall, neither for aesthetics nor for optimal adherence.

So much dirt floats around a construction site. What might that look like in our congregations and other Christian groups? Irritation builds up, or we start noticing that others aren't doing things our way. We focus on weaknesses instead of strengths.

Creator God who loves and saves us, thank You for building each of Your children into a holy temple where You can dwell. You've cleaned me and you're building me, but help me remember the ongoing need to keep clean. Forgive me for the gunk that accumulates so quickly, and help me keep working at it. Thinner layers are easier to scrub off, and they don't dim my shine as badly.

Anxiety-Busting

David said to the Philistine, "You come against me
with sword and spear and javelin, but I come against
you in the name of the LORD Almighty, the God of the
armies of Israel, whom you have defied."
1 Samuel 17:45, NIV

Other translations render "the LORD Almighty" as "the Lord of Hosts" or "the Lord of Armies." He is God, ruling over all.

When anxiety seeps into our spirits, we can fight it with deliberate focus on God and with determined praise for who He is and what He does.

Scripture is key, especially verses that remind us of His strength and authority. Remembering what He's done in the past is another good strategy. After all, He never changes or runs out of power. Worship music helps, because often He may pierce the oppression with a song.

These are battles we can't fight on our own, although we're called to give our best effort.

As we do our part, the Holy Spirit is so ready to meet us there. Not always right away, but if we persist He'll eventually make His presence known. He's there all along, but we can't grow if we don't practice depending on Him even when He's silent.

Mighty God, Lord of Hosts, thank You for the promise that You are with me. Thank You for Your light in my heart and Your grace that frees me. I'm under Your authority and Your protection. My times are in Your hands. Help me not to fear, but to trust and obey. And I praise You for the many times and ways You rescue me from anxiety and despair. You are good, and worthy of worship.

The Goal: No Fussing

Instead, I have calmed and quieted myself,
like a weaned child who no longer cries for its mother's
milk.
Yes, like a weaned child is my soul within me.
O Israel, put your hope in the LORD —
now and always.
Psalm 131:2-3, NLT

Some days we fight the good fight, and some days anxiety sneaks in there as fast as we push it out. Self-pity swirls into a whirlpool, and the best we can do by holding onto God is to keep from going down the funnel.

We try to anchor in the truth about God, but then we look back at the feelings and are undone.

Today's verses speak of where we need to be, resting in the Father's care.

A weaned child... able to sit on a parent's lap, or to play nearby, not fussing or seeing Mommy as only a source of "what I want."

Some parents can't provide, even healthy mother's milk if malnutrition is severe enough. Some parents won't provide. Won't love. We know God's not like that. He can meet our needs, when and how His wisdom knows is best. And He always loves us.

Abba God, Papa, whisper quiet to my soul so I can rest as if in Your arms, secure in Your love and provision without the incessant clamour of anxiety. I can't deny the realities and possibilities that tempt me to fret, but I can believe in You. Help me trust You more.

Never Forgetting the Good

Let all that I am praise the LORD;
with my whole heart, I will praise his holy name.
Let all that I am praise the LORD;
may I never forget the good things he does for me.
Psalm 103:1-2, NLT

When we're praising God, worshipping Him, we're most at peace. Self is lost in the wonder of who He is.

Ingratitude gets in the way and steals our focus, like the snake in the garden. There's so much to be thankful for, but we can forget it in the face of a perceived lack or slight.

Keeping a gratitude list helps, especially if there's a (short) daily quota, because it keeps us looking for the good instead of the bad.

Reading back through that list helps too. Remembering warms us and helps us praise God.

God my Provider, You give richly: not just materially but gifts that heal and grow my spirit. Thank You for the many ways You touch my life, sometimes so personally that no one else would recognize the love message in the touch. Grow me to praise You with all that I am. Let me thrive in Your care.

Convinced that God is Able

*[Abraham] was fully convinced that God is able to do
whatever he promises.*
Romans 4:21, NLT

Abraham's faith wasn't passive belief. It was belief with obedience. Active faith. Secure faith, anchored in God's character and ability.

Sometimes the tricky part is discerning what God has promised. Then there are other times when we see something we want in Scripture and interpret it to fit our desires.

But God has given plenty of legitimate promises — in writing — that we can rely on no matter what our circumstances.

He loves us (John 3:16). He will cleanse and forgive us when we bring our sins to Him (1 John 1:9). He will always be with us (Matthew 28:20). He will give wisdom when we ask (James 1:5). He's our source of mercy and grace in time of need (Hebrews 4:16).

And many more. These are things we can be fully convinced God can and will do. Remembering and relying on His promises changes how we react to our circumstances and lets us walk in victory instead of defeat.

God my Refuge, my Strong Tower, I would be nothing without You. You created me, You save me, and You sustain me. I believe; help my unbelief. Help me grow in faith to become fully confident like Abraham that You can, and You will, do all that You've promised, in Your way and in Your time.

Moment of Choice

Therefore, dear brothers and sisters, you have no
obligation to do what your sinful nature urges you to
do.
Romans 8:12, NLT

Paul is writing about how those who belong to Jesus are to "no longer follow our sinful nature but instead follow the Spirit" (Romans 8:4b, NLT). He says we're free from our old ways. Now we have to choose: will we stick with those destructive patterns, or will we obey the Holy Spirit?

As well as the "big ticket" sins, there are a lot of little things our sinful nature urges us to do: things we either don't notice as sin or that we think are just part of who we are. Things like grumbling or self-pity.

Even things that aren't really sin, but aren't good for us. Like that second — or third — chocolate chip cookie when we're trying to lose weight. Or "just one more chapter" when it's past bedtime.

We're told there's a moment of choice between stimulus and response, but it's easy to respond before we can think. May we learn to stop, look, and listen before acting.

God of grace and mercy, who ransomed me from sin and makes a way for me to be clean and holy in Your presence, open my eyes to the temptations I still give in to. Remind me that because of Jesus' sacrifice and resurrection I have absolutely no obligation to do what my sinful nature urges me to do. Give me a willing heart, and help me to choose those things that please You. Thank You for setting me free.

Prince of Peace

But he was pierced for our transgressions,
he was crushed for our iniquities;
the punishment that brought us peace was on him,
and by his wounds we are healed.
Isaiah 53:5, NIV

Jesus is the Prince of Peace.

Prince speaks to His authority. *Peace* is part of His character, but it's also something He gave His life to bring us.

Peace with God: We're adopted into God's family, loved and welcomed. He washed away the sin and shame and we don't need to hide anymore. Nor will God hide His face from us.

Peace with one another: We can overlook the surface irritants and choose to give grace to one another in the same way that it's been given to us. We can work together, united in belonging to the Prince of Peace, who enables — and commands — us to love one another.

Peace with ourselves: He knows our depths but loves and accepts us. We can accept ourselves. He has saved us and is saving us. We can cooperate with Him and rely on His promises.

God the Son, You are my Prince of Peace. Thank You for rescuing me. Thank You for making me whole and giving me peace with You, with others and with myself. Help me do all I can, strengthened by Your mighty power at work in me, to preserve and expand this peace. Help me be a peacemaker.

Not Just Going to Heaven

But he was pierced for our transgressions,
he was crushed for our iniquities;
the punishment that brought us peace was on him,
and by his wounds we are healed.
Isaiah 53:5, NIV

"Why should I believe in Jesus?"

"So you can be saved from your sins and go to Heaven when you die."

As Sunday school kids, that's how many of us thought. But there's so much more to it than that. Even "saved from your sins" means more than being forgiven. It means freedom from sin's domination and from the destructive mindsets we've accepted. Freedom from ourselves, too!

And healing for our brokenness. Peace for our anxious spirits. Forgiveness... and the strength to forgive. Most of all, it means a relationship with the God who formed the universe and who welcomes us like a longing parent welcomes a long-lost child.

He's *with* us. He's our strength for today and our hope for tomorrow. He won't leave us, always understands us, and His presence makes the difference in whatever we're going through.

Holy and merciful God, people were all damaged goods, without hope of healing. But Jesus came willingly to be our Saviour. Thank You for the grace to believe. Open my spirit to receive the full extent of the healing and restoration You want to work in my life, and help me to be a living example to those who still need to come to You.

Committed to God

I will also bless the foreigners who commit themselves
to the LORD,
who serve him and love his name,
who worship him and do not desecrate the Sabbath day
of rest,
and who hold fast to my covenant.
Isaiah 56:6, NLT

Have we committed ourselves to God — *bound* ourselves to Him, in some translations? We did at the moment of our salvation, but do we remember it and live it as strongly as we'd intended?

Committed to God: to belong to Him and to rely on His protection and grace.

Serving God: not to please ourselves, not to please others.

Loving His name: loving who He is, loving and proclaiming His character and reputation.

Worshipping Him: honouring, praising, obeying Him as God alone; keeping our minds and hearts fixed on Him.

Not desecrating the Sabbath: embracing and receiving the rest He gives. (For those who see the New Testament Sabbath rest as more than observing one day as holy, as a daily and ongoing rest, this is even more profound.)

Holding fast to His covenant (His new covenant, as established by the shed blood of Jesus): clinging to our salvation and walking in His light.

God who is worthy of worship and praise, God who saves us and changes us from foreigners to adopted daughters and sons, help me to fully commit myself to You. Help me serve and love You, worship You and live to Your glory. Help me live like the person You've called me to be, and keep my heart fixed on You.

Antidote for Discouragement

Let us run with perseverance the race marked out for
us, fixing our eyes on Jesus, the pioneer and perfecter
of faith. For the joy set before him he endured the
cross, scorning its shame, and sat down at the right
hand of the throne of God. Consider him who endured
such opposition from sinners, so that you will not grow
weary and lose heart.
Hebrews 12: 1b-3, NIV

Sometimes it feels like there's an overwhelming amount of pain in the world. Even if it's not touching us personally, we know it's touching plenty of others. The future looks dark, and it's getting darker.

The Last Trumpet might sound awfully good right about now. But it's not yet time, or our ears would be ringing.

There's still work to do, people to love, mercy to show. So how do we keep from "growing weary and losing heart"?

We look at how Jesus did it. He listened closely to the Father, and only did what He saw the Father doing. He knew the Cross was coming, but He stayed in the moment with the people around Him. He didn't try to carry the pain before its time. When it *was* time, He kept focused on His ultimate goal.

Father, this world will get worse before You make it better. I'm glad I don't know how bad things will get. And I'm glad I know You and Your promises for the end. Forgive me when I look at the circumstances and get weighted down. Train me to keep my eyes fixed on Jesus, my example and my Saviour, and to keep my heart fixed on You.

What Does Victory Mean?

But thank God! He gives us victory over sin and death
through our Lord Jesus Christ.
1 Corinthians 15:57, NLT

Jesus won the ultimate victory, and if we trust Him, we'll spend eternity with Him when we die. But in the here and now, what are some of the ways we have victory in Him?

In Christ, we can replace the devil's lies with truth. We can learn to see with His perspective instead of our own. We don't have to feel sorry for ourselves, and we find strength beyond our own.

We're forgiven when we sin, freed from the tyranny of sin, and we can be secure in His acceptance, instead of fearing rejection or failure.

We can love when it doesn't come naturally, give grace instead of retaliating, and we have access to the God of the universe, who loves us. We belong.

Merciful and holy God, thank You for rescuing me and for promising to never leave me nor reject me. Forgive me when I forget the benefits of being Your child, and help me learn to be secure in Your victory.

Self-pity or God-praise?

Are they servants of Christ? (I am out of my mind to
talk like this.) I am more. I have worked much harder,
been in prison more frequently, been flogged more
severely, and been exposed to death again and again.
2 Corinthians 11:23, NIV

The Corinthian believers have been listening to trendier leaders than Paul, and while those leaders may have a better delivery, they aren't delivering the truth. In this passage, Paul is reminding these Christians of his "credentials."

He's not talking like a victim, nor a beaten-down fighter. Instead, he's boasting about his persecutions. Not that he's proud of the suffering, as such.

He's saying "See how much Jesus trusts me — He knows I'll keep focused on Him, and others will hear." And "See how good He is to sustain me and to advance His kingdom even when its enemies throw everything they've got."

That's what happened in the jail in Philippi when Paul and Silas were singing praises to God. They showed how to "rejoice in the Lord always" (Philippians 4:4, NIV).

Praise and thanksgiving really do work when we want to keep our spirits set on God.

Father, Sustainer of our spirits, most of us haven't faced the abuse Paul did, and a lot of what we've endured hasn't been because of persecution. But we still need to keep our eyes on You and our hearts tuned in praise and worship. You are God. Help me anchor in You. Strengthen me so others will see Your goodness and love even when I'm in hard times.

Fear of the God Who Loves Us

Jesus said to the paralyzed man, "Be encouraged, my
child! Your sins are forgiven."

Then Jesus turned to the paralyzed man and said,
"Stand up, pick up your mat, and go home!"

Fear swept through the crowd as they saw this happen.
And they praised God for giving humans such
authority.
Matthew 9:2b, 6b, 8, NLT

Fear of the Lord is sometimes a difficult concept to understand, although the Bible says it's the basis for wisdom (Psalm 111:10).

People explain it as "reverence for the Lord," and that helps. Others say, "fear God or fear everything else." That makes it a bit clearer.

Look at the crowd's response in today's verse. Picture yourself in the crowd. Wouldn't you be afraid? This is power beyond our imagining. This is the God who is good, but who is not safe.

This is the God who is bigger than whatever situation threatens to paralyze us with fear. He doesn't guarantee to provide a miraculous way out, but He does promise to be with us. And with Him in trouble is better than on our own in a safer place.

Holy and mighty God, a glimpse of Your power could undo me, yet I'm drawn to Your presence. Help me understand and believe that I'm held in Your keeping, and that You are stronger than anything I could fear. Help me accept the paradox that in Your love and grace, You may not rescue me from what I fear, and help me trust that Your presence with me will somehow work even the darkness for good in Your time.

Waste or Worship?

*While [Jesus] was eating, a woman came in with a
beautiful alabaster jar of expensive perfume and poured
it over his head. The disciples were indignant when
they saw this. "What a waste!" they said.*
Matthew 26:7-8, NLT

Jesus had been telling the disciples that He was going to die. Of course they didn't understand. The human brain could never conceive of a plan on the scale of Jesus' sacrifice and resurrection.

They were good men, devoted to Jesus and learning His ways. Giving to the poor was important. They understood that, even if they didn't get the "coming death" part.

But they were so caught up in "the plan" as they knew it that they missed another thread in God's tapestry. God had a different assignment for this woman on this day, and they would have blocked it by "depending on their own understanding" (Proverbs 3:5, NLT).

Anointing Jesus this way expressed her love and gratitude, but it was also a visual prophecy like so many in the Old Testament. She demonstrated what was to come. And her tender gesture must have blessed Jesus' heart. He knew what was ahead.

God our Father, Master Artist, Your work is detailed beyond imagining. Help me listen closely to know Your leading, and help me obey with a willing heart. Give me courage when what You ask is different from others' expectations. And give me grace to recognize Your leading in others' lives when it doesn't look the same as the way You work in me. Thank You for the whole picture, which only You can see. Help me trust Your ways.

Performance-based Living

Watch out! Don't do your good deeds publicly, to be
admired by others, for you will lose the reward from
your Father in heaven.
Matthew 6:1, NLT

The warning here is more than just "live to please God and don't show off." It's also "don't be a people-pleaser."

It implies we're not to do good deeds to impress, but also not to appease or placate. Nor to live and act in fear of rejection, fear of not measuring up, fear of being yelled at or misunderstood.

The enemy of our souls would whisper lies and inflame our fears of failure and rejection, but this verse doesn't refer to a frowning God who will disqualify us from receiving something good if we've operated in people-pleaser mode. Or even if we've been showing off.

Our motives will cost us the reward we could have earned. It's an opportunity cost, to use an accounting term. It's not a punishment. God has the reward and wants to give it, but we have a part to play.

Holy and majestic God who hears my quietest prayers, forgive me for the times I've acted "to be seen by people" rather than to please Your heart. Thank You for saving me and for loving me too much to leave me in this damaged behaviour pattern. Thank You for today's and tomorrow's opportunities to do good with a God-ward heart and to earn that reward in the Holy Spirit's power. Thank You for the freedom that confidence in You brings, including freedom from fear of other people.

Doing Life God's Way

He led me to a place of safety;
he rescued me because he delights in me.
The LORD rewarded me for doing right;
he restored me because of my innocence.
Psalm 18:19-20, NLT

God had anointed David as the new king, to replace Saul. David believed it, but he wouldn't fight Saul, and refused to kill him when the chance presented itself. He did it God's way, trusted God to fulfil His promise, and refused to harm "the LORD's anointed one" (1 Samuel 24:10, NLT).

God had put Saul on the throne, so David waited for God to take him off.

This is the "doing right" and innocence David speaks of here. Everyone sins and misses the mark of what God has for us, and David wasn't claiming perfection. But in the long hiding from Saul, he resisted the temptation to do it his way and waited for God.

That's what God rewards. How we conduct ourselves on the journey is perhaps more important than reaching the end. There's more at stake than we see with human eyes.

Sovereign God who builds up and takes down, I praise You for the plans You have for each of us, plans for a future and a hope, plans of promise. In my times of stress, help me remember to choose Your way over any short-cuts or schemes that human nature may suggest. Help me live worthy of the Kingdom.

What's on Your Mind?

May the words of my mouth
and the meditation of my heart
be pleasing to you,
O LORD, my rock and my redeemer.
Psalm 19:14, NLT

This is a familiar passage often prayed before meetings or in other gatherings where we desire God to be honoured. In that context, it applies to "what we discuss and decide or plan here."

But what about all the other things in our hearts when we're alone?

Isn't that what *meditation* means, to focus on or rehearse? To dwell on? To, perhaps, stew over?

How many times do we let our thoughts swim with negatives and complaints? We wish a conversation could have gone differently, we pick at what we didn't like about Sunday service, we fret over grievances.

Not exactly the "Fix your thoughts on what is true, and honorable, and right, and pure, and lovely, and admirable. Think about things that are excellent and worthy of praise" (Philippians 4:8, NLT) that we're called to do.

Holy and good God, who searches my thoughts and knows my heart, forgive my sins and retrain me in Your ways. May the words of my mouth and the meditation of my heart be pleasing to You. And when they're not, please get my attention and bring me back on track. Don't let anything pull me away from nearness to You.

With Us is God

And be sure of this: I am with you always, even to the
end of the age.
Matthew 28:20b, NLT

Sometimes hearing a familiar concept re-worded or presented in a different way helps us take a fresh look — or listen.

We usually see *Immanuel* translated "God with us," but it can also be rendered as "with us is God."

Most of us are more used to hearing the traditional "God with us." It's familiar. Maybe we take it too much for granted.

"With us is God."

Because of that truth, we can be encouraged. Reassured. Comforted. Wherever we are, we're not alone or abandoned. Even if it's a hard place.

We can also be motivated: don't slack off, because He's here. We can't hide anything. Yes, He understands and forgives, but because we love Him, we don't want to disappoint Him.

God my Maker and my Saviour, ever-present with me, help me remember You are near. Help me take courage, and help me be alert and obedient. Teach me a healthy fear of You, and deliver me from the unhealthy fear that would ruin me. Help me love and serve You, and let others see Your love in me.

Where Our Hope Is

Let your unfailing love surround us, LORD,
for our hope is in you alone.
Psalm 33:22, NLT

How often can we honestly say our hope is in God alone?

We rely on what He's given: jobs, doctors, physical strength, and mental abilities. It would be silly not to make full use of them — after all, isn't that why He provided them?

But let's remember to look deeper and see where we're really anchoring our hope.

If some or all of our resources are taken away, God will still be God, still here, still loving and powerful.

Father, help me remember to put my hope and trust fully in You instead of in what You give. Teach me to recognize Your hand at work, and give me a grateful, praising heart for all You've done.

Because God Said So

For you have rescued me from death;
you have kept my feet from slipping.
So now I can walk in your presence, O God,
in your life-giving light.
Psalm 56:13, NLT

In this psalm David declares his trust in God and praises God for His promise. Twice he asks "What can men do to me?"

The first time, he follows with a list of what his enemies want to do to him. The danger is real. He asks God to prevent them from harming him. He reminds himself of how intimately God cares for him, and then he reaffirms his choice to trust in God.

Three times in the psalm, he refers to what God "has promised," likely about David becoming king.

At this point he's still on the run from King Saul and is in the hands of the Philistines. Logic and faith say he can't be killed before God accomplishes His purpose, so David has confidence that his enemies won't be allowed to kill him.

Most of us don't have a specific, personal promise from God guaranteeing we won't be harmed. We do have lots of promises, though. And if we don't have physical enemies, we still have spiritual ones that would bind or hamper us and keep us from the abundant life that God promises.

Father, Saviour, show me the individual promises to cling to for protection from the unseen forces, thoughts, and behaviour patterns that want to deny the new life You've promised to grow in me. Yes, they could do it — if not for Your promises. Help me be confident in You, help me walk in Your presence and in Your life-giving light.

The Best Response to Trouble

Be exalted, O God, above the highest heavens.
May your glory shine over all the earth.
Psalm 57:11, NLT

This is another David-hunted-by-Saul psalm. It's only 11 verses long, and twice David repeats the lines above.

He cries out to God for help, describing his danger and the strength of his enemies. Then he first calls for God to be exalted and glorified. The context implies "bring glory to Your name by defeating my powerful enemies."

When we look at troubles and dangers and ask God to be glorified, that's usually what we mean too.

But David keeps on writing. Now he's talking about his confidence in God, how he can praise God and how he'll thank Him. Present and future. Because of God's unfailing love and faithfulness.

Then he repeats "Be exalted... may your glory shine."

David's faith response, and his confident trust in God despite the circumstances, continue to exalt and glorify God. Isn't that something we can do, too?

Holy and majestic God Most High, be exalted. Let Your glory shine. May I see Your intervention in the troubles that shake me — and my world. Strengthen my faith so I can stand like David in hard times. Be exalted, let Your glory shine through me as Your child, as I trust You.

When Joy is Scarce

You satisfy me more than the richest feast.
I will praise you with songs of joy...
Because you are my helper,
I sing for joy in the shadow of your wings.
Psalm 63:5, 7 NLT

When joy is scarce in our hearts, it feels like David's "parched and weary land" (Psalm 63:1).

Today's two verses from Psalm 63 are a strong antidote, if we can let our minds and spirits truly believe them.

God satisfies. He is enough, and abundantly more than enough.

This negates the joy-drain of discontent. We need to practice intentional gratitude, not just for His gifts, but for who He is.

God helps. He is our ever-present helper and sustainer, and His strong hand holds us securely (Psalm 63:8).

This eliminates anxiety, if we really allow ourselves to believe it.

God, You are all I need. I believe. Help my unbelief. Help me realize, accept, and rely on the truth of who You are and what that means in my life. Help me be confident and secure in You, aware of the many ways You satisfy and delight.

Joy and Security

Because you are my helper,
I sing for joy in the shadow of your wings.
I cling to you;
your strong right hand holds me securely.
Psalm 63:7-8, NLT

Although this psalm is short, it's powerful. David is longing for God, and he's aware of his enemies pressing in, yet the verses overflow with words like *praise* and *joy* and *sing*. He has his faith perspective in place.

We may not always do it, but we know about pressing through in prayer, bringing God our fears and troubles. Leaving those troubles with Him. Praying until it becomes about Him rather than about us. Until we're worshipping. Praising.

That's what David's doing here. He hasn't forgotten the desert, or his enemies' plots. He's not denying or ignoring them. But he sees God. He knows God is enough.

He's not perching timidly in the shadow of God's wings, trembling in that strong hand because the danger might snatch him away. He has no thought that God might drop him or fail to protect him.

Our God, You are strong and mighty to save. You are my strong tower, my refuge, my shelter, and my Defender. You are my Good Shepherd. I know the words, but so often I don't act like I believe them. I run to You, but I keep watching my troubles as if they might break through Your defences. Faith tells me that can't happen. Help me listen and be confident in You.

Belonging

If the foot says, "I am not a part of the body because I
am not a hand," that does not make it any less a part of
the body.
1 Corinthians 12:15, NLT

One of the lies the enemy of our souls baits us with is "You don't belong."

Someone hurts our feelings. Or we don't get a joke, or everyone else seems to have it all together. We notice we're different. The lie slides right into our thoughts, and we cuddle up with it, nodding agreement. "That proves it. I really don't belong."

Paul's words in today's verse, about the foot and the ear saying they weren't part of the body, mean we should use the gifts God gave us and not compare ourselves with others. We shouldn't sulk and refuse to serve if someone else got the talent we wanted.

They also imply something else. If we fall for "I don't belong," then part of the body will be handicapped because we're disqualifying ourselves.

Of course we're all different. Even if some of us look the same on the outside. Different is good; we know that, and we don't want to be clones. But the deceiver's words can resonate with a fear of rejection, and maybe it's easier to tell ourselves we don't belong than to wait for someone else to say it.

The Bible says that we're each "fearfully and wonderfully made" (Psalm 139:14, KJV), and that God loves us.

Creator God, Your Word does not lie. How many ways do You have to say I have value in Your eyes before I can believe it? You also warn that we're in a spiritual battle and we need to use the weapons You've given us so we can stand. Help me be vigilant. Help me take every thought captive to Christ and speak Your truth to defeat the lies. I can't do this on my own, but Your Spirit in me can. Help me rely on You.

Stop, Look, and Listen for God

...they did not believe God
or trust him to care for them.
Psalm 78:22, NLT

The Psalmist is reviewing Israel's history, as a parable to teach the people. He looks at what God did on the journey out of Egypt and until the time of King David, and he looks at how the people repeatedly rebelled, "stubbornly tested God" (verse 18), and complained.

All God wanted them to do was believe, trust, and obey Him. You'd think He gave enough proof of His power and love that they could discern the pattern: God was leading, and He would meet their needs.

In these verses, they'd complained that God could give them water but couldn't feed them. He proved them wrong (verses 23-31). Again.

They had a cloud leading them, and they saw God's miracles.

Christians today have the Holy Spirit leading from within us, and we sometimes see His miracles too. If we pay attention, we see His touch on our lives. But these verses remind us how important it is to stop, look and listen for God, and to deliberately trust Him. It's how we're designed to live.

Holy and powerful God, how much easier it would have been for the Israelites if they'd been able to believe and to trust in You. You know my weaknesses, and that I'm no stronger than they were. Please give me faith to believe You, and help me choose to trust You.

It Takes Two

Teach me your ways, O LORD,
that I may live according to your truth!
Grant me purity of heart,
so that I may honor you.
Psalm 86:11, NLT

It takes two — God and the individual — to grow a Christian. God is the teacher, and we need to apply what we learn. We can't purify ourselves, but it's our job to honour Him with our lives.

Living according to His truth means believing Him, and that includes recognizing and rejecting negative thoughts. We choose to trust God because we've experienced His reality. He's been teaching us, and we've been discovering His character.

Purity matters, too. Not so we can look perfect and show everybody else up, but so we can honour the God who rescues and restores us. We can be living examples of what He can do.

God my Creator and Sustainer, when I was separated from You, You brought me near. It's only by Your goodness that I can stand in Your presence. Teach me Your ways, grant me purity of heart, and help me live according to Your truth and honour You.

Where the Heart Is

Lord, through all the generations
you have been our home!
Psalm 90:1, NLT

The New Living Translation labels this psalm "a prayer of Moses, the man of God." Moses, who led the Israelites out of slavery to wander in the wilderness en route to the Promised Land.

These people had no geographical home, but God's presence led them day and night. God spoke to them. God defeated their enemies, and provided food and water in the desert. He even kept their shoes from wearing out from all the walking.

Circumstances may have made it easier for Moses to see God as his home, but even though we have a warm, snug, physical home, perhaps shared with a loving family, God is our deeper home.

Creator and Sustainer God, I praise You that You never change. Thank You for being my home in the emotional and spiritual sense, my heart's home, my security and stability, where I can rest and thrive and shelter.

Living Rest

Those who live in the shelter of the Most High
will find rest in the shadow of the Almighty.
Psalm 91:1, NLT

Rest. Soul-rest, rest from anxiety and striving. The kind of rest implied in "Be still and know that I am God" (Psalm 46:10, NLT).

How do we get it?

We live. In God's care.

This isn't a pause or a passing-through. We need to consciously live... abide... dwell... in His shelter.

It requires gratitude, confidence in God, hope and trust in Him. It enables us to bring Him our needs as a child to a loving parent, with assurance that He listens, loves and knows best.

Loving God, Gentle Shepherd, help me live in Your shelter. Your power is great and You are all wise. Teach me who You are, so I can trust You more. Help me rest in Your care.

Transplanted to Flourish

For [the godly] are transplanted to the LORD's own
house.
They flourish in the courts of our God.
Even in old age they will still produce fruit;
they will remain vital and green.
Psalm 92:13-14, NLT

Transplanted trees usually come from the nursery (or forest) with their roots in a ball of dirt. Scrawny ones may be pulled out of poor soil with bare roots, or their roots may even need washing before being plunged into good ground.

It's amazing that God would take humans in all our messiness, clean us and label us "godly," and transplant us into His own house — into His presence.

May we not stand there, roots clenched tight into the clot of dirt they came with.

May we consciously poke our roots into the wide, deep, nourishing ground of God's presence. May we flourish. May we thrive.

God of grace and mercy, what can I say but "Thank You"? Help me grow into all You've designed me to be, with my confidence fully rooted in You.

Choosing to Believe God

The people refused to enter the pleasant land,
for they wouldn't believe his promise to care for them.
Psalm 106:24, NLT

The psalmist is recapping Israel's history, and this verse refers to the first time God brought them to the edge of the Promised Land, when they believed a frightening report of the dangers ahead instead of remembering how God had kept them safe thus far.

"They wouldn't believe His promise to care for them." That's not how they saw it. They'd probably say they were being realistic, facing facts. After all, the scouts reported giants in the land. What chance did they have?

They forgot they had God on their side. The same God who'd broken Pharaoh with plagues and destroyed his army after parting the Red Sea. The same God who'd given them water in the desert and daily bread from heaven.

The same God who disciplined them when they disobeyed or got too demanding.

They forgot. We do, too.

All-powerful and holy God, Your promises are true and Your hand is mighty to defend. Forgive me for the times I trust my own eyes and ears instead of trusting Your Word. Help me remember what You've revealed about Yourself, and help me choose to believe You.

Obeying Because We Trust

All [God] does is just and good,
and all his commandments are trustworthy.
They are forever true,
to be obeyed faithfully and with integrity.
Psalm 111:7-8, NLT

We may struggle with obeying God, but we never need worry about the quality of His leadership. He's not like a human leader who may be mistaken or manipulative.

When we think of "all His commandments," let's look at the Ten Commandments and Jesus' teachings, not the hundreds of legalistic, man-made rules the old teachers of the law made to teach people how to apply the law.

Some of His principles seem upside-down to our thinking: give to receive, die to live, humble yourself to be exalted. They don't look sensible to our eyes, but they work. Will we choose to trust what God says, or what we see?

God, You are enthroned above the heavens, yet Your Spirit dwells in my heart. You've proven Your character, authority, and goodness time and again. Help me choose to trust and obey the commandments and principles You've set out, because I trust that You are good.

The Kindness of God

What can I offer the LORD
for all he has done for me?
I will lift up the cup of salvation
and praise the LORD's name for saving me.
I will keep my promises to the LORD
in the presence of all his people.
Psalm 116:12-14, NLT

God answered the psalmist's desperate prayer. There's no way he can repay his Rescuer, except with his life. How then will he live?

He'll accept and embrace the salvation, not holding it off because he's not worthy and can't earn it. Neither will he keep it to himself. He'll declare God's praises publicly so others will know His character.

And he'll keep whatever promises and vows he makes to the Lord. This isn't so much about bargains he may have tried to make with God in the troubled time. It's about integrity in his ongoing relationship with God and in the presence of witnesses.

He also commits to be part of corporate worship as well as private worship. Despite any irritating, flawed or hypocritical people in his faith community, he won't walk away.

His example of faithfulness and his declarations of praise will encourage others' faith, and theirs will encourage his.

God, You are Creator and Sustainer, Saviour and King. Your kindness reaches for me even while I'm running away from You. Soften the hearts of those who know You and of those who don't, and help us all to look to You for help. Yes, I can fear Your discipline, but it's when I experience Your love and Your mercy that my heart is undone. I love You because You loved me first. Help me live in light of Your love.

Not About Us

But Samuel replied,
"What is more pleasing to the LORD:
your burnt offerings and sacrifices
or your obedience to his voice?
Listen! Obedience is better than sacrifice,
and submission is better than offering the fat of rams."
1 Samuel 15:22, NLT

What is it about humans that we always want to make it about us? And about outward, not inward, and doing, not being?

Too often our first line of thought is "what do I want/think/feel about this?" If Jesus is really Lord in our lives, the better question is "what does God want/think/feel about this?"

Self-focus is insidious. It's silly, really, because when we know God's way is best, why do we so quickly shift focus to what we want? When we focus on our own opinions and feelings, we miss the better things God has for us. And we're not pleasant to be around.

Focusing on (and surrendering to) His way brings joy, contentment, and a contagious sense of wellbeing. A much better choice... if only it were easier to keep this perspective!

Without this heart-choice — spirit-choice — we'll either be doing the wrong thing or doing the right thing for the wrong reason. We can even turn the pursuit of holiness into being about us.

God my King, Your wisdom and power, kindness and justice make You the perfect ruler. Forgive me when I try to re-take control of my life, and draw me back to full surrender to You. There is none other like You, none other worthy to be God. Remind me who You are, and help me to trust and obey. Help me worship You with my life.

Obedient Thoughts

We take captive every thought to make it obedient to
Christ.
2 Corinthians 10:5b, NIV

There's more to this verse than avoiding sinful or tempting thoughts, as important as that is. There are at least three other types of thoughts that need to be kept in line:

Thoughts of self-focus, self-centredness, or self-pity. When we're preoccupied with our own opinions, choices, and preferences, we can't hear His.

Thoughts that ramble instead of being attuned to God's leading. When we let our minds wander, even in safe places, we've lost focus and aren't following our Shepherd.

Thoughts that yammer on and distract us from His voice. We need to still our thoughts and listen to God.

Creator God, You know my weakness and how easily my thoughts slip away from the paths You'd like them to be in. Without Your Spirit to remind and guide me, I don't have a chance of keeping my thoughts obedient. Thank You for Your grace that helps me. Give me a teachable mind and an attitude of obedient perseverance, and grow me in Your ways.

Joy Under Pressure

As pressure and stress bear down on me,
I find joy in your commands.
Psalm 119:143, NLT

Despite the pressure and stress we may experience, there's joy to be found in reminding ourselves that God is the ultimate authority. We can trust Him to care for us, and ask Him for equipping wisdom or deliverance.

It's not us against the universe. God is bigger than the problem. Focusing on His way builds an attitude of God-trust instead of futile human striving or fighting the circumstances. His code of conduct helps us know what to do, how to act in difficult situations.

While there's no joy looking at stress, or in legalism, there's deep joy in belonging to God. Keeping His Law, precepts, and principles as the Spirit enables us keeps the barriers down between us.

Doing it God's way brings joy and life in the midst of stress. What's not to like?

God all-wise and loving, I can't do this on my own, and that's one reason You gave the Law in the first place, to help us see our need. Help me learn and understand, and through Your Holy Spirit keep me focused and following. Thank You for the joy and life You give.

What if Jesus Hadn't Come?

What if the LORD had not been on our side?
Psalm 124:1a, NLT

What if the Lord had not been on our side? What if Jesus hadn't come?

Things are dark, but they'd be so much darker without the Holy Spirit working in and through His followers.

We wouldn't have His presence with us in the happy and the sad.

Despair and hopelessness would be everywhere — if God hadn't already brought final judgment.

We wouldn't know as much of what God is like, or how to walk with Him, because Jesus showed us both. And how could we walk with Him? We'd still be alienated from Him by our own choices. We'd be cut off from Him in our sin, blinded and miserable.

But He took our side — He came — and so we live.

God who is Maker, Redeemer, and Sustainer, thank You for Jesus' life, His willing sacrifice and daring rescue, for His rising, His gift to us of the Holy Spirit, and for His coming again. Help me live in praise, gratitude and confidence in Your care. Help me love You in response to Your great love for me.

Rock-Solid Security

Those who trust in the LORD are as secure as Mount
Zion;
they will not be defeated but will endure forever.
Psalm 125:1, NLT

Trusting God brings security. We won't be defeated. That's not to say we won't have pain and trouble, but it's a reminder of the real battle, the long-term spiritual one.

Whatever our hard times, it's easier to focus on the externals: the disease, rebellious child, unemployment. The things outside our control.

We're not responsible for the externals. We're responsible for our hearts, our focus, our faith.

Defeat is when we get our eyes off God. Victory is continuing to trust in spite of what we see, hear, feel, experience.

We can pray for healing, common sense, provision. But we also need to pray for ourselves, to remain strong in our private tests.

This is our temptation, our battle: will we continue to trust? This is where God makes a way, if we'll only look for it.

Faithful God, You've promised to never leave me, and to always make a way out from under the temptations I face. You want me to stand victorious in Your strength, for Your glory and my wellbeing. Help me keep my focus on You despite whatever may go on around me.

To See God

Where there is no vision, the people perish:
but he that keepeth the law, happy is he.
Proverbs 29:18, KJV

This verse is often quoted in terms of direction and planning, of a corporate sense of purpose. But there's more to vision than just seeing the next step in God's plan.

There's seeing Him.

Not literally — not yet — but seeing, believing, accepting His revelation of who He is. His character. His attributes. His promises, laws, and requirements.

Do we really know Him? Or are we distracted by the pain or pleasure in our own small lives?

Too often the problems look bigger than the God who can solve them. Or we pray for help but don't really believe things will change, because we don't see them changing.

Instead, we need to see God — to know Him rather than just knowing about Him. To believe Him instead of believing whatever stress is currently staring us down.

Holy and mighty God, You spoke the universe into being, and You proved Yourself as Israel's King and Defender. You haven't changed. Reveal Yourself today. I live among people who reject You and who are indeed casting off restraint and running wild. Guide me. Strengthen me. Give me a glimpse of who You really are, so I can stand in firm confidence in You, so that others will see You too.

What Pleases God?

He takes no pleasure in the strength of a horse
or in human might.
No, the LORD's delight is in those who fear him,
those who put their hope in his unfailing love.
Psalm 147:10-11, NLT

God restores the nation of Israel but also heals the broken-hearted. He names each star and feeds baby ravens.

He does it all without needing our help, although the Bible makes it clear that He invites and empowers us to participate in His work.

God is big, vast beyond our knowing. His power can't be thwarted, nor His mercy exhausted. What does He ask us to do? Save ourselves? Restore and bind up ourselves? Name the stars and feed the wildlife?

Some of those things we will do, and it will please Him. We'll care for one another and for creation. That's important. And He likely doesn't mind that we name the stars, even though His names for them are truer.

But it's not our strength, accomplishments or actions that delight God. It's our heart-responses to Him — responses of healthy fear of His power and hope in His unfailing love.

Majestic Creator God, there is none like You. You give me so much — including salvation — that I could never earn nor repay. Instead of trying to do the impossible, help me respond in reverent fear and hope. You say it pleases You, so help me to live this way more and more. And help me to show my love for You in how I treat others.

To Know God

Jesus answered: "Don't you know me, Philip, even
after I have been among you such a long time? Anyone
who has seen me has seen the Father. How can you
say, 'Show us the Father'?"
John 14:9, NIV

Have you heard the anecdote about three blind people encountering an elephant for the first time?

The first one, touching the trunk, said the creature was skinny, long, and floppy. The one at the elephant's side insisted it was huge like a house, while the third one stood at the patient animal's foreleg and thought maybe it was a tree.

God is so much bigger than we can comprehend, and the silly story illustrates the danger of insisting we know all about Him based on what we've personally encountered.

We have the Bible to teach us about Him, but we need to be careful to read all of it instead of focusing on what we "get" or what makes us feel good.

And we have Jesus, who reveals the Father's character. That makes the four Gospels extra valuable for study.

Majestic and holy God, the better I know You the more I can trust You. And the more my spirit will surrender to You in worship. You alone are holy, all-wise, our Redeemer and our Judge. You are more than I can comprehend, yet You reveal Yourself to me. Open the eyes of my heart to the truth of who You are, and help me to live a life of worship.

A Symphony of Praise

Let them all praise the name of the LORD.
For his name is very great;
his glory towers over the earth and heaven!
Psalm 148:13, NLT

The final pages of the Book of Psalms resound with calls to praise, for what God does and for who He is.

From the most powerful people to the least, praise the Lord! But the praise doesn't stop there. Psalm 148 calls for praise from the armies of heaven and small, scurrying animals; from created things, wind, and weather.

It's a symphony of praise, with each aspect of creation adding its own part. Those who can sing, speak, or make noise contribute audibly. The trees and mountains may do their parts simply by existing.

Imagine what this would sound and look like in the heavenly realms: everything reflecting praise and glory to God.

Psalm 147 says it's good, delightful, fitting to sing praises to God. It brings perspective (as we remind ourselves of His power and His care) and contentment (we are safe in His hands). It's what we were made for. The better we know God, the more we'll overflow with praise to Him.

Awesome and holy God, teach me to live so that every action and word reflects my confidence in You — my reliance on You and my praise of who You are. Thank You for giving me a part in the symphony of Your praise.

Cheerful Hearts

A cheerful heart is good medicine,
but a broken spirit saps a person's strength.
Proverbs 17:22, NLT

Nobody takes medicine when they're well, but we usually have a few spiritual "germs" in our systems that need fighting.

We're called to take every thought captive under Christ's authority, focus on praising God, and not dwell on the negatives. But we can't manufacture a cheerful heart or mend a broken spirit.

Who gives us a cheerful heart? Who binds up our broken spirits? It's God.

Our part is to cultivate an openness to Him, to receive what He has for us, to discover Him to be our source of healing and light. And to choose to obey.

After all, according to the King James translation, Jesus said, "In the world ye shall have tribulation: but be of good cheer; I have overcome the world" (John 16:33).

Father God, my Healer and Sustainer, grant me a cheerful heart — based on Your goodness, not on my circumstances. Let it be a tonic when I'm in good space, and medicine when times are hard. And when my spirit cracks and breaks, please bind me up and renew me, heal my heart, and plant cheer in it again to make me strong.

Quiet Times With God

My child, eat honey, for it is good,
and the honeycomb is sweet to the taste.
In the same way, wisdom is sweet to your soul.
If you find it, you will have a bright future,
and your hopes will not be cut short.
Proverbs 24:13-14, NLT

The Bible's invitations to wisdom are free to those who will seek God and draw near to Him. They're not conditional on our latent intelligence or on our spotless pasts, but they're based on God and His love for us.

In these verses we're encouraged to look for wisdom, rather than waiting for it to magically appear. The honeycomb illustration implies an eager, childlike search for something we know we'll like.

Where do we find wisdom? From God, and through His Book. We need a daily quiet time with Him, to read, pray, listen, and learn. It's not enough to know *about* Him. We need to *know Him*.

If we can take time to stop and pray, we'll find the rest of the day goes smoother. Not that we can bribe God into giving us pleasant days, but if we're aligned with His Spirit, we're better prepared to face what comes.

Father God, what a privilege it is to spend time with You. Help me make this a priority in my daily life, not as an obligation but as a respite, a delight, and a time of refreshing and nourishing. Thank You for Your grace and Your love for me.

Taking God for Granted

Yes, they knew God, but they wouldn't worship him as
God or even give him thanks. And they began to think
up foolish ideas of what God was like. As a result, their
minds became dark and confused.

Romans 1:21, NLT

Knowing God but not worshipping Him or being thankful leads to terrible depths.

The context here is people who turn away from God. They know about Him but don't care. How many turned away on purpose, and how many drifted away because they weren't paying attention?

We all know of good people who believe in God but don't seem to think about Him.

Sure, He's there to turn to in a crunch, but what if their spirits harden and they won't call out to Him for help? What if they believe the enemy's lies about God and decide there's no point?

And what about those of us who know and love God? This is a warning for us too, not to take Him for granted and let our relationship stagnate. It takes discipline and intentional effort to keep a strong, daily connection with our God. There are so many distractions and drains on our time.

Father, I don't want to slide away from You even a little distance. You are life itself. There's so much more of You to know; draw me deeper into relationship with You. Let me know You better, so I can more fully trust and obey You. And please, by Your grace, draw back the ones who are slipping away. Help them see, help them choose Your life. Our whole world needs You, Lord. We're no good on our own. Open eyes, soften hearts, draw many to Yourself.

Our Shepherd

He guides me along right paths,
bringing honor to his name.
Psalm 23:3b, NLT

Psalm 23 is probably the best-known psalm, and it's such a comfort, whether we're in the green meadows or in the narrow valley of the shadow.

Our Shepherd is with us, resourceful to nourish us, powerful to defend and rescue, wise in His leading, and rewarding us for following.

We can get to thinking it's all about us.

Today's verse reminds us of the bigger picture: the psalm — and life — is about revealing the character and nature of our Shepherd. It's about Him.

Thank You, God, for how You care for me. You provide, protect, guide and reward. The way You treat me reveals more about You than it does about me. You are the Holy One, worthy of all honour and praise. Help me follow obediently, not just to stay safe, but to give You glory.

Believing the Lord

And Abram believed the LORD, and the LORD counted
him as righteous because of his faith.
Genesis 15:6, NLT

Abram believed God. Sometimes it's that simple.

By now in Abram's journey with God, he's seen God protect and provide for his household in amazing ways. He's had conversations with God and recognizes God's voice.

Here, he's been lamenting to God that all the riches he's acquired are hollow. He has no son to inherit them, and they'll pass to a servant. He's honest with God about his pain.

God (who's just been accused of not providing Abram a son) says that not only will Abram have a son, he'll have as many descendants as there are stars in the sky.

Abram knows the facts. He's old. His wife Sarai is old. If they haven't conceived by now, it's not happening. Abram knows God. What God says, God does. And Abram knows God's voice.

Abram believes. And that's all God wants here: believing faith.

Holy, Creator God, Your ways are beyond knowing. You've already proven Your trustworthiness, power, and love. You speak in many ways through the Bible and through the Holy Spirit. Teach me to recognize Your voice, and help me to believe what You say. Your Word says so much about how You see us, what You promise us, and who You want us to be. Help me to trust and obey.

God's Good News

For I am not ashamed of this Good News about Christ.
It is the power of God at work, saving everyone who
believes — the Jew first and also the Gentile. This
Good News tells us how God makes us right in his
sight.
Romans 1:16-17a, NLT

Sometimes it's hard for Christians to share our faith because we forget it's not our job to "close the deal" on a person's salvation. It's God's job to soften people's hearts and open them to hear the truth about Jesus, and it's God's job to give them the faith and courage to accept that truth.

Our role is to be open to sharing what we know. If people have questions, we need to be able to give an answer about our hope and faith (1 Peter 3:15).

Think for a minute about this good news: It tells what God has done for all people, all over the world.

We didn't even know He'd done it until after the fact. We need to believe it and obey Jesus (Romans 1:5). It's the power of God at work. It saves everyone who believes it, it tells how God makes us right with Himself, and it's only by faith (Romans 1:17).

Doesn't that put a bit more light in your spirit, just thinking about it? Doesn't it sound like something worth sharing?

Holy and Majestic God, thank You again for the gift of Your Son Jesus, who came to reveal who You are and to make people right with You. None of us could earn Your approval, but You did this for us, in all our messes, to rescue and redeem us. Remind me of the power of Jesus' death and resurrection. Remind me of our hope. And help me to share the good news with those who need to hear it, in ways that will reach their hearts.

Putting Our Faith in Jesus

We are made right with God by placing our faith in
Jesus Christ. And this is true for everyone who
believes, no matter who we are.
Romans 3:22, NLT

"Placing our faith in Jesus Christ" is more than intellectual belief, more than a casual agreement.

It's an active trust, the same as we would rely on to sit in a chair or step onto a bridge. We place our faith in Jesus Christ.

It means following His way instead of living for ourselves, walking with Him each day and in each situation, and relying on His leading, equipping, presence, and protection.

It means trusting Him to work things out as He chooses, trusting the goodness of His character, and living to bring glory to God the Father.

Holy and majestic God, there is none like You. Thank You for making a way for me to be right with You through faith in Jesus. Thank You for His death and resurrection, the most costly gift I've ever been offered. Thank You for the faith to believe. Help me to embrace this faith actively and fully and to let faith in Jesus change the way I live each moment, to Your glory.

When Jesus Prays For Us

Simon, Simon, Satan has asked to sift each of you like wheat. But I have pleaded in prayer for you, Simon, that your faith should not fail. So when you have repented and turned to me again, strengthen your brothers.
Luke 22:31-32, NLT

This is Jesus talking. He who has the power to stop storms, banish demons and raise the dead. Yet all He does here is pray for the fallout. Couldn't He have rejected Satan's request? Placed a special protection around the disciples?

Of course He could. The fact that He didn't shows that, as with Job, the trial would be permitted because it would ultimately accomplish God's purposes in the lives of His dearly loved people.

So He let it happen. It can happen to us too.

Sometimes, as with Peter's denial, it's about our failure.

Sometimes, like with Job, it's things outside our control: circumstances and others' actions.

Either way, if we surrender it to God, He can use it to shape and grow us into the image of His Son.

And Jesus intercedes for us (Romans 8:34). Just as He did for Peter.

Father God, I affirm Your sovereignty. Nothing can touch me outside of Your will. Your plans for me are good. I rely on the intercession of Your Son, and I ask for grace to cooperate with Your Holy Spirit who lives in me, so that whatever the day holds, I can offer it to You in worship and conduct myself in a manner worthy of Your Name.

Day 198

Let God Make it Plain

Let all who are spiritually mature agree on these things.
If you disagree on some point, I believe God will make
it plain to you.
Philippians 3:15, NLT

Paul used his position of authority to single out sin and call for church discipline, but when it came to teaching, he gave the truth and stopped at that. He prayed for believers to grow in understanding (Colossians 1:9-14), but he didn't bully or badger or fret to get people's agreement.

God has been so patient in bringing each of us to understand elements of His truth and to learn to live them. We still have much to learn — about God and about life in general.

Just as we're on the journey, so are our brothers and sisters in Christ. So are our family and friends.

Paul's example here is freeing. We can pray, speak when appropriate, and remember that God is even more invested in revealing His truth to each heart.

God who is Truth, in whom is no shadow of lie or deceit, thank You for drawing me to know You and Your ways. Because You know each person so intimately, You know the best way and timing to make Your truth plain. Make me receptive so I can learn quickly, and grant me patience with myself and with others in the process. Help me trust You to be about Your work. Nudge me when You have a word or deed for me to contribute, and nudge me even more when I'm to keep my hands and voice out of the way.

When Our Role is to Pray and Wait

When he finally came to his senses, he said to himself,
"At home even the hired servants have food enough to
spare, and here I am dying of hunger! I will go home to
my father..."
Luke 15:17-18a NLT

If there's something our loved ones need to learn or change in their thinking, we can trust God to make it plain to them. He works in the lives of believers (including our own lives!), but also in those who don't yet know Jesus.

That's a huge comfort as we pray for people who are outside of relationship with God. And it makes perfect sense. After all, it's God who initiates the contact, who softens hearts and gives faith.

When the young man in the parable left home, his father's only option was to pray. Jesus didn't say he did, but it's implied by how he was watching and waiting for his son's return. We don't know how long he waited, either.

The father knew the trouble his son could get into, and he presumably prayed for physical and spiritual protection. He would have also prayed for God to change the young man's heart and bring him home.

God our Father, thank You for revealing Your love, shining Your light of truth on my life, and giving me freedom to choose You. Help me as I pray for those I love who don't yet trust You. Help me pray in love, power, and confidence, and help me wait for Your perfect timing as You draw them to know You. You love them even more than I do, and in this I will rest.

Is Your Loyalty Divided?

If you need wisdom, ask our generous God, and he will
give it to you... But when you ask him, be sure that
your faith is in God alone. Do not waver, for a person
with divided loyalty... should not expect to receive
anything from the Lord. Their loyalty is divided
between God and the world, and they are unstable in
everything they do.
James 1:5-8, NLT

Reading these verses in other translations, it's easy to think "do not waver" means "don't doubt," and that can leave us feeling a bit uncertain.

After all, despite our best efforts, doubt can flicker in our prayers. God knows that. Remember the father with the demon-possessed son? "I do believe, but help me overcome my unbelief!" (Mark 9:24, NLT).

But this translation makes the real issue clear. Are we asking God for wisdom, leading, direction, but still holding onto worldly wisdom as a backup? No wonder it doesn't work. If our loyalty is divided between God and the world, we're sunk.

That's not to say God doesn't want us to use our common sense, any more than He doesn't want us to avail ourselves of doctors or other resources.

But He does want us to look first to Him, to His power and His ways, and to obey what He says, even if it's counter-intuitive from a natural human perspective.

Remember His instruction for the Israelites to march around the walls of Jericho (Joshua 6:20)? God's way works, because *He* works. We need to trust. And to commit.

Holy and all-powerful God, help me to fully embrace You as my source of all help and resources. Grow my faith so I can trust and obey You — fully and completely.

Trouble or Opportunity?

Dear brothers and sisters, when troubles come your
way, consider it an opportunity for great joy. For you
know that when your faith is tested, your endurance
has a chance to grow.
James 1:2-3, NLT

If we were to read this aloud, most of us would probably emphasize the word "troubles." Perhaps James begins his letter this way to restore perspective away from *troubles* and onto *opportunity, joy, faith, chance,* and *grow.*

He's not telling his readers anything new. He says they already know it. We do too.

But we start focusing on our troubles and we forget. We want to solve our problems, avoid the pain, steer out of the storm into safe harbour. James reminds us that the trouble, whatever its source, can be an opportunity for God to grow us.

Trouble as a test of faith isn't about do we pass or fail, do we have faith or not.

James is writing to people who believe in Jesus. The test is to determine and reveal the quality and strength of our faith, not to disqualify us but to help us grow.

We can think of it in terms of spiritual exercise. The more we use our "faith muscles," the stronger they become, and the more coordination and balance we develop.

Father God, help me develop the joy James talks about: growth and maturity in my faith. When I rely on You more than on myself, it draws me nearer to You and lets me experience more of Your strength in my life. Thank You for Your grace and mercy, and for Your loving presence that never leaves me.

Loyalty to God

Pure and genuine religion in the sight of God the
Father means caring for orphans and widows in their
distress and refusing to let the world corrupt you.
James 1:27, NLT

The most obvious meaning of "refusing to let the world corrupt you" is to not buy into, approve, or indulge in the many things society flaunts that God's Word tells us to avoid.

In the choice between human ways and God's, wisdom always follows God. After all, we humans can get ourselves into a heap of trouble.

But the implication here, the deeper level, is one of allegiance: of loyalty to God and living life His way.

We may abstain from harmful behaviour and thoughts, but if we allow society and those around us to hold a greater influence over our thoughts, decisions, or actions, we're giving "the world" an authority in our lives that rightfully belongs to God.

We need to be considerate of others' feelings, and God often speaks through the people in our lives whether they know Him or not, but our loyalty belongs to God.

He's the one we need to go to first, because of His authority, His wisdom, and His genuine care for us.

God who is my Good Shepherd, forgive me for so often living a divided loyalty that makes me unstable in all I do. Help me focus on You in love and in worship. Work Your Word and Your way in and through me, so that I become more like Your Son. Grow me into a loyal citizen of Your Kingdom.

Wisdom: More than Choices

But the wisdom from above is first of all pure. It is also
peace loving, gentle at all times, and willing to yield to
others. It is full of mercy and good deeds. It shows no
favouritism and is always sincere.
James 3:17, NLT

When we ask God for wisdom, it's usually because we need to know what to do or what decision to make. The same when we consult the wise people in our lives. It's always about knowledge and choices.

Today's verse, and perhaps the whole of James' letter, says wisdom is about living wisely.

Living wisely as James defines it will result in wise choices because the wise Christian is living in obedience to the Master's ways.

This wisdom is the opposite of self-focused ambition and selfishness. It's loyalty to God, following His path. It's bringing the human spirit in line under the Holy Spirit, submitting our wills to His and following Him instead of pushing ahead.

If we can live like this, we'll find ourselves making the wise decisions we wanted in the first place, because we'll be in tune with God.

God who is fully wise, Shepherd who is fully good, lead me in Your ways and train me in Your precepts. In You I find wisdom, health, and strength. I'm no good on my own. Help me stay in Your presence, where I can thrive.

Enemies of God?

You adulterers! Don't you realize that friendship with
the world makes you an enemy of God? I say it again:
If you want to be a friend of the world, you make
yourself an enemy of God.
James 4:4, NLT

James uses strong language in this passage to make us see the seriousness of divided loyalty. We live in the world, but as Christians we're to live by God's wisdom and not by following the world's way.

"World" has two meanings here. We live in the physical world and are called to bring God's love to our fellow inhabitants, but we're also called to demonstrate a way of life that doesn't match the natural, unredeemed human mindset.

It's not about being *against* the world. It's about being *for* God, choosing to stay close to Him, guarding our relationship with Him above all else. It's about faithfulness. Loyalty. Loving this God who loves us so much more.

The more we resist the desires and thought patterns that would damage our intimacy with God, the more we can grow in the abundant life He wants to give us.

We want it all — want it both ways — and we fool ourselves that it's okay. But it's stunting our spiritual lives, making us poor examples of what God offers, and it's making us much less than God designed us to be. And it's offensive to Him.

Holy God, You love us but You require our full allegiance. Please forgive my times of disloyalty and help me live for You. Take Your rightful place in my heart, exalted and adored, and help me conduct myself in a manner worthy of the hope and salvation You've so freely given.

When Faith Affects Our Lives

Now someone may argue, "Some people have faith;
others have good deeds." But I say, "How can you
show me your faith if you don't have good deeds? I will
show you my faith by my good deeds."
James 2:18, NLT

The good deeds James is asking for are to grow naturally out of applying faith in Jesus to our daily lives. There's no eternal value in good work without a heart for God. People judge by appearances and actions, but God looks at the heart.

If our faith is growing, it will cause visible changes in our lives. We'll learn to rely more on God in our daily thoughts, responsibilities, and experiences. That's one reason a daily quiet time with God is so vital.

Remember James' words on accepting the word of God planted in our hearts (James 1:21). Prayer, listening, and reading the Bible are key ingredients in a growing faith.

In our culture of busyness, over-calendaring, and of being always "on call" to texts, emails, and more, the danger is that there's no time for God.

We're busy, distracted, and it's easy to take God for granted. But if we don't read His Word, don't spend time getting to know Him, how will we know what's true? How will we know how to live, or have the confidence that He can — and wants to — help us?

God my Creator, who knows my heart, help me be intentional in taking time with You. Give me a longing to know You better and to please You. Give me wisdom in how to use my time so I can do what You've given me to do and yet grow in relationship with You and with those You've given me. Give me faith, and work that faith out in my life in good works — not for You but because of You.

Joy and Strength

This is a sacred day before our Lord. Don't be dejected
and sad, for the joy of the Lord is your strength!
Nehemiah 8:10b, NLT

A group of the exiled Israelites have returned to Jerusalem to rebuild the Temple and the city wall. Ezra the scribe has read to them the Law of the Lord.

They've listened to God's life-rules and they see where they've gone a different way. They're sorry for what they've done wrong. They may be scared, too.

God hauled the entire nation off to Babylon for 70 years because of repeated sin, and here they are, newly back in the land and already messing up. Will He send them away again? Or worse?

Might they also be discouraged? How could they ever live up to God's expectations in the Law? Maybe that's why Nehemiah tells them "the joy of the Lord is your strength."

He says it here to a people weeping for their moral and spiritual weakness, and it shows that God's strength is for more than rebuilding Temples and walls — it's for rebuilding human lives.

Creator God, You are holy and just. I can't stand in Your presence except through Jesus' blood. I can't please You on my own, but how grateful I am that the joy of You can be my strength, and Christ in me is my hope of glory. Draw me to live ever closer to You, in the light of Your love.

Christians and Temples

"We promise together not to neglect the Temple of our
God."
Nehemiah 10:39b, NLT

The returned Israelite exiles have vowed to keep themselves pure, to live God's way, and to provide all that's needed for the upkeep of the Temple and its ongoing offerings.

The Temple is where they worship God, where they're forgiven and restored. Where they go for wisdom. It's the symbol of their relationship with God.

The Apostle Paul wrote, "Don't you realize that your body is the temple of the Holy Spirit, who lives in you and was given to you by God?" (1 Corinthians 6:19a, NLT).

We're responsible to keep our bodies pure and healthy, and to maintain our spirits.

"The church" is the people of Christ, not the buildings in which we meet, but we do need to care for our corporate worship sites, since they're visible signs of our worship. More than that, we need to care for one another.

Jesus said, "Your love for one another will prove to the world that you are my disciples" (John 13:35, NLT). We need to guard our relationships with God, to put Him first in worship, and to offer ourselves as living sacrifices to Him.

God who longs to reconcile all people to Himself, You are holy. I am not. Yet You designed me for relationship with You and I'm not complete without it. Rekindle the intensity of my first love for You. Draw me nearer, and remind me how vital it is to stay close to You. Help me to live for You and to love others and to keep my "temple" in good order.

Remembering God: Hope and Worship

So each generation should set its hope anew on God,
not forgetting his glorious miracles
and obeying his commands.
Psalm 78:7, NLT

When the people of Israel "set their hope anew" on Him, they thrived.

When they forgot what God had done — and He did some highly memorable miracles — or when they stopped believing or rationalized it away, the psalmist describes them as "stubborn, rebellious, and unfaithful, refusing to give their hearts to God" (Psalm 78:8, NLT).

The same goes for us today, and for our children and their children.

We have the miracles — and commands — of God preserved in the Bible. We have the testimonies of other Christians in person or in print. We have our personal encounters with the Lord of Heaven.

We need to remember, and to set our hearts and our hopes anew on God no matter what circumstances surround us. We need to pass our stories on to the next generation, but that generation is responsible to take them personally.

Faith isn't a history lesson, or literature, myth, or fairy tale. Theoretical nods to God don't do much except set us up to fall.

Father God, You have drawn me to Yourself with a love stronger than I can know. Refresh my faith, rekindle my first love for You, and work in my loved ones' spirits to awaken them to Your love too. Let them not refuse to give their hearts to You. Let none of us be lost.

The Tenacity of God

Long ago the LORD said to Israel:
"I have loved you, my people, with an everlasting love.
With unfailing love I have drawn you to myself.
Jeremiah 31:3, NLT

So much of what we do is what Eugene Peterson calls "a long obedience in the same direction." It can be a slog, but something drives us to keep on, to refuse to quit. If we don't do our part, who will?

We need tenacity in our faith, to keep believing and obeying in the dry times. To keep applying the lessons God teaches until we finally "get" them — or at least "get" one step and graduate to the next. We need it in our relationships, in our responsibilities, our jobs.

Spiritual maturity grows from a reliance on God's character, His strength and His love. His desire to draw all people into relationship with Himself, no matter how much we resist and try to go our own way.

He can be trusted. His love doesn't get tired of reaching for the wayward and the stubborn. The Bible warns that there will be a day when His invitation ends, but there's still a bit of time.

God calls His people to be holy, because He is holy. Compassionate, because He is compassionate. Patient, kind, loving, merciful, just... because those attributes reflect His character.

God of the highest heavens, who stoops to dwell in human hearts, You keep Your promises, You are patient beyond belief, You work to bring Your plans to fulfillment despite the knots we tie. Help me to be a person of tenacity because You are a God of tenacity. Draw me to Yourself, help me hold onto You as You hold me in the shelter of Your strong hand. And help me live confident in your everlasting love.

God's Urgency

How often I have wanted to gather your children
together as a hen protects her chicks beneath her wings,
but you wouldn't let me.
Matthew 23:37, NLT

Jesus came because we needed rescuing. He had compassion on us. The Good Shepherd saw our need and longed to meet it.

Hear His longing in our opening verse, where He laments over the city of Jerusalem. He's lamenting still today, calling out to so many lost and confused souls who don't even realize their state.

Sometimes we can catch an echo of his heart... the Creator, the King, calling... almost begging... for souls to turn His way. It matters that much to Him. *We* matter that much to Him. And it feels like time's running out.

We can't convince people to trust their hearts to Jesus. That's His work. But we can pray for them, we can demonstrate His care for them, and we can speak a few words when they're open to hear.

Fierce and gentle Shepherd, call Your lambs and help them to listen. Rescue them from where they're trapped, from menacing predators, and let them experience the true and good care that only You can give. Show me how to pray for those You give me, and help me love them as You love them.

Why We Need to Know God

He will flatter and win over those who have violated
the covenant. But the people who know their God will
be strong and will resist him.
Daniel 11:32, NLT

This is part of Daniel's prophecy about a future king who will conquer and destroy many nations and intend great harm to God's chosen people. It also has a lesson for Christians today, in our own circumstances.

We have an enemy too — the enemy of our souls. How do we stand against the opposition and persuasion he sows?

Daniel tells us how. We have to know our God: His character, His ways, His commands. We need to know His ultimate power.

Events unfold according to God's timing. (The phrase "the appointed time" occurs three times in Daniel 11.) And we need to know that He is bigger than our circumstances and thoughts. Focusing on this perspective keeps us from letting our problems loom larger than life.

How well do we know God? Biblical literacy is on the decline, and many people's idea of God comes from a mix of Hollywood, hearsay, and maybe even heresy, depending on who they've been listening to.

To truly know God, we need to go to the source: the Bible. And we need to ask Him to reveal Himself in it.

God who is the Author and the Finisher of my faith, who reaches into my tangled life to rescue and redeem me, help me to know You better. Help me live relying on Your character and following Your ways, so I can recognize and resist deception.

Counting Our Blessings

Trust in the LORD with all your heart;
do not depend on your own understanding.
Seek his will in all you do,
and he will show you which path to take.
Proverbs 3:5-6, NLT

It all comes back to trusting God and not ourselves — trusting Him with everything that we are

The NIV renders "Seek His will in all you do" as "In all your ways submit to Him," and the King James Version says "In all thy ways acknowledge Him."

The other translations suggest the intent of "acknowledge Him" is "submit to Him" or "seek His will," and again that needs to be part of the wholehearted trust the psalmist is calling for.

But "acknowledge Him" can be a little bit more.

For one thing, it includes gratitude. God blesses us in so many ways, with good things and best of all with His presence even when things aren't so good. Whether we list them in a gratitude journal or simply whisper thanks, let's notice.

God my abundant Provider, who lavishes gifts upon me, open my eyes to see, my ears to hear, my heart to receive and to overflow with praise and adoration to You, the Giver of all good gifts. The Giver of life and hope and salvation.

What Idols Obsess Us?

Then I said to them, "Each of you, get rid of the vile
images you are so obsessed with. Do not defile
yourselves with the idols of Egypt, for I am the Lord
your God."
Ezekiel 20:7, NLT

Time after time, God has proved His existence, His power, and His supremacy to the Israelites.

Yet here He accuses the people of being obsessed with idols. The NLT footnote for the word "idol" in this verse suggests the original word refers to dung. So these idols are not only worthless and powerless, but defiling to an Israelite. They don't just distract from God, they separate from Him.

We wonder why the Israelites would bother with idols. Yet don't we do the same?

What might we have brought "out of Egypt" when Jesus saved us? Performance, people pleasing, possessions? Often the worst is an ugly clay idol called *self*.

It's not very big or powerful, but we give it a lot more attention than we should. That attention rightly belongs to the One who rescued us — who is still rescuing us.

God my Redeemer, my Rescuer, how can I still be obsessed with such futile and defiling things when You have brought me out of slavery to sin and into Your kingdom of life? Continue Your saving work in me, and keep me in Your grace. Help me recognize when I look away from You to the idols in my life. Help me control my thoughts and spirit and turn back to You, the true, life-giving God.

A Willing Spirit

Restore to me the joy of your salvation
and grant me a willing spirit, to sustain me.
Psalm 51:12, NIV

"I don't really want to do that."

It's easy to look at our responsibilities or opportunities that way. Who really wants to drag their tired body out of bed too early to face the day? Or pick up toddlers' toys one more time. Make that difficult phone call. Go to the dentist.

There are things we choose not to do, but there are plenty that we need to go ahead with.

The "I don't want to" attitude can even slip into our relationships, or the job we love, or our ministry. It steals our joy.

Conscious gratitude helps: finding what we appreciate in the situations and deciding to thank God for His presence even in what we don't like.

We may need to echo King David's prayer: "Grant me a willing spirit, to sustain me." It's the way back to joy.

Holy God, Giver of life and mercy, complaining is offensive to You. Please forgive me for the attitude of self-focus that grows so easily, and wash me clean. It's about You after all, not about me. Grant me gratitude, restore the joy of my salvation when it slips, and give me a willing heart to sustain me in Your service.

Glory, Not Shame

Therefore, give the people of Israel this message from
the Sovereign LORD: I am bringing you back, but not
because you deserve it. I am doing it to protect my holy
name, on which you brought shame while you were
scattered among the nations.
Ezekiel 36:22, NLT

Israel's ungodly behaviour caused the Babylonian exile in the first place.

Set apart to be a holy people, to live in fellowship with God as a light to the people around them, they copied their neighbours instead. They abandoned the Living God for idols of stone and wood.

God stated His case through the prophets — repeatedly — and then followed through on the exile as He'd said. He promised it would end, and the people could come home after 70 years (Jeremiah 29:10).

Now they were coming home, but not because they learned their lesson and turned back to God. They were still bringing shame on His name in exile. Still living by their own understanding and desires, instead of wholeheartedly following His ways. And don't we do the same, to a lesser extent?

We need what God promises His people later in this chapter: clean, responsive hearts, and His Spirit within us. Then we need to listen to and rely on His Spirit.

Holy and mighty God, You've given me the Holy Spirit as a guarantee of my salvation. Forgive my waywardness, and draw me to love You more. Help me spend time with You to discover more of who You are. Forgive me for when I've brought shame on Your name. Help me live in confident trust in Your character and Your love, so that others will see that You are my Good Shepherd.

To Know God

I will be faithful to you and make you mine,
and you will finally know me as the LORD.
Hosea 2:20, NLT

The theme of knowing God threads through the Bible. In Daniel we see that it's the people who know God who will resist the evil leader's flattery. And Ezekiel is filled with "then they/then you will know that I am God." Hosea carries on with the trend.

Knowing God — knowing His character as revealed in the Bible and in our lives — is key to trusting Him, to staying faithful to Him, and as in the Daniel quote, to standing against the inroads of evil.

Our world is in a mess. Many people don't know God. Some who knew seem to have forgotten. And lots of people think they know who He is, but their ideas come from rumour and speculation.

Holy and righteous God, help me believe that You are who You say You are. Forgive me for any false beliefs I've accepted, and open me to know You in spirit and in truth — and to live for Your glory. And please reveal Yourself to a hurting world of people who don't even know that they don't know who You are.

Grace, Mercy, and Peace

I am writing to Timothy, my true son in the faith.
May God the Father and Christ Jesus our Lord give
you grace, mercy, and peace.
1 Timothy 1:2, NLT

Paul begins most of his letters with a variant of these words, before getting into the meat of what he has to say. It sounds like an overall blessing, kind of a loving way to say "hello."

What if it's more than that? His letters are very specific in terms of teaching and instruction. He doesn't seem the type to open with generic fluff.

Instead of a pleasantry, perhaps this prayer for "grace, mercy and peace" is a carefully-targeted prayer for Timothy's needs.

The letter goes on to advise Timothy in his conduct and duties, but the "working out" won't be effective without the inner working of the Holy Spirit in answer to Paul's request here.

We often pray for detailed needs and results, and rightly so. But let's take Paul's prayer as a reminder to ask for these essential gifts of God — grace, mercy, peace — as well. Often we don't know how to pray, or we think we do but our ideas may not match God's.

Paul reassures us that it's not a cop-out to pray for these larger, intangible blessings that will work themselves out in lives and in situations according to God's sovereign will and purposes. It may instead be the foundation for what comes next.

God who is the source of grace, mercy, and peace, please pour these gifts on me so I can understand and obey the teaching of Your Word. Thank You for the reminder that what I do in my own strength won't amount to much. I need Your touch, and You so readily give it when I remember to ask. Grant me Your blessing, I pray.

Hope Giver

This letter is from Paul, an apostle of Christ Jesus,
appointed by the command of God our Savior and
Christ Jesus, who gives us hope.
1 Timothy 1:1, NLT

"Christ Jesus, who gives us hope." Let that steep a bit in your mind.

Jesus gives us hope of healing, growth, and new life — and of Heaven. He gives hope that we'll make it when life is hard, and that we'll conduct ourselves in ways that are pleasing to God.

Only in Him to we have hope of doing what He gives us to do: "I can do everything through Christ, who gives me strength" (Philippians 4:13, NLT).

He's also our hope of glory — His glory (His character) shining through us.

That's a lot of hope, and some days we need it all.

God of grace and mercy, You are my strong tower and my hope. Increase my faith and help me seize hold of the hope You offer. Let me live in confidence in You, expecting to see Your work in my life and in the lives of others. Not as I might want to see it, but as You want to unfold it. For the sake of Your glory.

God's Strength for God's Work

I thank Christ Jesus our Lord, who has given me
strength to do his work. He considered me trustworthy
and appointed me to serve him...
1 Timothy 1:12, NLT

Jesus gives Paul the strength, and considers him trustworthy despite Paul's past.

And the work assigned is Jesus' work, not Paul's. Not mine. Not yours.

In Paul's case, it's high-profile, dangerous work. For most of us, it's not.

We're parents, employees or employers, citizens, neighbours, friends, shoppers, etc. It's still more than we can handle in our own strength, and we need to rely on the strength and grace that God provides.

We're Christ's ambassadors, just like Paul.

If we keep the trust and conduct ourselves in a manner worthy of the Gospel, relying on Jesus' strength and leading, we're doing His work of revealing God's reality to those around us.

That's a high calling indeed.

Holy One who saves me, You send me just as You sent Jesus, to let the world see that You are God, and that You are good. Help me walk by faith, not by sight. Help me rely on Your strength, not my own, and help me live for the sake of Your glory, not mine. Thank You for calling me to work with You in reaching the world.

Life. God Promised.

This letter is from Paul, chosen by the will of God to
be an apostle of Christ Jesus. I have been sent out to
tell others about the life he has promised through faith
in Christ Jesus.
2 Timothy 1:1, NLT

Accepting Christ gives us more than eternal life with God when we die. It gives us new life in the here and now. It's a spiritual rebirth, so we can grow in relationship with God.

He hears our prayers and responds to us. As the Good Shepherd, He directs and protects us, and leads us into opportunities to serve Him, be they big or small.

Sometimes in worship we sing "I will never be the same," but often we seem the same as we were before Christ. We're not the same — we're spiritually alive now — but sometimes it can hide pretty deep. After all, we're works in progress and sometimes the old "stuff" surfaces.

Believing the promise is key. God keeps His promises, but if we don't believe them, we can't receive them.

It's promised through faith. We can't earn this new life by working harder or working smarter. We need to believe what God says. When we don't feel any different, we can remind ourselves of His promises and pray "Lord, I believe. Help my unbelief" (Mark 9:24, NLT).

God who saved me and gave me new life, You know my weakness and You know the plans You have for me — plans to give me a future and a hope. Help me trust You, Lord. Help me grow in You. Thank You for giving me new life.

Flee. Pursue. Enjoy.

Run from anything that stimulates youthful lusts.
Instead, pursue righteous living, faithfulness, love, and
peace. Enjoy the companionship of those who call on
the Lord with pure hearts.
2 Timothy 2:22, NLT

The Apostle Paul's words to Timothy are ones we need to hear today in our fragmented, too-busy world.

Run from — the NIV says *flee* — "anything that stimulates youthful lusts." This includes more than just provocatively-dressed women wreaking havoc with men's hormones.

It's anything that catches our eye, ear, or heart and we *want* it. For those of us who aren't young anymore, it can even be things that promise to help us feel, look, or act young again.

"Pursue righteous living, faithfulness, love and peace." Those things don't grow without an investment of our cooperation and effort, even though God is the Master Gardener.

Enjoy the companionship of other Christians. As we spend less time in meaningful church experiences, and we find fewer believers in the workplace and neighbourhood, we're losing our support system.

We need the companionship, encouragement and challenges of other Christians. We are, after all, a body. Not a collection of single units.

Dear Father, please help me recognize when to run away — to run to You. Strengthen me to pursue the life You've designed me to live. Remind me of the importance of Christian companions. I pray for those who know You but have drifted away from church and Christian community, that You will bring Christians into their lives and help them recognize their need for fellowship and unity. Lord, we are weakest alone, and You call us to be strong in You and to not give up meeting together. Remind me when I forget, and please forgive my forgetting.

Faith, Patience, Love, and Endurance

But you, Timothy, certainly know what I teach, and
how I live, and what my purpose in life is. You know
my faith, my patience, my love, and my endurance.
2 Timothy 3:10, NLT

Paul's faith was more than intellectual belief. He lived it, and died for it. He definitely knew "the secret of living [and being content] in every situation" (Philippians 4:12, NLT).

He suffered frequent persecution and abuse for his faith. Perhaps this is where his patience appeared: in endurance and in persisting in relying on God.

His love doesn't sound like the soft, huggy kind, but his letters reveal a passionate commitment to the well-being and growth of Christians everywhere.

He thanks God for them, he prays for them, and he fights for them.

Sovereign God, You were with Paul and You are with me today. Help me learn from Paul's example. Help me remember and rely on Your presence and power. Lord, I believe. Help my unbelief in those times when I don't anchor to You. Help me choose to praise You no matter what, and to keep my eyes on You instead of on the problems.

What Holds You Together?

The Son radiates God's own glory and expresses the
very character of God, and he sustains everything by
the mighty power of his command. When he had
cleansed us from our sins, he sat down in the place of
honor at the right hand of the majestic God in heaven.
Hebrews 1:3, NLT

Jesus sustains everything. He holds it all together: atoms and solar systems, swirling in their created dance. He draws it out, lets it continue and resonate like a lasting chord played on a piano.

When life feels like it's spinning out of control — or when we feel like *we* are — this promise can be our anchor.

We might not like what's going on, and maybe we can't see any sense or any good in it, but it doesn't have to break us.

We are held. Together.

When we want to quit, the choice is ours. But if we choose to pray for help, to stand and trust God to sustain us, we will see Him at work.

Majestic and glorious God, You made heaven and earth and still You choose to care for me. You sustain and nurture me and draw me into relationship with Yourself so I can thrive. When chaos makes me doubt, help my unbelief. Strengthen my faith and help me choose to rely on You. Thank You for Your promise to never fail or abandon me.

Listening? Or Drifting?

So we must listen very carefully to the truth we have
heard, or we may drift away from it.
Hebrews 2:1, NLT

The writer of Hebrews has been refuting a false teaching that has crept into the church. It sounds like some form of angel-worship, but the warning applies just as well today and to a variety of falsehoods.

We can be led astray by error, or by lies. We need careful attention to the truth to keep us anchored.

One of the best ways to stay focused on the truth is to make Bible reading and prayer a daily part of our lives.

Five minutes... fifty... God is more concerned with the quality of the time than its duration. And it doesn't need to be one lump sum, either. Some people stop regularly throughout the day to say a quick prayer or to listen to His voice.

The point is to be intentional, and sincere. We don't want to — don't dare to — drift away from the truth.

God who reveals Himself through His Word and His Spirit, so many people don't think there's time to spend with You each day. They don't see the need, or the danger, but You've warned us. Please stir each heart that believes in You, draw each one to desire You. Draw my heart, too. Don't let me drift from the truth I've received.

Unbelief, or Rest?

So we see that because of their unbelief they were not
able to enter his rest.
Hebrews 3:19, NLT

"They" were the Israelites, led by Moses. The people who heard God's voice on the mountain and begged in terror not to hear it again. The people who experienced the plagues in Egypt, the parting of the Red Sea, the manna in the desert. The people who swore to follow and obey God.

Hebrews 3:16-18 says they rebelled, made God angry, sinned. Disobeyed Him. Not just with the golden calf, but by refusing to enter the Promised Land because they trusted their fears more than they trusted God.

A lot of their disobedience came from unbelief. Aren't we the same?

Sometimes we don't believe because either we don't want to obey or we don't want to let go of our own ways or understandings.

But sometimes we don't believe because we're afraid. That's when we need to pray, "Lord, I believe. Help my unbelief" (Mark 9:24).

God knows our weakness, and He wants us to get it right. He wants us to enter His rest, that's why He invited us. We only need to ask.

Thank You, God, that You don't disqualify me for my weakness, but You invite me to ask for help. Thank You for such grace and love to help me, again and again, when I'm in need. Help me remember to ask You — help me believe and obey.

Into the Inner Sanctuary

This hope is a strong and trustworthy anchor for our
souls. It leads us through the curtain into God's inner
sanctuary. Jesus has already gone in there for us. He
has become our eternal High Priest in the order of
Melchizedek.
Hebrews 6:19-20, NLT

The hope this verse mentions is the hope of our salvation, of eternal life in restored relationship with God.

Think about the Temple imagery for a minute: only the High Priest was permitted to enter the Most Holy Place, and only once a year. First he offered sacrifices for his own sins, and then, once clean, for the sins of the people.

There were special clothes to wear, special rituals of preparation. His robes had bells, and he wore a rope around one ankle in case he committed an offence and was struck dead, so the other priests could pull him out. This was serious business.

And now, Jesus has gone into this place of most intimate communion with God, once for all to atone for our sins... and once we've received this *we're invited through the curtain ourselves*.

Into God's inner sanctuary. Into His presence. With no guilt, no fear of destruction. What a gift is ours!

Holy and righteous God, I could never be worthy to even crawl into Your presence on my own merit, but You have made a way to wash me clean so I can come to You boldly and with confidence — and with reverent fear. Thank You for restoring me, for loving and rescuing me. Let me not neglect the privilege of spending time with You.

What Are You Looking At?

And Moses answered, "Look at me. I stutter. Why
would Pharaoh listen to me?"

GOD told Moses, "Look at me. I'll make you as a god to
Pharaoh and your brother Aaron will be your prophet."
Exodus 6:30-7:1, MSG

Poor Moses, no wonder he felt overwhelmed from the moment God first called him. Exiled from Egypt as a murderer, living as a shepherd, and he had trouble speaking. Hardly an ideal mouthpiece for the Almighty. Good thing he had no idea how the people would behave once he got them out!

Moses: Look at me! Everyone's mad at me. I can't even speak clearly! I can't do this — it's hopeless!

God: Look at Me.

We likely haven't been assigned such an enormous task, although sometimes it feels that way. But don't we respond the same way? Look at me, my weakness... the obstacles...?

Can you hear God's whisper? *Look at Me.*

God, You are mighty to save and powerful to change hearts and circumstances. I praise You for dramatic miracles like the Israelites saw in the Egyptian exodus. I praise You for invisible miracles that strengthen my spirit and enable me to serve You faithfully in the day-to-day of life. Forgive me when I look too long at my weakness. Teach me to look at You, Your strength and Your promises. Let everyone see the difference You make in me.

Getting It. Remembering It.

And Israel looked at the Egyptian dead, washed up on
the shore of the sea, and realized the tremendous power
that GOD brought against the Egyptians. The people
were in reverent awe before GOD and trusted in GOD
and his servant Moses.
Exodus 14:31, MSG

The people finally get it. They've seen God in action: the ten plagues that broke Egypt, and now the dramatic parting of the Red Sea and destruction of the Egyptian army.

How else could they respond but in worship and reverent awe? And by trusting God and the man He chose as their leader?

Sadly, it doesn't last long. Before the end of the next chapter, they're complaining there's no safe drinking water (Exodus 15:24), as if the God who's leading them might have run out of resources.

Living on this side of the Cross, Christians have the Holy Spirit in us, a personal and more intimate connection with God.

You'd think we'd stay close. He shouldn't have to keep calling us back like He did the people of Israel. Isn't it good that He does it, though? He doesn't just dust off His hands and walk away. He loves us, and He woos us back.

Saviour God, patient and abundant in mercy, forgive me for the many ways I let myself get distracted from You. Draw me close to You, and teach me to keep looking at You in love and awe. I'm incomplete apart from You, and unable to be Your light in the world. Grow me in faithfulness and in truth, into the child You've called me to be.

Will We Wait?

> When the people realized that Moses was taking
> forever in coming down off the mountain, they rallied
> around Aaron and said, "Do something. Make gods for
> us who will lead us. That Moses, the man who got us
> out of Egypt — who knows what's happened to him?"
> Exodus 32:1, MSG

Moses has gone up on Mount Sinai in personal conversation with God. The same God who so dramatically brought the people out of their slavery in Egypt. The same God whose thunder and lightning from the mountain made them plead for Him to talk only to Moses — not to address them directly.

On the mountain, God has been revealing to Moses how the people are to live, how they can remain in His holy presence. Below the mountain, the people make this ridiculous request to Aaron — and he goes along with them.

They're so close to intimacy with God and they throw it away, unknowing. Are we any different?

We may not go looking for other gods, but don't we chase other answers to our problems, other advice, when maybe if we waited for God's timing and His communication we'd be far better off?

He *is* our Good Shepherd, after all.

Holy and mighty God, You keep reaching out to draw me to Yourself, and I get distracted and pursue everything but You. Thank You for Your grace that forgives, and that keeps calling me. Make me a child after Your own heart, quiet and able to wait for Your voice. Let me truly live with You and not just go through the motions.

Come Clean. Quick.

When you are guilty, immediately confess the sin that
you've committed.
Leviticus 5:5, MSG

We're human. For all the good things that means, it also means we're not perfect. Despite our best intentions, sometimes we mess up. We don't measure up to the righteous standard of living God intends for us.

The early chapters of Leviticus are all about sacrifices to atone for the people's sin, and God spends a lot of time and detail explaining to the people what not to do. Some of it should be pretty obvious, but there you have it.

Chapters 4 and 5 deal with what happens when someone unintentionally sins. They've done something wrong with no malice aforethought. We do that too. And sometimes we do the premeditated wrongs.

In either case, the remedy is clear: immediately confess it to God. He knows anyway. It's already put a rift between us.

If it's an ongoing situation, ask for His wisdom in how to get back on target. And remember that He's faithful to His promises. He will forgive us, clean us up, and restore us.

We need to act immediately. Things won't get better, the problem won't go away, if we stall. We'll just make ourselves increasingly miserable as we widen the gulf between our spirits and the God who wants to hold us close.

God who saves me, Your forgiveness and grace are more than I can comprehend, and they're beyond my capacity to earn. Thank You for extending mercy again and again. Please grow me to maturity in my faith, into righteousness and holiness, so I can please You. Please forgive me when I fail, and help me cry out to You quickly for restoration.

Therefore We KNOW

The LORD's promises are pure,
like silver refined in a furnace,
purified seven times over.
Therefore, LORD, we know you will protect the
oppressed,
preserving them forever from this lying generation,
Psalm 12:6-7, NLT

The context in these verses comes from verse 5, where God says He has seen and heard the suffering of the poor and helpless and He will rescue them. And so, verse 7 says that's what the people know He will do.

The same logic holds for us today: Because God's promises are pure, we know He will keep them.

That doesn't mean we can pick something out of the Bible and expect God to fulfil it our way and on our timetable. There are plenty of promises we can claim in confidence, though.

Jesus will be with us always (Matthew 28:20). If we confess our sins, He is faithful to forgive them and to cleanse us (1 John 1:9). He has begun a good work in us and He will finish the job (Philippians 1:6).

"The LORD's promises are pure... Therefore, LORD, we know you will..." Doesn't that encourage you? When doubts come, when we're tired and worn, we can stand on what we know: that God will keep His word.

Mighty God, Your promises are pure and true and thoroughly tested. There is no doubt, no defect or weakness in them. Help me therefore to believe and to declare that I know You will keep them. Remind me of the ones I need to rely on at any given moment. Thank You that Your promises are guaranteed by Your character, which cannot change. Let me rest in that fact.

Learn to Live

In this way you will learn to live in deep reverence
before GOD, your God, as long as you live.
Deuteronomy 14:23b, MSG

The Book of Deuteronomy contains Moses' parting instructions to the people of Israel: how to live clean lives and worship God.

The laws, the schedule of sacrifices... some of the details don't make a lot of sense to us, and some of the dietary restrictions would cut us off from food we love.

But here's the point: Moses says this is how they'll learn to live in deep reverence before God. Isn't that what we, as Christians, want?

Rigidity and legalism are not healthy, but deep reverence for God is.

What we can take from these chapters is the importance of intentional living.

Within the flexibility of being led by God's agenda and not our own, we can practice certain habits: daily time with God in prayer, reading His Word — the manual — and asking for His leading and guidance in the day.

We can learn to rely on His grace and presence, and to live with Him in the moment instead of racing ahead.

Mighty and majestic God, You are worthy of worship, honour and adoration. You could demand those things, but instead You invite them. Help me draw near to You. Open my eyes and heart to be intentional in living with you — living for You. Then I will truly learn how to live.

Remember, and Give

Don't for a minute forget that you were once slaves in
Egypt and GOD, your God, redeemed you from that
slave world.
Deuteronomy 15:15a, MSG

In his letter to the Corinthians, Paul challenges them to remember their humble origins (1 Corinthians 1:26). His point is that we can't boast in our own abilities. We're saved and empowered by God.

Moses uses the same "remember your past" to say something different yet related. His focus here is more on gratitude, and on generosity. Because we've been given much, we're to freely give much.

This isn't about remembering past bondage and dirt to weigh us down. That is the enemy's tactic, but it's never God's plan. It's about remembering what God has done in freeing us from that past.

We need to remember what God has done for us... steep in it... let it shape and change us... so we can live grateful lives trusting God and giving to others as He has given to us.

Having been set free, we are to set others free. Having been given much, we are to give much. We can do this secure in the knowledge that He who provided for us will not run out of provision.

Heavenly and holy Father God, I need fear no lack, because You are the God of abundant supply. You have saved me and treated me well when I didn't deserve it. Warm my heart with love and gratitude, and help me treat others as You have treated me. Help me remember and rely on Your goodness so that I can live as a giver, not a hoarder.

Light in the Tunnel

Even though I walk
through the darkest valley,
I will fear no evil,
for you are with me;
your rod and your staff,
they comfort me.
You prepare a table before me
in the presence of my enemies.
You anoint my head with oil;
my cup overflows.
Psalm 23:4-5 NIV

Many translations broaden the KJV's "valley of the shadow of death" to be a dark valley of any kind, where we may be in danger or may just be slogging and struggling.

Isn't that where the enemies are? Not when we come out the other side, but in that valley? Where the Shepherd keeps His staff handy to protect us?

When the going is hard and we're desperate for a light at the end of the valley-tunnel, remember that our Shepherd — the Light of the world — is with us.

Sooner or later we'll glimpse the end. Then we'll reach it. But even now, when we despair of going on, here in the presence of our enemies — illness, grief, negativity, fear, family, work, whatever valley we're in — maybe our Shepherd is setting a table for us.

Maybe He's whispering, "Sit for a minute and eat. Rest and catch your breath. I AM here."

Jesus, my gentle but strong Shepherd, remind me of Your presence in the light and in the dark. Help me rely on Your love and care. You know my needs and the needs of those I love. Help me trust You to meet them. Even in the valleys, with enemies all around.

What's in the Heart

For out of the abundance of the heart the mouth
speaks.
Matthew 12:34b, NKJV

"Nothing ever goes my way. Why should anything good happen, anyway? I knew it was too good to be true. I should have known it wouldn't work out."

Ever said — or thought — anything like that? Most of us have, and it reveals things we don't want in our hearts: doubt, lack of faith, negativity, discontent, a complaining attitude... and at the very root, a suspicion that God isn't such a good Shepherd after all.

Nothing we'd espouse under ordinary circumstances, but when push comes to shove, the thoughts are there. Clamping our lips shut saves others from hearing it, but Jesus is right. It's a heart matter.

We don't have to believe the lies, the fear and the negatives. We can choose to believe God's promises and rely on His love.

But it takes work. It takes catching these unwanted thoughts and replacing them with truth.

In New Testament language, it takes putting on the armour of God: especially the shield of faith, helmet of salvation, sword of the Spirit, and the belt of truth to hold the breastplate in place.

And it takes speaking God's truth aloud to replace the negatives we've whispered so long.

God my loving Father, You see my heart and yet You work to save me. Help me rely on Your promise to forgive me when I confess and to make a way for me to escape temptation's power. Grant me faith to truly rely on You, to fully believe Your love and Your care, to live in such a way that others will see I do indeed have a Good Shepherd.

Free From Fear

I prayed to the LORD, and he answered me.
He freed me from all my fears.
Psalm 34:4, NLT

God kept David safe and got him out of the Philistines' clutches (1 Samuel 21:10-14), but David knew King Saul still wanted to kill him. And David had an honourable streak that wouldn't let him kill Saul first.

David's *reason* for fear — Saul — was very much alive and well. But David declared that he'd been *set free from all his fears*.

That suggests an important distinction. Maybe it echoes another David-psalm where he rejoices that his Shepherd is even with him in the dark valley under death's shadow (Psalm 23).

The danger hadn't changed, but David had. Fear didn't own him anymore. This wasn't David's first experience with God's trustworthiness. Growing up, he faced down lions and other predators. Then he acted in faith to kill the giant, Goliath (1 Samuel 17).

Even when we can't change our circumstances, we can change how we respond. We can choose to rely on our strong God. It isn't easy, and it's not a one-time deal for most of us. It often starts with bringing God our fears, and saying "Lord, I believe. Help my unbelief" (Mark 9:24, NKJV).

We will still feel fear. But we don't need to be afraid, bound by that fear. Our God is bigger.

God, my strong and mighty refuge, You promised to never leave me, and to shepherd and shield me. Whether you lead me through easy terrain or dangerous paths, help me remember that You are with me. Help me trust Your love. I know that doesn't mean I'll live a pain-free, happy life, but whatever happens, You will be with me to carry me through, to Your glory and ultimately for my good.

Spending Our Time

We are merely moving shadows,
and all our busy rushing ends in nothing.
We heap up wealth,
not knowing who will spend it.
And so, LORD, where do I put my hope?
My only hope is in you.
Psalm 39:6-7, NLT

Deep in our spirits, if we pause long enough to listen, don't we know the truth of these verses?

Whether we're heaping up wealth like the psalmist's example, stacking up accomplishments, or just trying to keep ahead of the demands of the day, we can be caught in this frenetic cycle of producing more. At the end of our lives, what really matters?

Yes, we need to provide for our families, be faithful to our employers or our callings, but aren't these means to an end? Isn't it really about the relationships: with family, friends, strangers... with God?

We were made for activity, work, and responsibility, but not to worship these things. Let's pray with David, "LORD, remind me how brief my time on earth will be" (Psalm 39: 4a, NLT). And, Lord, open our eyes to the best way to spend that time — and with whom.

In each day, Lord, each moment, remind me that You are present. Help me learn to love and enjoy You — and the people in my life — in the process of doing life. Help me learn to be, not just to do.

Living God's Way

The word of GOD came to Solomon saying, "About
this Temple you are building — what's important is
that you *live* the way I've set out for you and *do* what I
tell you, following my instructions carefully and
obediently. Then I'll complete in you the promise I
made to David your father. I'll personally take up my
residence among the Israelites — I won't desert my
people Israel."
1 Kings 6:11-13, MSG

For New Testament Christians, God keeps this promise to personally
take up His residence among us by placing His Spirit inside us.

Because of our sins, we're even less worthy of His presence than
Solomon's beautiful Temple building — except that Jesus has washed
us and is in the process of re-creating us into His image.

And so, since we're so richly blessed, we need to do what God said: live
the way He sets out for us, do what He tells us, and follow His
instructions.

Rigidity here would be to miss the point. We're to live carefully and
obediently. Lovingly. Trusting our Good Shepherd.

It's about staying close to Him instead of wandering away. Believing He
is strong and loving to care for us. Relying on His wisdom and guidance.

*Holy and majestic God, my mind can't comprehend how One such as
You could dwell in someone such as I — but You do it anyway. Thank
You for making me worthy, and thank You for the gift of Your presence.
Help me know and rely on You and to live a life worthy of Your Name.*

Overloaded

"I've been working my heart out for the GOD-of-the-
Angel-Armies," said Elijah. "The people of Israel have
abandoned your covenant, destroyed the places of
worship, and murdered your prophets. I'm the only one
left, and now they're trying to kill me."
1 Kings 19:10, MSG

Elijah's conversation with God comes after one of his most public exploits, when he taunted the prophets of Baal in a public showdown. Yet here he is, not long afterwards, running scared from evil Queen Jezebel.

Surely the God of fire and miracles could handle a vicious queen and her henchmen, but Elijah isn't thinking about God. Look at what he says — and he says it twice in the chapter. He's thinking about himself. The mighty prophet of God is having a self-pity party.

We don't dare point any fingers. Most of us have been there, and for far less reason. Commentators say Elijah was depressed, or that it was the crash after a victorious high. Maybe so. But maybe it's more than that. Did Elijah start wearing too much of the responsibility?

It was God's power that burned the drenched sacrifice on the rebuilt stone altar, but did Elijah get too involved in shouting at the priests of Baal? Did he start taking the fight too personally? Don't we do that sometimes? God's doing His part, but all of a sudden we're carrying loads He never asked us to carry?

In his hurt, Elijah shows us what to do. He goes to God. He gets alone with God, and even though he spills out his whole "poor me" rant, Elijah hears God. God meets him there. And Elijah doesn't leave that place until God sends him out.

Mighty and holy God, sometimes I start looking at the work more than at the One who sends me. In Your patient mercy, please help me see when I go off-track, and please draw me back to Yourself to sit in quiet and renew my spirit. Teach me to trust You in all things instead of trying to forge ahead in my own power. Teach me to rest in You.

How to Thrive

But I am like an olive tree, thriving in the house of
God.
I will always trust in God's unfailing love.
Psalm 52:8, NLT

What's the context of this psalm? David is warning an enemy that he will get what's coming from God for his evil deeds. Not in the sense of retaliation, but cause and effect: the man's crimes will meet justice.

David isn't bitter about the betrayal — if he were, he wouldn't be thriving in God's presence. Instead, David is trusting in God's unfailing love to care for him.

What would that look like in our lives, if we always trusted in God's love? And if we trusted in the rest of His character attributes?

Instead of bitterness and blame, we'd have peace. Yes, God will judge the offender if that person doesn't come to Him for forgiveness. But closer to home, God will be enough for us.

Instead of self-pity, we'd have security. Jesus loves us. He'll never abandon us. Instead of fear or anxiety, we'd have assurance. The all-powerful God of the universe has a plan for us. We may not see how He'll do it, but He will work all things out for good in the end.

If we could live this way, it would be thriving indeed.

Merciful God whose love is unfailing and extravagant, help me in my limited belief. Increase my faith, increase my desire for Your presence. Teach me to thrive in You and to always trust You.

Is God Enough?

"Why are you crying, Hannah?" Elkanah would ask.
"Why aren't you eating? Why be downhearted just
because you have no children? You have me — isn't
that better than having ten sons?"
1 Samuel 1:8, NLT

This sounds incredibly insensitive. How could Elkanah not understand the pain of Hannah's longing? Not pick up on her rival's smugness? In a culture that measured a woman's worth by her fertility, Hannah was barren, and her husband's other wife twisted that knife as often as possible.

But what if Elkanah and Hannah are a picture of God and us? Don't we often hold onto other desires — real, deep and painful — instead of being satisfied by all that God is? The irony is, we can't discover His depths while we're focused on what we don't have.

Not that we should minimize our longings. Love, employment, children, whatever it is that's the empty place in our hearts, these things matter.

Some longings, like Hannah's, are God-planted. He'll fulfil those. Others, equally strong, He won't. And we won't know why. Or which are which, until some come to fruition.

Whatever happens, we need to trust His unfailing love. We need to let God be enough for us in the now.

God my Provider, Sustainer and Redeemer, forgive me if I've let unmet longings take my heart away from You. Teach me to trust Your unfailing love, and open my spirit to realize that You are enough. Please fill what's empty in me and help me trust You with the desires of my heart.

Choosing to Trust God

In God, whose word I praise —
in God I trust and am not afraid.
What can mere mortals do to me?
Psalm 56:4, NIV

Did you ever struggle with this verse? We know our fellow humans can do some terrible things. How could we not fear the worst-case scenarios? Sometimes God lets these things happen, even to His own.

Let's look at the context of the verse, though. This is David writing, David who has been promised *by God* that he will be Israel's next king.

At this point in his life, he's on the run from the present king, Saul. Yes, David is afraid. Saul has a large, well-equipped army, and he only wants one thing: David, dead.

But God has promised. Because of that, David can reassure himself. Clearly, Saul isn't as strong as God, and God's plans will be fulfilled. In light of that, what can mere mortals do to him?

What has God promised you? Where is He directing you? What obstacles are blocking your path, where you can pray in confidence for God's intervention in His best timing and in His own way?

Even without physical enemies, the "stuff" in life looms large, and pressures can hunt us like King Saul chased David. In our families, work and volunteer duties, home care, and many other areas — we can pray in confidence that, if we're in God's will, His purpose for us will be fulfilled.

God who keeps His promises and whose purposes will be fulfilled, I praise and thank You for the privilege of being Your child and of living for Your glory. Forgive my doubts and stumbling, and remind me that Your plans for me are good. Help me see where I've accepted fear or defeat when You wanted me to take courage in Your strength. Lord, I believe. Help my unbelief.

When Life Piles Up Around Us

I cry out to God Most High,
to God who will fulfill his purpose for me.
Psalm 57:2, NLT

God may not have revealed a great purpose for you, like He did for David, the shepherd boy and future king. Nonetheless, God has plans for your life.

We're each to live for His glory, and therefore it's reasonable to pray that He will be glorified through our lives and in (or despite) our circumstances.

Do you have a family? Friends? His purpose there is that you love, care for, and support them. A home? That requires care too. Employment? Responsibilities? They are opportunities to serve diligently, as if God were the boss (which He is). A spiritual gift? It needs to be used God's way.

When you look at what He's given you, does it feel overwhelming? Like there's more to do than time to do it? Sometimes the pressures pile up and threaten an avalanche.

But God will fulfill His purpose despite the opposition — be it Saul's soldiers chasing David, or our crowded schedules. Like David, we need to trust and pray — and act as led — not to cower, whimper, and give up.

God, You hold all time in Your hands. Give me faith to believe Your promise to never leave me and to fulfill Your purpose for me. Grant wisdom in how to spend my days and meet my responsibilities. Help me obey Your leading instead of going my own way. Help me to focus, and to serve You in all I do.

"Use This"

Give your burdens to the LORD,
and he will take care of you.
He will not permit the godly to slip and fall.
Psalm 55:22, NLT

Attitude. Heaviness of spirit. Frustration. Sadness. Some days we struggle with these things. They rise up and make it hard to live a life worthy of the gospel. Even minor situations amplify them, and we risk having a meltdown or snapping at (or crying on) the people around us.

Then there are the bigger situations — actual crises — health, obstacles, bad news. External things we can't do anything about to help the people in pain or to salvage whatever plans have been overturned.

God can teach us to pray "Use this" — to give the burdens to Him, repeatedly, with the plea that He will use even these to reveal His glory.

The Bible, and the personal stories of believers through the centuries, prove God can do this. Instead of rolling over and giving up in these experiences, we need to keep our eyes on the King and look in faith to see what He will do.

God, I know and believe there is none like You, none more powerful, wise or loving. I believe Your promise to sustain and care for me. You can do more than I can ever imagine. Help me trust You to use every aspect of my life for Your glory. Let me not hold back or give up. Please strengthen my faith so I can stand.

A Quiet Moment With God

Step out of the traffic! Take a long,
loving look at me, your High God,
above politics, above everything.
Psalm 46:10, MSG

Traffic noise: motors, horns, someone's booming stereo. Dust. Exhaust fumes. Movement everywhere. We get used to navigating life in the middle of it all. This verse invites us to take a time out.

In our relationship with God, we can get caught up in the "traffic" of daily life, the things we're doing *for* God.

Sometimes we drift into managing our responsibilities in our own strength (we all have stories of how well that works — not!). But even when we're praying about it, committing the day and its needs to God, working *with* Him as well as for Him, it can get to be all about the work. The responsibilities.

Yes, we want to please God. We love Him, and He's given us so much. But it's easy to forget that this isn't *all* He wants. It isn't even the most important part.

God wants quality time with us. Just like a husband and wife, or friends who work or study together, we can't let it all be about doing — even when there are a million things to do. We need to pull back, "step out of traffic," and "be still and know" that He is God.

Let's slow down and enjoy that quiet time. Reflect more on who God is. Worship. Enjoy His presence. Maybe with a worship song to help us focus, or maybe in silence.

God my Creator and Shepherd, teach me to be still and to know that You are God. Help me abide in You, delighting in Your presence. Forgive me for what I've missed in my frantic pace. Help me work diligently for You and in Your strength, but help me first and foremost to set my heart on You and to let everything else flow out of that relationship.

God Isn't Finished With Us Yet

Listen! The LORD's arm is not too weak to save you,
nor is his ear too deaf to hear you call.
Isaiah 59:1, NLT

In our God-ignoring culture, sometimes even Christians don't seem awake to the importance of living God's way.

We don't dare go back to legalism, but often we as God's people don't look much different in our attitudes and behaviours than the people who don't know Him. As if God's call to holy living was only a suggestion, or as if His definitions have changed over time.

We need to live by God's standards in a way that's both genuine and approachable.

For some of us, that means remembering that Jesus is rightfully Lord of our lives and has a claim on our behaviour. For others, it means risking transparency so our non-Christian friends can see we're different. For all of us, it means guarding our relationship with God and growing deeper in relationship with Him.

No matter how bleak North American culture is today, it's not over, and it's not hopeless. In the long history of God and humans, this has happened many times. God can bring us back to where we need to be.

He's done it before, and His strength has not weakened over time. It doesn't end with us and our efforts. This is God's work, and our weakness isn't enough to eclipse His strength.

Mighty and holy God, it's a good thing You know human weaknesses — and an even better thing that You are mighty to save and longing to forgive. Speak to each one of us. Speak to me. Reveal anything that needs to change. I am very much a work in progress, and I need Your help. Restore, revive, renew me, and make me useful to Your Kingdom. Though I fail, let none be lost because of it. Have mercy on the hurting, and draw them to Yourself. Thank You for Your plan as revealed through the Cross, and for what You will do.

Helper AND Ruler

You who fear GOD, trust in GOD!
— trust your Helper! trust your Ruler!
Psalm 115:11, MSG

We're likely more familiar with this verse in other versions of the Bible. The NIV, NLT and KJV all use the words "help/helper" and "shield."

Often we gravitate to descriptions of God as our refuge, fortress, shield.

That may say something about fear and a need for security, who knows? But in The Message, the names "Helper" and "Ruler" raise a question.

Do we focus too much on God as our helper — to the point where we think of Him as a co-labourer or even an assistant — and forget that He is also our ruler and King?

Jesus is rightfully Lord of our lives, and He has a claim on our behaviour. That claim extends to our hearts and attitudes as well.

Holy and all-powerful God, I could never please You on my own, never be who You want or do what You ask. Thank You for the Holy Spirit in me as my Helper and Comforter. Forgive me for those times I forget that You are the Boss. You are my Ruler, my King. Under Your authority, I thrive.

In Stress, Remember God

GOD's strong name is our help,
the same GOD who made heaven and earth.
Psalm 124:8, MSG

This psalm is a celebration of God rescuing Israel from their enemies. They had no other hope, no chance. Without God, they'd have been destroyed.

We have life-or-death crises too. More frequently, we have lesser struggles that can still overwhelm us.

This verse offers two strategies to help us hold onto God by faith:

Remember God's strong name. His name reveals His character. It's who He is. Healer. Provider. Ruler. Deliverer.

Remember God's acts. He made heaven and earth. He parted the Red Sea and the Jordan River. He sent His Son to die for us and break the power of sin and death.

God is, and has done, so much more than this. And He hasn't aged or gotten tired. He's the same now, and He'll be the same tomorrow.

Strong and compassionate God, help me find confidence in Your unchanging nature. I praise You for who You are and what You've done, and for what You will do. Please strengthen my faith and help me rely on Your unfailing love.

The Desires of Our Hearts

For the LORD has chosen Jerusalem;
he has desired it for his home.
Psalm 132:13, NLT

God, who needs nothing that we can make for Him, wanted to establish His presence with His people.

Psalm 37:4 says that God gives us the desires of our hearts. He planted the desire in David, and in Solomon, who actually built the Temple. It was their desire, but it was God's first.

That reminds us how important it is to listen to God, to take time alone with Him in quiet. What dream or vision might He want to plant?

It also means we need to remember that any desire He may give us is ultimately His. We don't dare re-shape it or get possessive over it. David's role wasn't to build the Temple, but to gather the resources and prepare his son Solomon to be the builder.

Knowing a longing like this comes from God releases us to trust that He'll accomplish it as He fully envisions. This may be different from what we expect, since we may see only a portion of the whole.

Do you have a longing that wells up from such a deep place inside that sometimes it hurts? Stay close to God, listen to Him, and wait for His timing. He knows what He's doing.

Our God, Your ways and thoughts are beyond what I can comprehend, and yet You choose to involve me in accomplishing Your purposes. Thank You for the desires You plant in my heart, the ways You draw me into Your work. Help me listen and follow You, not turning aside and not running ahead. Help me remember that this is for Your glory, and not mine.

A Prayer For Every Day

Finish what you started in me, GOD.
Your love is eternal — don't quit on me now.
Psalm 138:8, MSG

Wouldn't this be a great prayer to memorize? To print out and stick on the bathroom mirror, on the car dashboard or somewhere else you'd see it every day?

Listen to the trust in these words. David knows that God has started a work in him. Because God started the work, David can count on it, and so can we, as believers in Jesus.

God's love is eternal. That includes His patience, His wisdom and His creativity. We often lament that we're slow learners with God.

Let's draw closer to Him in trusting surrender, so that He can work unhindered, but let's also relax and rejoice in the knowledge that His timing is perfect.

God never quits. He finishes what He starts. We have His promise.

As we pray "Don't quit on me now," what we're really expressing is the confidence that He won't quit on us — now or ever.

Wonderful and all-powerful God, because of Your great love You've begun a work in me. Thank You that You finish what You start, and that Your love is eternal. I rejoice in Your promise to never leave nor forsake me. Help me cooperate with You in the renovation of who I am — because of whose I am.

Kingdom Corners

Listen for GOD's voice in everything you do,
everywhere you go;
he's the one who will keep you on track.
Don't assume that you know it all.
Proverbs 3:6-7a, MSG

In the big things, the scary things, the God-sized things, it's easy to remember to rely on God's strength. We pray, we listen, we don't dare risk moving ahead on our own.

What about the little things? The daily routines, small decisions, mundane chores. They're the ones we often handle solo, using the skill and common sense that God gave us.

The problem is, these minor duties (including our day jobs) can fill our time and our thoughts until they're all we see. We miss what else God might want to do through, with, or for us.

Or we begin to own responsibility for the little things, but not in a good way. We decide what's good enough or how to allocate our time among various tasks. We take charge of this corner of the Kingdom.

The Kingdom. It all comes back to remembering who's the King. And that He's a good one, with good plans for us.

We also need to remember that our small corners are part of His Kingdom, with all the privileges and responsibilities that entails.

Holy and magnificent God, forgive me for the ways I complicate life and make it more difficult and less joyful than You intend. You know my weakness, and yet You love me. Give me clear perspective of Your sovereignty and of my place in Your Kingdom. Help me serve You with a willing heart, glad in the knowledge that You're in charge and not me.

Continual Praise

Enter his gates with thanksgiving;
go into his courts with praise.
Give thanks to him and praise his name.
Psalm 100:4, NLT

When the Israelites went to the Temple, they brought sacrifices: animals, birds, grain, oil, wine. They were giving back to God through a variety of offerings.

We bring our financial gifts and sometimes ministry gifts. We bring our hearts. But our thanksgiving to God, our praise of His character and His deeds, are acceptable sacrifices as well.

Just like the animal sacrifices were to be pure and without blemish, we need to offer God our best praise, our best thanksgiving. That means spending time with Him in prayer, reading the Bible, and keeping our eyes open to spot the good things He does in our lives.

It means offering the sacrifice when life is easy, and when life is hard. Not that we pretend everything's happy, but that we're honest about the pain while continuing to declare God's unchanging nature and His unfailing love.

David did this, in many of his psalms. It's a "required" sacrifice, but not to stoke God's ego. It's required for our sakes — as an antidote to how quickly we let the blessings or trials block our sight of the One who loves us.

Praise and thanksgiving ground us. They restore our focus and our perspective.

God my Creator, Saviour, and Sustainer, I could never thank You enough for all You've done, and there aren't enough words to tell how great You are. Please move my heart to praise and gratitude as part of my worship. Remind me this isn't optional, and thank You for the benefits I'll receive in my spirit as I draw nearer to You in obedience.

Do You Fear Bad News?

They do not fear bad news;
they confidently trust the Lord to care for them.
Psalm 112:7, NLT

Fear of lack. Fear of loss. It creates an underlying anxiety that leaches away our joy and strength. It diminishes our daily quality of life. We can end up living in tension, on alert, ready for something bad to happen, whether it's financial, physical, or relational.

If our vague fear doesn't materialize, we've carried the burden for nothing. And if it does, our strength is too depleted to face it well.

Things happen, despite our best care. Other things don't, either because God intervened or because they were only fear-whispers from the enemy of our souls.

Our best defence is to position ourselves securely in the care of our God and Refuge. We need to draw close to Him and stay close. As we get to know Him, we develop confidence in His character and power, and we learn to delight in living His way.

It's a life-long process, but the more we do this, the easier it is to do. We see evidence of God's care, and it grows our faith.

In those moments when our faith is shaky, we can go back to a beloved prayer from the New Testament: "Lord, I believe. Help my unbelief" (Mark 9:24, NKJV).

God my Shelter in the storms of life, You know my needs and You know the plans You have to work for good in all things. As a shepherd cares for the sheep, please care for me. Help me recognize Your voice and trust Your care. When I waver, help my unbelief.

Lord, I Want to See

If people can't see what God is doing,
they stumble all over themselves;
But when they attend to what he reveals,
they are most blessed.
Proverbs 29:18, MSG

We see with our natural eyes, and we "see" our perspectives and interpretations, and all of this gets in the way of our discerning what God is doing — and what God sees.

In ourselves: "Search me, oh God, and know my heart..." (Psalm 139:23a, NIV) is a key prayer.

God already knows us. Do we know ourselves? He won't overwhelm us by showing us everything He wants to fix, but He'll let us see what He wants to work on now. And it's never to diminish us, but always as an invitation to let Him work.

In others: It's so easy to justify why we do the things we do, yet to make assumptions about the motivations of others, especially when they irritate us. Unless we take time to know them, we have no idea what's happening under the surface of their lives.

In the world: Much of what we hear is slanted by the media or by individual opinion. Again, even if we get the unbiased truth, it's still surface information. God knows the details, and He knows His plans.

Seeing what God is doing helps us to pray. It also helps us live confidently in Him despite the circumstances. When we attend to what He reveals — when we see, hear, pay attention, and adjust our actions accordingly — we are most blessed. Because then we're closest to His heart.

God my great Shepherd, my King and Sustainer, open my eyes to the many ways You touch my life. Forgive me when I get discouraged by what I see, and open my eyes to what You see and what You're doing. Forgive me for not looking past the surface of the people I meet. Give me Your vision, so I can better serve and reflect You in my life.

The One Opinion of You that Matters

The fear of human opinion disables;
trusting in GOD protects you from that.
Proverbs 29:25, MSG

"Disable" is a strong word. Even though many levels of disability don't incapacitate a person, they do affect and interfere in some way with that person's ability to function. And some disabilities increase over time.

We all know how fear of others' opinions can cause us to self-censor, to put up walls or wear masks, to hide our true thoughts and feelings. In contrast, certain people make us feel safe to be ourselves.

No matter what people say or think about us, whether they misunderstand us or see the truth, God loves us

In His eyes, we have such great value that Jesus came to rescue us from life (and death) cut off from relationship with God.

We can trust His love. We can trust the things He says in the Bible. Things like "If we confess our sins, he is faithful and just and will forgive us our sins and purify us from all unrighteousness" (1 John 1:9, NIV). And "I am with you always" (Matthew 28:20, NIV).

Rejection, snide remarks, and misunderstanding from others will always hurt. But security in God's love can keep us from being disabled by the fear of human opinion.

Our best defence is to get closer to Him.

God my gentle Shepherd, You understand the pain of rejection. You know my fears. When others hurt me, help me anchor in Your deep love. Help me remember — and believe — what You say about me. Help me pay more attention to Your opinion of me than to those of the people around me. Help me live confidently in Your care.

Idols Aren't Wooden Anymore

*An idol is nothing but a tree chopped down,
then shaped by a woodsman's ax.
Jeremiah 10:3b, MSG*

In 21st century North America, the idea of calling an inanimate object "god" sounds foolish. We'd never worship something like that. Not in the sense of offering sacrifices to it, or of praying for its help.

But what if an idol is anything that takes first place in our lives, anything that replaces or reduces our adoration of our Saviour?

Maybe we've just build more sophisticated ones. Not out of wood or metal, but out of our wants and needs. Cars, houses, technology. Mates, children, pets.

God deserves first place in our hearts, minds and spirits.

When we align under His authority, we can rest in His sufficiency and His presence. With Him, we can pass through the hard times and come out the other side, even if that other side isn't until we die.

It all comes back to trusting God. Putting Him first. Checking our other affections to be sure they haven't begun to crowd Him out. Restoring our perspective wherever it's needed.

Holy God, You alone are worthy of my worship, praise and adoration. You're the giver of all good things. Forgive me for the times I've allowed good things to usurp Your place in my heart. Help me to appreciate Your gifts but to worship You, the Giver.

Signpost Life

I myself am GOD, your God: Keep my statutes and live
by my laws. Keep my Sabbaths as holy rest days,
signposts between me and you, signalling that I am
GOD, your God.
Ezekiel 20:19-20, MSG

As Christians, we live under grace. It's not about trying to earn our salvation or to appease God so He won't zap us.

But God is a holy God, and our behaviour matters to Him.

We can please Him, or we can offend Him. With all He's done to save us, isn't the best response a life that honours and obeys Him? A life lived in loving trust?

That's the kind of life that keeps us close to God instead of putting up spiritual barriers. And in a culture that has little use for God's statutes, laws or Sabbaths, it's a life that shows others that our God is different. He is good. He's worth following.

Holy God, I could never earn Your approval, but Jesus does, and as a believer, I stand clothed in Him. Thank You. Please free me from any lingering doubt of Your acceptance, and give me a heart that longs to please Your heart — in my words and in my actions. May others catch glimpses of Your character in my life.

The Long View

I pray that your love will overflow more and more, and
that you will keep on growing in knowledge and
understanding.
Philippians 1:9, NLT

This is Paul's deepest longing for these people he loves. They're enduring hard times, but he asks for love and growth — not for relief from suffering, for health, protection, or happiness. In verse 6, he expresses confidence that God will use even these times to complete what He has started in them.

He's praying they'll hold firm for their lifetimes, or until Christ's return, whichever comes first (Philippians 1:10). Either way, Paul is taking the long view, and the highest thing he can ask for them is that they'll bring much glory and praise to God (Philippians 1:11).

For ourselves, and for our loved ones, it's so easy to be distracted by the circumstances. To beg for relief. Rescue.

Those desires aren't wrong, but let's look at both the immediate need and the bigger picture. Let's pour out our hearts while remembering Jesus' prayer, "Nevertheless, not My will but Yours be done" (Luke 22:42, NKJV). To pray, "Use this."

Our prayers need to include the emotional and spiritual with the physical. We pray for love, encouragement, hope, and endurance, remembering that the ultimate goal is growth for us and glory for Him.

Mighty and loving God, help me be willing to endure hard times if that's what's needed for others to see Your goodness in how You sustain me. Help me not to be too quick to rescue others, if You might have a lesson for them in their struggles. Show me how to be Your hands and feet, Your voice of encouragement. Grow me in faith and trust, for the long view.

Encouragement for the Struggle

For I know that as you pray for me and the Spirit of
Jesus Christ helps me, this will lead to my deliverance.
Philippians 1:19, NLT

Paul has already been delivered, in the sense of being rescued from the penalty of sin. In context here, he's in prison and some of his enemies are trying to make that even harder for him. Likely the deliverance he's thinking of is release from his chains.

If we belong to Jesus, we're free from the power of sin and death, but there are still "chains" in our lives, binding us in ways that keep us from growing into all God intends us to be.

Attitudes, fears, memories... maybe we struggle with them and get discouraged.

This can be our verse of hope. We can ask at least one trusted friend to pray, and we can remind ourselves that the Holy Spirit *is* at work in us. No matter what we feel.

Holy Spirit, please help me believe that You are at work in me. Help me cooperate with that work, and help me persevere without giving up. Protect me from discouragement. Thank You for the promise of deliverance. And thank You for Your grace.

Because You Belong to the Lord

Now I appeal to Euodia and Syntyche. Please, because
you belong to the Lord, settle your disagreement.
Philippians 4:2, NLT

"Because you belong to the Lord." We forget this perspective, forget that belonging to the Lord is supposed to make a difference in our behaviours and our motivations. Not so we can earn more love (or more salvation) — we can't — but because we love this God who loved us first.

Euodia and Syntyche have had a serious falling out. The friction is hurting the local body of believers, and it's also giving ammunition to the scoffers who say all this love-and-unity stuff is too good to be true.

In every group of believers, there will be differences of opinion. Even conflicts. And our enemy loves to get us focused on anything that can divide us.

The good news is, God can use these opportunities as ways to demonstrate His kingdom living, if we'll rely on Him.

It's not about us. It's about God — the news of what He's done for us and His power to save us from ourselves.

We don't have the luxury of indulging in hurt feelings and splits. If we can make reconciliation more important than restitution or revenge, the world will recognize something — Someone — holy at work.

Our God, You ask the impossible, but all things are possible with You. Conflict is part of living. Please help me conduct myself in a manner worthy of the Gospel. Give me willingness and power to forgive, and remind me that forgiving doesn't mean the "other side" is necessarily right. Help me to love those who have hurt me, and to pray for their good. Please intervene in disputes among Your children. Help each to understand the other, and to see where confession, change, and courage are needed. I ask this for the sake of Your Kingdom and Your reputation in this world.

Short on Motivation?

For God is working in you, giving you the desire and
the power to do what pleases him.
Philippians 2:13, NLT

This verse talks about those activities and roles that God leads (or pushes) us into, where we rely on His power and we're motivated by a passion from Him.

But it goes deeper than that. As well as the key activities, our days are full of the mundane and the routine: opportunities to please God, to show the results of our salvation.

Those moments often escape our notice, but it's the small things that add up over time.

We need to depend on God working in us, giving us the desire and the power to do what pleases Him in the day-to-day.

Do we ask Him, every morning? Do we remember, when we're knee-deep in routine?

God my Maker, my Shepherd, You plan good things for me. On my own I have nothing that could please You. Open my eyes to see what You see, and give me the desire to please You in the big and in the small. Help me live for You in love and in trust.

Service and Offering

But I will rejoice even if I lose my life, pouring it out
like a liquid offering to God, just like your faithful
service is an offering to God. And I want all of you to
share that joy.
Philippians 2:17, NLT

Our "service" isn't just what we do in church, or our volunteer activities. It's also how we care for and interact with others on a daily basis. Do we make eye contact with the sales clerk, show courtesy in driving, remember to say thank you?

Service: not serving self. Being mindful of God in our behaviour, attitudes, and choices.

Offering: More than the rote giving of funds on a Sunday morning. It's yielding our whole selves to His will, holding nothing back, in the example of Jesus Himself (Phil. 2:5-11).

Maybe that sounds dramatic. Over the top. Too hard for us. But break it down to the small choices in each day: Will we choose God's way, or our way? Grudgingly, or with a willing heart?

Mighty and loving God, You ask me to give my all. You're worthy of my all, and I owe You my life. You know how tightly I hold on, though. Help me surrender myself to You daily — moment by moment, even — because You are a good God. You love me. And You've paid my ransom.

Fixing Our Thoughts

Fix your thoughts on what is true, and honorable, and
right, and pure, and lovely, and admirable. Think about
things that are excellent and worthy of praise. Keep
putting into practice all you learned and received from
me — everything you heard from me and saw me
doing. Then the God of peace will be with you.
Philippians 4:8b-9, NLT

It's so easy to dwell on the negatives. The hurts or injustices. Sometimes we do it because we're sulking or just plain cantankerous, but it's often out of fear (what's this world coming to?) or discouragement. After all, we see so much, so often; it wears us down.

The Christians in Philippi were experiencing persecution, and their beloved Paul was in prison. His letter encouraged them to keep focused on Jesus as their help and their hope. With Christ as their anchor, they needed to keep their broader focus positive and filled with gratitude.

This verse doesn't ask us to deny the bad things in our lives. The context of Paul's letter makes that clear.

But after acknowledging the circumstances and bringing our needs to God in grateful prayer that He cares and will help (Philippians 4:6), we're not to stay focused on the needs or the waiting.

We're to cultivate an awareness of the good, in the middle of the struggle. If we focus on the darkness, it swells to fill our vision. If we focus on the light, with our Saviour at its centre, the darkness reduces to its true size. A size which is smaller than God.

Mighty and compassionate God, protect and deliver me from spirits of discouragement, despair, and hopelessness. Remind me that You are greater than my hardships, and that Your creative grace can take even the worst and bring something positive from it. Doubt would tell me that's impossible, so please help my unbelief.

Staying True

Therefore, my dear brothers and sisters, stay true to the
Lord. I love you and long to see you, dear friends, for
you are my joy and the crown I receive for my work.
Philippians 4:1, NLT

Staying true to an invisible God is hard, if we let our personal time with Him slip. Life and busyness have a way of eroding that time, and without a vibrant, intimate connection with God, our loyalty drifts. We aren't as faithful, or as faith-filled. We depend less on God and more on ourselves.

"True" also means *focused, fixed on* — like our direction is "true" if we're on the correct course.

This verse calls us to more than loyalty and faithfulness, to be true to God and not turn away or betray Him, although it clearly says that as well.

It echoes a repeated theme of Scripture: to keep our eyes on God and keep pressing on to know Him better. He is our Sustainer and Shepherd in the journey, but He is also our goal — and our prize.

Focusing on Him prevents dwelling on the circumstances or on our differences. It gives unity to believers as well as personal balance, growth, and faith.

Lord of all, help me seek You ahead of all else. Amid all the good You've given me, help me prize You most and desire You most. Help me to stay true to You. May my life show others that You're truly worthy of worship.

Growing and Building

And now, just as you accepted Christ Jesus as your
Lord, you must continue to follow him. Let your roots
grow down into him, and let your lives be built on him.
Then your faith will grow strong in the truth you were
taught, and you will overflow with thankfulness.
Colossians 2:6-7, NLT

If we truly accept Jesus as Lord and Saviour, it's more than a head thing.

We've escaped sin's domination by coming into His kingdom and putting ourselves into His care. We're under His authority, and we need to follow Him, by obeying what He says, and by following His example of living surrendered to God the Father.

Deep roots and a solid foundation are images of strength, and our strength is found in Jesus. The deeper we root, the more securely we're built on His foundation, the stronger we'll be.

Our faith will mature. And our gratitude will abound.

This is the rich and satisfying life Jesus promised (John 10:10, NLT). And it has nothing to do with our circumstances.

It's available to all believers, even if it'll take a lifetime of practice to grow into it. The investment is worthwhile. It's what we were made for.

Gracious God, thank You for saving me from sin — and from myself. Please help me to stay close to You and to cooperate as You grow me to be more like Your Son Jesus. Thank You for this new chance at life.

Devoted to Prayer

Devote yourselves to prayer with an alert mind and a
thankful heart.
Colossians 4:2, NLT

If we devote ourselves to prayer, it will become an essential part of our daily lives. We'll find a quiet time to be alone with the Lord to worship, to listen, and to speak. We'll also carry the attitude of prayer with us through the day.

With a mindset of prayer, trouble won't be something to fight, to complain, or fret about. We can lift every struggle to God, as often as needed.

Good things won't be sources of pride or security, or possessiveness. We can thank the Giver and listen for how He might want to use them for His greater good.

Thankfulness in everything doesn't mean we're happy about the bad things. It means we're thankful for a God who invites us to bring Him every need, who has a good plan and the power to complete it, and who loves and never leaves us.

Looking at this from a human perspective, we could dismiss it as impossible. Ridiculous. A fantasy. But on the other hand, wouldn't you love to be able to live that way? Think of the deep-down sense of peace and security, no matter what life might throw at us.

We can't just say "Yes, God, I'll live like this," and be suddenly changed, although He may make a dramatic shift that gets us well on the way. This is a lifetime's learning, a maturing into life with Jesus. It will take practice, and there'll be setbacks, but the Holy Spirit within us can change us — if we'll cooperate.

Father God, You know how many times prayer is not my first response, or how I'll give you a problem and then take it back to carry on my own. This isn't the life of glad, dependent obedience that You want to grow in me. Please help me learn to bring everything to You and to listen to You. Teach me to devote myself to prayer — to communicate with You — and to be alert and thankful.

Bring Out the Best

Look for the best in each other, and always do your best
to bring it out.
1 Thessalonians 5:15b, MSG

"Look for the best..." for God-given potential, even if faintly visible. For spiritual gifts and natural talents.

Bringing it out in the best way starts with prayer: asking God what to say (or what to pray without even approaching the person). Asking God what He wants to do, and waiting for His timing.

Then, we may point out the ability or potential we see, and encourage the person to volunteer at the level of his or her ability. Maybe introduce a beginner to someone experienced in that area.

Beginner or seasoned worker, everyone is still a work in progress.

How do we bring out the best? We celebrate the good, we are careful in correction, we encourage growth. Quality of work matters, but a genuine and God-serving heart is an essential part of "the best." So let's encourage one another's hearts, spiritual lives, and attitudes, as well as the outward working of one another's potential.

In our relationships with non-Christians, this would also include being alert to signs of spiritual seeking or longing for truth. The best way to bring it out will be by living our own faith authentically and sharing a word or two as God makes a way. What better way to follow Jesus in our daily lives?

God who gives talents and gifts according to Your own wisdom and for Your glory in building up of the body of believers, thank You for what You want to do in and through each of Your children. Open me to recognize the best in others, and show me how best to bring that out. Forgive me for the times I look through human eyes, short-sighted and biased — and sometimes grumpy. Help me to see what You see, and to desire what You desire.

When God Does Something Good

"How kind the Lord is!" [Elizabeth] exclaimed. "He
has taken away my disgrace of having no children."
Luke 1:25, NLT

North American culture today doesn't equate a woman's worth with her fertility, but for women in Bible times, failure to produce a child, especially a male heir, was a source of shame.

Elizabeth is old by this point, well past natural childbearing age. God surprises her with a miracle pregnancy as announced by an angel to her husband, Zechariah (Luke 1:5-25), and she is purely grateful.

She alludes to the long disappointment in her life, but she's not bitter. She sees how God's gift is meeting that hurt. She sees the power of God. And she accepts His timing.

"How kind the Lord is!" If God chooses to meet our unmet longings — or if He chooses not to — He is still kind and good. He is still enough. He still does good things for us.

Let's keep our eyes and hearts open to notice what He does. Let's respond like Elizabeth, with gratitude and trust. Not with "well, it took You long enough!" Not with complaints to taint the thanks. Neither with mindless acceptance or casual indifference — nor a sense of entitlement.

Let's respond with worship and gratitude, acknowledging God's goodness and mercy, and knowing that while He doesn't owe us anything, He loves us enough that He gave His own Son to rescue and redeem us.

Loving Father God, how good You are! How kind indeed. Grow in me an awareness of Your care and a humble gratitude for Your many gifts. Teach me, like Elizabeth, to respond with praise, adoration, and trust.

Free, or Tyrannized?

Since Jesus went through everything you're going
through and more, learn to think like him. Think of
your sufferings as a weaning from that old sinful habit
of always expecting to get your own way. Then you'll
be able to live out your days free to pursue what God
wants instead of being tyrannized by what you want.
1 Peter 4:1-2, MSG

These are good verses to memorize for perspective. Whether we're suffering or simply living amid the day-to-day opportunities for self-indulgence, may we be alert to notice the choices. And may we choose growth.

"That old sinful habit of always expecting to get your own way." Peter says it plainly, and it's deeply ingrained in each of us. Especially in a North American culture that assumes it's our right to have what we want.

"*Free* to pursue what God wants instead of being *tyrannized* by what you want." The better we know God, the more sure we can be that what He wants is better and more healthy than what we want, as well as it being for our ultimate good.

Perhaps the key is in the first part of this passage: learning to think like Jesus. Renewing our minds, as Paul says in Romans 12. And diligently cooperating in the "weaning" from self-focus.

The Christian life is a process. We're not just saved and instantly complete. We need to mature. The New Testament letters emphasize our responsibility to grow.

Holy and gracious God, thank You for rescuing me from the penalty of sin and for rescuing me from myself. I could never earn Your grace, and You give it freely. Help me be diligent in working with You to break the sinful habits that linger in my life, so I can grow in spiritual maturity and in intimacy with You.

Belief and Trust

"Lord," he said, "if you are willing, you can heal me
and make me clean."

Jesus reached out and touched him. "I am willing," he
said. "Be healed!" And instantly the leprosy
disappeared.
Luke 5:12b-13, NLT

Imagine the fervent, desperate hope in the leper's voice, and in his heart.

There was no cure for the disease at the time, and Luke calls it an "advanced case." He might have be missing fingers, toes, part of his nose. Jesus touches him — touches a potentially contagious untouchable. And Jesus heals him. Instantly.

Two things stand out in this man's example: his *belief* and his *trust*. He has no doubt that Jesus has the power and authority to heal and cleanse him.

"*If* You are willing" suggests that he knows not everyone who asks gets healed. Even if he doesn't know that, we do. We need to pray "if You are willing, You can..." but we can't let the "if" become doubt of God's goodness.

"If You're willing" must never become "If You're good" or "If You love me," or even "If I deserve it." It simply means "You can, so I'm asking, but I don't know Your full plan." And we need to trust His heart, however He answers.

Almighty and all-wise God, Your plans and purposes are beyond my understanding, but You have clearly revealed Your heart in Jesus' life and death. You've revealed Your power in His resurrection. If You are willing — if You choose — You can do anything. Forgive me for the times I doubt Your power, and for the times I doubt Your love. Help my unbelief. Teach me to trust You and to live and pray with confidence in Your care.

Taking God Seriously

So why do you keep calling me "Lord, Lord!" when you
don't do what I say?
Luke 6:46, NLT

Jesus' miracles proved His power, authority, and compassion. His message was direct and understandable, except when cloaked in parables. People flocked to Him.

Yet here, after a very practical sermon, He accuses them of not doing what He says. And He warns that putting His words into practice will be the difference between stability and disaster (Luke 6:46-49).

He's just told them to love, bless, do good, not to judge or condemn, to forgive, and to be generous to friend and enemy alike. He's told them to live like Himself, minus the miracles.

God tells us how to live, and He means what He says.

We need to take Him seriously, for our own health (He designed us and knows us best), as examples to show His love and care and righteousness, and to keep close to Him instead of drifting away. We can't do it on our own, but He knows that, and He's given us the Holy Spirit to help us.

God my Creator and Redeemer, what is it I'm not doing that You say? Help me hear and obey, for my own sake and for the sake of Your Kingdom — and to please Your heart. Forgive me for the times I've lived as if obedience were optional. Help me submit fully to Your authority in my life, with complete trust in Your goodness.

Jesus' Authority

I know this because I am under the authority of my
superior officers, and I have authority over my soldiers.
I only need to say, "Go," and they go, or "Come," and
they come. And if I say to my slaves, "Do this," they
do it.
Luke 7:8, NLT

The Roman officer believed that Jesus' word at a distance was enough to heal his dying slave, because he understood how authority works. And he believed Jesus had the authority to heal.

Jesus has authority over us by right of creation and by right of rescue. He is our Good Shepherd, and He knows what's best. He has the power and the heart to care for us.

Jesus has authority over everything. The Bible shows that not only did sickness and oppression leave at His command, but He calmed storms, raised the dead, even provided a coin in a fish's mouth to pay a local tax.

He spoke wisdom straight from God the Father.

We can trust His authority, and His heart.

God who is Father, Son and Holy Spirit, strengthen my faith. Help me rely on You and trust Your authority. Help me obey You in love and in confidence in who You are.

Keep Listening

So pay attention to how you hear. To those who listen
to my teaching, more understanding will be given. But
for those who are not listening, even what they think
they understand will be taken away from them.
Luke 8:18, NLT

Jesus' warning here is why we need to read the Bible — daily — and to ask God to open our ears and teach us. It's why we need to spend time with other Christians, not just socializing but also sharing what we've seen God do and what we're learning.

Reading the Bible doesn't have to be hard. Pick an understandable translation, and begin your reading time with a prayer that God will teach you. He loves to answer that kind of prayer!

Prayer isn't hard either. It's being quiet with God, listening as well as speaking. It's spending time with Him, with a willing spirit, ready to adore and obey. It's relationship time, just like with our loved ones.

We dare not risk losing our closeness with God just because we haven't taken time or have been too busy for Him.

Oddly enough, a few minutes with Him at the beginning of the day can make the rest of it fall into place better than expected. After all, He *is* our Shepherd and *does* give us strength and wisdom when we ask.

God my loving Father, my strong and caring Shepherd, what a privilege to be in relationship with You. Forgive me for the times I allow myself to drift away, and please restore me to intimacy with You. Help me be intentional in spending time with You, and to listen and obey.

A Teaching Moment

The disciples went and woke him up, shouting,
"Master, Master, we're going to drown!"

When Jesus woke up, he rebuked the wind and the
raging waves. Suddenly the storm stopped and all was
calm.
Luke 8:24, NLT

We know from the Gospels that Jesus rose early to pray and sometimes stayed up late praying. Preaching, teaching, and healing would have been exhausting. Yet this is His only recorded nap.

Perhaps He intentionally slept during this storm, as part of the day's lesson for His disciples. Not that they recognize it as a teaching moment. They're panicking, shouting. Expecting to die.

After He calms the storm, Jesus asks, "Where is your faith?" And Luke says the disciples are "terrified and amazed" at what He has done (Luke 8:25, NLT).

The passage carries an undertone of, "Why were you freaking out? All you had to do was ask." His question isn't about blame, or about their lack of faith. It's to show them faith applies even here.

By this point in their relationship, the disciples have heard Jesus' authority when He taught. They've seen miracles: healings, demons cast out, a supernatural catch of fish. Even a raising from the dead. But this new crisis seems so immediate — so personal — and they don't think to ask Jesus for help.

Like the disciples, we need to not only remember what Jesus has done in the past, but remember His power. His presence. And ask for His help.

God, You are a patient teacher, yet so many times I don't learn. Open my heart, mind, and spirit to receive what You want me to know. Help me remember what You've shown me in the past, and give me confidence in Your presence and Your power, whatever comes my way.

Terrified and Amazed. In a Good Way.

The disciples were terrified and amazed. "Who is this
man?" they asked each other. "When he gives a
command, even the wind and waves obey him!"
Luke 8:25b, NLT

When was the last time you were terrified and amazed by God?

Not fearing He would nail you with a lightning bolt. Overwhelmed by awareness of how much power is His. Of what He does. Of how much He loves us.

God is infinitely great, yet we're invited to come into His presence. This is the same God who thundered on the mountain in the Old Testament, whose presence terrified the high priests.

He is no less powerful by giving us a way back into His presence. (He is, after all, the same God who walked in the Garden of Eden with Adam and Eve.)

We don't often see "big" proof of His power, but He is working in and around each one of His children right now. It's easy to miss if we don't keep our eyes open. Even then, it's easy to see His touch as evidence of love and care but to miss the power behind it.

Awareness of His power increases our confidence in Him. It reminds us that obedience is not negotiable. And it stirs us to worship.

Holy and majestic God, all power and authority are Yours. Forgive me for forgetting, for settling for less than full worship of all You are. Help me take time to reflect on all of Your attributes, so I can grow in faith.

Hypocrisy vs. Holiness

Beware of the yeast of the Pharisees — their hypocrisy.
The time is coming when everything that is covered up
will be revealed, and all that is secret will be made
known to all.
Luke 12:1a-2, NLT

Jesus often called out the Pharisees for their showy ways and love of public admiration, and for the burdens they laid on the people performance-wise. Now He's warning His disciples about the Pharisees' contagious example.

The message for today's generation of the church, which has its own stain of hypocrisy, is this: Do the outward acts, the tithing and good deeds (the Book of James has a lot to say about that) but "do not neglect the more important things" (Luke 11:42, NLT).

What's more important than doing? Being. Being right with God. Close to Him, our spirits lined up with His, listening to Him and obeying. Worshipping. Living confidently in His care.

If inward purity is important — and it is — and if we're cultivating "the more important thing" of a close relationship with God, it's bound to show in our character and in our actions.

Not that we'll be perfect. When we slip up, it may look like hypocrisy, but it won't be. It'll be a humbling opportunity to be open with the people around us about our — and everyone's — need to rely fully on God's grace, forgiveness, and strength.

We can't allow fear of failure to keep us from shining for God, but we must be careful to shine to please an audience of One. Not for the people around us.

Father God, You call me to grow in the image of Your Son, whose righteousness grew from His relationship with You. The outward life is easier for me to measure, but You see my heart. Call me deeper in faith, love, and obedience, purify and renovate me within, so that what comes out of me will be pleasing to You.

Time-Sensitive Invitation

O Jerusalem, Jerusalem, the city that kills the prophets
and stones God's messengers! How often I have
wanted to gather your children together as a hen
protects her chicks beneath her wings, but you
wouldn't let me.
Luke 13:34, NLT

"You wouldn't let Me."

Those are some of the saddest words in the Bible. Jesus makes the invitation, but it's up to us to accept Him.

By this point in the narrative of the Gospel of Luke, Jesus is moving toward Jerusalem for the last time, and His teaching has taken on an urgency. Luke 13 warns repeatedly that time is running out, for Jesus' hearers and for people today.

Those who don't turn from their old ways and "work hard to enter the narrow door" (Luke 13:24, NLT) — those who won't come on God's terms instead of insisting on their own interpretations — will one day find it's too late.

There is restricted access to a relationship with God in the Kingdom of Heaven. There will be a cut-off time, an expiry to the invitation.

But the invitation is extended to everyone. "He does not want anyone to be destroyed, but wants everyone to repent" (2 Peter 3:9b, NLT).

Holy God, my finite mind can't grasp the enormity of sin or the vastness of Your love. Thank You for the grace of Jesus, and please give me faith to cling to You. Help me recognize when others are responding to Your Spirit's call, and give me wisdom and willingness to speak or to be silent as You lead. May I do nothing to hinder anyone's coming to You.

Saying Thank You

One of them, when he saw that he was healed, came
back to Jesus, shouting, "Praise God!"
Luke 17:15, NLT

Ten lepers — contagious, shunned and ritually unclean — had called to Jesus from a respectful distance, begging to be healed.

Their faith must have been strong, because Jesus didn't invite them nearer, or touch them. He simply told them to go and present themselves to the priests, to be permitted back into the community.

Luke says that "as they went, they were cleansed of their leprosy" (Luke 17:14b, NLT). Their act of obedient faith allowed them to receive what they'd pleaded for.

Only one came back to say thank you. And he was a Samaritan. Not that a Samaritan shouldn't have come back, but where were the Jews whom Jesus had just healed?

Those who'd had the most exposure to Jesus, the most benefit from His teaching, responded with less gratitude than the man from outside Jesus' main teaching focus.

There are a few other examples of this throughout the gospels, and it's not to put down the Jews. It's to show Jesus' wider focus, and to call those of us who have been blessed with hearing Him to not take Him for granted.

What have you asked Jesus for today? Or what have you seen Him do? Remember to say thank You.

God who saved me and restored me to Yourself, if You did nothing else, I could still never thank You enough for the gift of salvation. But You do so many other things for me as well. Open my eyes to see Your hand in my life, and give me a sensitive spirit to respond with heart-felt gratitude and praise. Thank You for all You do, and for who You are.

Squandering the Inheritance

All these years I've slaved for you and never once
refused to do a single thing you told me to. And in all
that time you never gave me even one young goat for a
feast with my friends. Yet when this son of yours
comes back after squandering your money on
prostitutes, you celebrate by killing the fattened calf!
Luke 15:29-30, NLT

Can't you hear the bitterness in the older brother's voice as he accuses his father? Yes, the younger brother did squander his share of the inheritance, advanced to him by his still-living father. But the father had divided his estate between the two sons, and the older one was squandering his share too, in a different way. Because *he didn't realize it was his*. He hadn't *received* it.

Have we, as Christians, fully received the inheritance God gave us when He saved us? Not the treasures we're called to be storing up in Heaven, but those things we forget to notice, or don't fully believe are ours.

The promises that are already ours: forgiveness, abundant life, the fruit of the Spirit that will grow as we work out our salvation: "love, joy, peace, patience, kindness, goodness, faithfulness, gentleness, and self-control" (Galatians 5:22-23, NLT).

The little gifts in each day: sunbeams (or fat, gorgeous snowflakes), a loved one's smile, the perfect parking spot when we're running late, a cup of tea steeped just right.

The wealth of God's presence with us in the now.

Lord Jesus, You know how many days I just push through, head down, missing the tangible gifts You've strewn across my path and the more valuable spiritual gifts I need only stop and receive. I'm helpless to live the abundant life on my own, and that's how You designed it. Teach me to be mindful of Your presence and my need, whether I'm quiet before You or attending daily duties. Open my eyes to see, ears to hear, and heart to receive all that You have for me.

Receiving Like a Child

I tell you the truth, anyone who doesn't receive the
Kingdom of God like a child will never enter it.
Luke 18:17, NLT

Have you watched a child receive a gift lately?

If this is an emotionally healthy child, raised with love and care, there's no doubting, no hanging back. (How many of us as adults stop and say, "You shouldn't have," or ask, "Are you sure?")

The child's eyes light up. If she's young enough, she likely squeals or bounces up and down. Older, learning the restraint that snares most of us, she'll still give some subtle hint of excitement.

Hands reach for the gift. Test its weight. Shake it a little, listening for clues. Tear open the paper or pull the tissue from the top of the bag.

If it's something she likes, the child radiates pleasure. (God is not giving us dental floss or socks — this is the Kingdom of Heaven that Jesus is talking about in today's verse.)

Something the child *really* likes? She'll probably take it everywhere, even sleep with it. Tell her friends, show them... maybe even share, it if it's not breakable.

The only gift that would go back in the package, shoved in a corner of the closet, would be something she didn't care about. But even a child's favourite gift today would eventually be replaced by a future novelty. Not so the Kingdom of Heaven.

Gracious and loving God, You offer me the Kingdom of Heaven — the best gift of all. The more I explore it, the more I'll appreciate it. Help me to truly believe it's for me, and embrace and cherish it. Help me spend the rest of my life growing in relationship with You and not holding back because I'm afraid to receive.

More Than a Miracle-Worker

"Lord," he said, "I want to see!"

And Jesus said, "All right, receive your sight! Your
faith has healed you."
Luke 18:41b-42, NLT

On the way to Jericho, Jesus responds to a blind beggar's plea. While the crowd tries to shush the man, Jesus stops and commands him to be brought near. He invites (or commands) the beggar to make his petition, a petition Jesus grants with an authoritative response and with none of the touching or further instructions He often gives.

Instead of a dusty road, the actions bring a picture of an elegant throne room. This is a King's response to a subject's plea.

When the blind man asks about the crowd noise, the people say "Jesus the Nazarene" (or "Jesus of Nazareth") is passing by. Excitement fills the air. This is the miracle-worker.

The beggar calls Him a different name: "Jesus, Son of David." From what he's heard about Jesus, this man's spirit knows the truth. Jesus isn't just a travelling healer. Jesus is the promised King. The Messiah.

Jesus responds in kingly fashion here to meet the man where he is and reinforce his belief, but also to give the crowd a chance to realize there's more to discover.

What difference would it make in our prayer lives if we remembered we're approaching the King, the One who welcomes us and who has complete authority to meet our needs?

Jesus, Saviour, Son of David. You are my King, who came in the flesh and defeated death and hell. You save me when I cry out to You, even though I have nothing to offer but myself. Thank You for such grace, power, and love. Strengthen my faith to believe that You are fully approachable and fully able to meet my deepest needs.

Pride? Or Jesus?

When Jesus came by, he looked up at Zacchaeus and
called him by name. "Zacchaeus!" he said. "Quick,
come down! I must be a guest in your home today."
Luke 19:5, NLT

Zacchaeus was the chief tax collector, an occupation that brought great wealth and greater condemnation from his fellow Jews. It made him a Roman collaborator, one in a position to cheat his own people.

We'd expect a man like that to take his dignity most seriously. Everyone around would want to cut him down, so wouldn't he project an indestructible image?

Yet he's so desperate to see Jesus that he forgets appearances, runs ahead of the procession, and climbs a tree to get one glimpse of Him. Is he up the tree to hide? Or is Jesus' route so crowded with citizens that the branches are a short man's only option?

Picture an extravagantly-clad little man dashing through the crowded street and scuttling up the tree. His self-importance is forgotten in the desire — the need — to see Jesus. In proof of that, when Jesus calls him out of the tree, Zacchaeus takes Him home "in great excitement and joy" (Luke 19:6, NLT). There's no blustering or posturing from wounded pride.

Instead, imagine Zacchaeus' happiness. Cut off from his people, only dining with those his money can impress, suddenly he's offered the chance to host this famous miracle-worker and teacher — and Jesus is accepting him, not condemning.

Zacchaeus throws away his self-made status to meet Jesus. What do we cling to that keeps us from fully entering into relationship with Jesus? Is it worth the cost?

God our Maker, thank You that Jesus makes a way for each one of us to know Him. Help me give my all for the privilege of living in Your presence — not letting anything hold me back.

Waiting Quietly

Let all that I am wait quietly before God,
for my hope is in him.
Psalm 62:5, NLT

David wrote these words about a time of great pressure, reminding himself and his people to look to God for help instead of relying on others or on their own assets. The "trust God" theme is so important that it's written twice: before and after David's list of troubles.

Waiting quietly before God speaks to the state of our hearts and spirits. It's a choice to control what could easily be frantic desperation, and to bring our fears to God instead.

It's not passively sitting and waiting for God to fix everything, but it's acknowledging that God will be the one to make a way and to protect. And it's being open to recognize that way when it comes. It's also realizing whose power will ultimately bring victory — God's, not ours.

Are you in a good place today? No particular stresses or battles? This verse is just as relevant.

The sheep in the quiet meadow can enjoy it more when she fully trusts the Shepherd. (At least that would be true if sheep had thoughts, feelings, and anxieties.) Happy, secure, restful times need an awareness of God just as much as the crises.

God my gentle yet strong Shepherd, when I'm at peace or in turmoil, give me grace to choose to quiet myself and wait in hope before You. Help me fully rely on Your love, wisdom, and power, for my own sake and so that others will see Your goodness.

Who Does It Look Like We're Living For?

So we are Christ's ambassadors; God is making his
appeal through us. We speak for Christ when we plead,
"Come back to God!"
2 Corinthians 5:20, NLT

As "ambassadors for Christ," we need to choose His will and His way over our own, and do it cheerfully, not grudgingly, because we love Him and it's a joy to do whatever we can to stay close to Him.

When we cultivate an attitude of trust in God, of gratitude and peace, it's not simply for our own spiritual wellbeing. Others will see that in the good and in the bad, we choose to rely on God, and that He is enough.

Jesus is our model, as well as the One we're to represent. His countenance, conduct, and demeanour all reflected God. He didn't go around with a moping, frowning face. He didn't deny His pain, either — just took it to the Father.

He spoke truth gently to the hurting, and He listened first to discern their true needs. He reserved His blunt talk for leaders He needed to call out. He didn't complain about people behind their backs. He didn't gossip, stew in resentment, or indulge in any of the attitudes that so often beset us.

He didn't condemn sinners, but invited them into new life. And He showed them that the new life was good.

We're not perfect, but the more we rely on the Holy Spirit within us, the more effective ambassadors we'll be.

Father, sometimes I get tired, or frustrated, or fearful. Help me remember that if I indulge in cranky or moody behaviour, it reflects poorly on You. Help me press into You, my Rock and my Redeemer, and live authentically so that others will see how trusting You makes a difference.

Obstacles or Stepping Stones?

For we have heard how the LORD made a dry path for
you through the Red Sea when you left Egypt. And we
know what you did to Sihon and Og, the two Amorite
kings east of the Jordan River, whose people you
completely destroyed.
Joshua 2:10, NLT

En route to the Promised Land, Israel encountered two kings who refused to allow them to pass. Each king attacked, and was killed along with all his people.

Imagine the Israelites, thinking they were on the road to their blessing, confronted by an army. Twice. The way was blocked. Soldiers pointed weapons at them. Do you think they were discouraged? Frustrated?

Every time God intervened for Israel was a chance for them to develop confidence in His power. He was proving Himself to them. He gave them victory, and brought them to the Jordan's banks with the river in full flood.

Today's verse was spoken by a citizen of Jericho (Rahab) when the Israelite spies went to scout the city. Word of God's mighty power had spread.

The obstacles, like the Red Sea, the two kings, and the Jordan River, weren't random challenges to make Israel's life harder. They were stepping-stones to not only build up God's people's faith but to show others His power.

Can we look at the issues and setbacks in our lives this way? Learn to trust God to meet them, and recognize that however impossible they seem now, God can use them if we'll only trust Him? Can we press on in the strength He gives, without grumbling or despair? Even with hope?

God my Provider and my King, forgive me when I look at the obstacles and forget about Your unseen power and Your love for me. Where You lead, You will make a way. Increase my faith, and help me choose to rely on you. Strengthen me to take captive my fears, doubts, and complaints, and open my eyes to see what You will do.

Expectations and Limitations — and Freedom

But the people who know their God will be strong and
will resist him.
Daniel 11:32b, NLT

The context of this verse is a prophecy about a future king who will "flatter and win over those who have violated the covenant" (Daniel 11:32a, NLT). What protects God's people from this enemy? They know Him, and they act on that knowledge. They rely on Him.

Today we also have an enemy who wants to defeat us, either through appealing to our self-focus or through undermining our awareness of who we are in Christ.

What limitations or expectations have we accepted? From whom? Or what are we measuring ourselves against? How does this impact what God might want to do through us?

If we know Him — and choose to believe what we know about Him — we can live by His grace and strength instead of holding back in fear of what others might say.

Here's where today's verse applies. We know who the Liar is, who wants to get our eyes off of God. Those lies include things like "you're not good/smart/old/young/gifted (etc.) enough."

If we know and believe our God, we can resist the lies with truth. "For I can do everything [that God asks me to do] through Christ, who gives me strength" (Philippians 4:13, NLT).

Gracious Father, draw me closer to Your heart and deeper into Your Word. Give me faith and courage to choose to believe You and to resist the lies that diminish me. Show me where I've accepted limitations instead of stepping out for You. Forgive me, and give me new chances to live for Your glory.

Revealing Jesus

I did not recognize him as the Messiah, but I have been
baptizing with water so that he might be revealed to
Israel.
John 1:31, NLT

John says that Jesus "has revealed God to us" (John 1:18, NLT). We who
believe in Him are called to reveal Jesus to those around us just as
surely as John the Baptist was called to prepare the way.

Each of us will have a different way of revealing Jesus to the world. John
the Baptist called the people en masse to repentance, confronting their
sin so they'd be ready to receive salvation.

Most of us, unless we're in some kind of public ministry, are likely called
to reveal Jesus one-on-one. That doesn't mean practicing John's
approach on a smaller scale, pointing out our friends' sins and calling
them to repent.

It means revealing Jesus through our lives, caring for others in a manner
worthy of the Gospel. Listening. Seeing. Helping. Encouraging. Yes, it
may mean asking honest questions about life choices that don't honour
God, but only as and when He leads.

It's important to remember that the Jews of John's day thought they
were already serving God. John showed them the gaps. If the people in
our lives aren't interested in following God, what's the point of us
pushing them to obey Him? First they need to discover who He is and
why His way matters.

*Saviour God, You are my one true Hope. You have drawn me to Yourself,
and You're drawing others. You do the saving, but I have a part to play
in showing how good You are and how practical Your love is. Open my
eyes to the opportunities You give to shine for You, and help me share
what You've given me. It's too good to keep to myself.*

God at Work

And we know that in all things God works for the good
of those who love him, who have been called according
to his purpose.
Romans 8:28, NIV

Many of us know and rely on verses like this in times of trouble. The NIV footnotes offer an alternate wording:

"... that in all things God works together with those who love him to bring about what is good — with those who..." (Romans 8:28, NIV).

In all things, God works with us "to bring about what is good." This alternate wording opens a whole new vista. It changes the focus from how God will look after *us* to how He will care for *others through us*.

Yes, we have personal stresses and difficulties, and yes, God is our Hope and our Helper. We can trust that He will work to make all things good in His way and His time.

But it's easy to become selfishly absorbed in our own circumstances and overlook the needs around us. Or to see those needs and be too overwhelmed to know how to start making a difference.

The idea of God working together with us is biblically sound — as long as we remember that He's in charge. We're to act as His hands and feet and to represent Him.

Christ in us empowers us and uses our small actions to achieve His larger goals. This verse turns our eyes to others, and takes away our fear of not being able to make a difference. Of course we're not enough on our own. God never intended us to act solo.

God my Saviour and Redeemer, You created everything in the beginning, and You're still at work creating beauty from our broken pieces and our messes. Thank You that I can join You in Your work, and that it's not my responsibility to fix anything. My responsibility is only to show up with willing hands and an obedient heart, and to share what You give me with those I meet. Help me do this, so that others will experience Your great love.

Our Point of View and God's

*"You can't become famous if you hide like this! If you
can do such wonderful things, show yourself to the
world!" For even his brothers didn't believe in him.*
John 7:4-5, NLT

Jesus' brothers clearly believed in His power, but didn't "believe" in the sense of recognizing Him as the promised Messiah. Without that crucial piece of understanding, the future they saw for Jesus wasn't in line with the Father's actual plan. Jesus, who always listened to the Father and did what He said, knew the path ahead of Him and chose His actions accordingly.

Jesus' brothers' advice was aimed at reaching a different goal. So was Peter's, when he rebuked Jesus for saying He had to die. Jesus' strongly-worded response included this assessment: "You are seeing things merely from a human point of view, not from God's" (Matthew 16:23b, NLT).

Today, Christians know Jesus is our Saviour, who gave His life and rose again to restore us to relationship with Him. But don't we still ask or expect things that aren't in His plan? In our limited perspective, we forget that we don't have the full picture. Sometimes we ask selfishly, but sometimes we're sure we know what's best.

Those are the hard times, when God doesn't answer as we expect because He sees and knows more. He sees the future, and the ripple effects from the need we've been praying about. He sees how to better use this time of struggle.

When we don't understand, it has to come back to trusting the God who does understand. The better we know His character, the easier it is to trust Him and to surrender to His will and His way.

Creator God, Saviour and Sustainer, help me surrender every aspect of my life into Your capable hands. Open me to see more of what You see, and give me the faith to trust You even when I can't see.

Half Right is Half Wrong

But how could he be [the Messiah]? For we know
where this man comes from. When the Messiah comes,
he will simply appear; no one will know where he
comes from.
John 7:27, NLT

The common people thought Jesus would just "appear" — they wouldn't know where He came from. John 7:41-42 shows that the religious leaders knew He'd be born in Bethlehem, which is why they had so much trouble with His coming from Nazareth. Perhaps they should have thought to ask Him where He'd been born.

Today's verse highlights the importance of spending time in God's Word and in prayerful study to know what it really says.

Remember the Bereans, in Acts 17:11, when Paul told them about Jesus? They looked into the holy writings for themselves instead of believing or disbelieving based on his word alone.

The religious leaders' response later in the chapter stresses the equal importance of realizing we may still not have the full picture, no matter how much head knowledge we have. We can't assume we know it all.

Seekers after God's truth need to do three things: First, we can't rely on hearsay and assumptions; we need to learn for ourselves. Second, we need to ask honest questions, in prayer and of those who believe. Third, we must live daily in trust and obedience, keeping close to God and growing closer.

We don't want to have it half right and miss the Saviour.

Awesome and holy God, although Jesus came as "God with skin on," there's so much more to You than I can grasp. Yet You do reveal Yourself as I spend time with You and surrender my life to Your care. Give me a hunger to know You better, and a heart to love and obey You. Where I have misconceptions or false assumptions, open my eyes to the truth.

Seeing One Another

So we have stopped evaluating others from a human
point of view. At one time we thought of Christ
merely from a human point of view. How differently
we know him now! This means that anyone who
belongs to Christ has become a new person. The old
life is gone; a new life has begun!
2 Corinthians 5:16-17, NLT

When we look at our brothers and sisters in Christ, do we remember they're new people? Or do we focus on the bits of their old nature still clinging to the edges of their newness?

When conflicts arise and difficulties spring up, do we band together, united by a common love of Jesus? Or do we pick at one another, take sides, form factions? Allow bitter roots to grow?

Despite differences of opinion, we who are born again spiritually are new people, citizens of God's kingdom. We see Jesus differently, as believers. We need to see each other differently as well.

What if we consciously chose to look for signs of new life in one another instead of focusing on the negatives? To pray for one another instead of putting up walls? To pray *with* one another until we found common ground?

Not that we'd agree about everything, but could we hear and understand one another? Love and forgive, even if life moved us in different directions?

God our Saviour and Redeemer, You call each of us to reconciliation to Yourself and with one another. Forgive me when I allow the mess of living to obscure the new life You gave me. Help me recognize and confess, daily or even more frequently, those things that dim my light. Help me stay as close as possible to You, so I won't poison myself or others. Give me Your love for my Christian brothers and sisters so that those around us will recognize something that only You can do.

Beyond "Why?"

"It was not because of his sins or his parents' sins,"
Jesus answered. "This happened so the power of God
could be seen in him."
John 9:3, NLT

Jesus and his disciples encountered a man who'd been born blind, and the disciples asked about the cause. Apparently in the culture of the time, anything like this was considered a direct result of someone's sin.

When we encounter difficult situations, how often do we ask if it's because of something that person, or another, did? Or if we're the ones with the trouble, how often do we ask "What have I done?" or "Why me?" Or we sulk at God and say it's not fair? We're still focusing on the individual with the need. Still looking for a cause.

Jesus doesn't say trouble is never self-inflicted, never reaping what we've sown. But He clearly says those aren't the only reasons. "This happened so the power of God could be seen in him."

Instead of asking why, let's ask the bigger question: God, what do You want to do in this situation?

Jesus isn't saying God caused the initial problem so the people would see how good He is when He solved it. But there are plenty of things He chooses to allow, things we don't like but that He wants to use for greater good.

What difference would it make in our outlook if we asked about God's solution instead of about the problem?

Mighty and merciful God, Your thoughts and ways are beyond comprehension, but I know You are good. You proved Your love through the Cross, and Your power through the Resurrection. Forgive me for looking too long at my problems. Teach me to bring them to You in trust, looking for Your help.

Abraham's Example

Abraham never wavered in believing God's promise. In
fact, his faith grew stronger, and in this he brought
glory to God.
Romans 4:20, NLT

Abraham believed God. He obeyed, went where he was told, and tried to live a righteous life, but it was his faith that made him "the father of all who believe" (Romans 4:16, NLT).

Perhaps the hardest thing for him to believe was God's promise to give him and his wife a son. Especially when the years kept passing with no sign of pregnancy. Humanly speaking, it was impossible for this elderly, childless couple to reproduce.

But "Abraham never wavered in believing God's promise... his faith grew stronger." He didn't know how, or when, or even why (except that God said so). But he knew who would make it happen.

God gives some people "impossible" promises, but He gives all of us the promises in His word. Promises like "I am with you always" (Matthew 28:20, NLT), and "whoever believes in him [Jesus] will... have eternal life" (John 3:16, NLT).

Abraham's example shows us how — and why — to live by faith, in the big challenges and the small ones. Our purpose is to bring glory to God.

That doesn't have to involve doing great things. Sometimes the greatest thing is just to hold on to our faith and to act in obedience.

Father God, help me to trust You with my honest questions. Grant me the faith to keep relying on Your promises, no matter what. Help me trust You and wait for what You will do. Help me hold on to You and know that You are holding on to me. Your grip is sure.

Take Heart

I have told you all this so that you may have peace in
me. Here on earth you will have many trials and
sorrows. But take heart, because I have overcome the
world.
John 16:33, NLT

If we look around, there is plenty to discourage us. Despite global progress, people still suffer. And many of us live in cultures that are increasingly open about their godlessness, illustrating Paul's words to the Romans about how, when people turned away from God, He let them have what they wanted (Romans 1:18-32).

Closer to home, there may be financial pressures. Health, employment, relationship concerns. Each one of us likely has at least one thing pressing heavily on our heart. Through it all, we need to keep ourselves rooted in Jesus, depending on Him.

That's hard, though. Over time, the weight seems to increase, and we may not see the Lord doing anything. We can believe the suffering more than the Saviour.

Life is truly "a long obedience in the same direction," and the closer we are to Jesus, the better off we'll be.

We can do that by spending more time in worship, remembering who God is and how much He loves us. Reminding ourselves of what He's done in the past, to reassure our faith that He's still at work.

Faithful and all-wise God, so often I strain to see the end of the story when You're still working in the middle of it. Help me trust You in the waiting. Help me worship. Remind me who You are, and give me the faith I need. Grow the fruit of the Holy Spirit in me, including patience and faithfulness. Enable me to conduct myself in a manner worthy of the Gospel.

When We Get Into Trouble

"Didn't I see you out there in the olive grove with
Jesus?"
Again Peter denied it. And immediately a rooster
crowed.
John 18:26b-27, NLT

Peter loved Jesus. He wholeheartedly meant his earlier vow that he'd never deny his Lord (Matthew 26:31-35).

Yet here he was, doing that very thing. Matthew's account says Peter's denial was so intense it involved cursing. And that when the rooster crowed and he realized what he'd done, he fled, "weeping bitterly" (Matthew 26:69-75).

Why did he do it? Was he afraid? Or was he trying to stay "under cover" in case there was a chance to rescue Jesus?

Whatever his motivation, Peter's denial came because he was acting on his own initiative and in his own strength. Isn't that when we get into trouble, too?

Our best intentions can blow up in our faces. Peter's experience reminds us how important it is to learn to listen to and rely on the Lord. He also reminds us of Jesus' loving forgiveness when we mess up (see John 21).

My God and Saviour, Your grace to forgive is beyond human understanding, but I receive it gladly and rely on it often. Teach me to walk closer to You, to trust You instead of myself. Slow me down to listen before I leap. Make me a believer after Your own heart.

Waiting as Worship

Wait for the LORD;
be strong and take heart
and wait for the LORD.
Psalm 27:14, NIV

Waiting. It's a challenge. We who hope in God wait for Him to act, to speak, to comfort.

There's an element of strain in that. "When, Lord? How long?"

When we give in to that strain, we miss part of the waiting. We miss simply waiting for (or with) God. Being with Him, even when we can't sense His presence. He's with us — He promised, and we can depend on that, whatever we feel.

His timing won't speed up if we're peering at the horizon and begging, "Are we there yet?" When we do that, we miss what He has for us in the now. Maybe it's rest. Maybe it's a quiet word He wants to drop into our spirits. It could be an opportunity we'll miss if we're looking too far ahead.

Most of all, we miss His presence. Especially in the stressful times, His presence is subtle, easy to miss. And it's what we most need.

Quieting ourselves before God, entrusting our needs to Him and abiding in Him, is trust. It's an act of worship. It honours Him for who He is, not for what He can do for us.

Oh God, You see my hurts, needs and fears. Forgive me when I come clamouring to You with requests without taking time to appreciate You for who You are. Whisper into my spirit and teach me to worship You in trust and adoration. Help me set my heart on You, no matter what goes on in and around me. You are my greatest treasure and my deepest need.

Pain and Endurance

We can rejoice, too, when we run into problems and
trials, for we know that they help us develop
endurance.
Romans 5:3, NLT

Most people's natural reaction to problems and trials is a plea to get us out of there. We don't like pain, and it's often a signal of danger (think about touching a hot stove, or feeling symptoms of a health problem).

In a fallen world, pain is inevitable. Nobody wants it, but God can use even this. Let's not waste it.

Today's verse reminds us to invite God to work in our problems and to "help us develop endurance."

It shifts our focus from the trouble itself to God. Not that it diminishes the pain, but it restores perspective. We're not alone. The God of the universe is with us. He cares for us, and He is our best and only hope.

Instead of slipping into self-defence mode, can we learn to ask, "what will God do here?" Can we look for His help in anticipation and trust, instead of watching fearfully for disaster?

The Message actually uses the words "alert expectancy" as we look "for whatever God will do next" (Romans 5:3-5, MSG). That's hard to live up to, most days. But wouldn't it be great?

God my Strength and Shield, when You let me go through trials, help me remember that You are there with me. Help me keep my eyes on You. Teach me to look in alert expectancy for "whatever You will do" and to remember that however huge the crisis, You can give me what I need to endure it.

Opportunity or Threat?

Dear brothers and sisters, when troubles of any kind
come your way, consider it an opportunity for great
joy.
James 1:2, NLT

Often we have the child's response (mentally) of cowering and shrinking. Of thinking the trouble is too big, and fearing it will overwhelm us. Of seeing a threat. Or we raise our defences, as if it's a win-or-lose struggle that we can't afford to lose.

James gives us a much broader perspective. Of course the pain and risk of trouble is great. (In verse 12 he talks about how "God blesses those who patiently endure.") But James reveals a higher level of stakes.

Trouble isn't one more bout with a larger danger that will eventually overcome us, as if life is really out to get us. It's is one more opportunity to grow spiritually and to deepen our relationship with the God who loves us.

It's not a case of "fight until you can't get up." James says trouble tests our faith. To that he adds:

"For you know that when your faith is tested, your endurance has a chance to grow. So let it grow, for when your endurance is fully developed, you will be perfect and complete, needing nothing" (James 1:3-4, NLT).

How can we reach a perfect state of needing nothing? Only by becoming fully reliant on our God, who is all-sufficient for any trouble that threatens us. Will that happen this side of Heaven? Maybe not, but we can grow toward it.

God who loves and shepherds me, please open me to see opportunity where my natural self sees only threats. Help me allow the troubles in my life to help develop my endurance. Give me the faith to trust You, so I can experience Your all-sufficient care for me.

A Slave of God

This letter is from James, a slave of God and of the
Lord Jesus Christ.
James 1:1a, NLT

The word "slave" meant something different to James than it does in a North American context. In identifying himself this way, he's not saying he's dehumanized, abused, a victim, or in any way to be pitied or rescued.

He's a willing slave. There existed in Bible times men or women who could have been freed but who chose to commit to a lifetime's service to their master. Imagine how good a person this type of master would be.

If we look at this in the context of service to a good master, and with the slave being like a servant, worker, or employee, what does it imply for our faith walk?

We serve out of love, wholeheartedly, remembering that we're under authority and also under protection.

We know we're provided for, both our physical needs and the provisions we need to do our assigned tasks. Obedience is expected, without whining or attitude. Thinking is expected too, with questions as needed; arguing and back-talk are not. Work is also expected, so our service isn't doing God a favour.

Bottom line: it's not about us. Plenty to think about, isn't it?

God Most High, as a believer, I'm Your servant and ambassador, but You also call me Your child and heir. Help me grow in relationship with You so I can conduct myself in a manner worthy of Your great Name, serving in such a way that others will discover how good You are.

God: Love and Power

Then he asked them, "Why are you afraid? Do you still
have no faith?"

The disciples were absolutely terrified. "Who is this
man?" they asked each other. "Even the wind and
waves obey him!"
Mark 4:40-41, NLT

At first glance it looks like Jesus was asking why the disciples were afraid of the storm, as in, why hadn't they trusted Him to save them? Why hadn't they simply asked for His help instead of panicking?

But this "Why are you afraid?" came after He had stilled the storm, when they were terrified of what they'd just seen Him do.

In North America these days, we don't often see God reveal a glimpse of His power in this way. It's easy to forget the magnitude of who God is and to get comfortable with the idea of a "safe" Saviour.

Yes, we *are* safe with Him, held in His loving care, secure that nothing can separate us from His love. We can rely on our Good Shepherd. He is good. But as C.S. Lewis said, He's not safe. Not tame.

A safe, tame, containable God couldn't protect us in life's storms. Couldn't walk through the turbulence to reach us. Couldn't defeat the power of hell to rescue and redeem us.

We can take great comfort in His care, and rest in Him, secure in the knowledge of His limitless power.

Holy and mighty God, Your love assures me that You want to care for me. Your power proves that You can. I need fear neither Your abandonment nor Your failure, because both are impossible. Impress this on my spirit, and draw me to worship You in trust and adoration.

Not Obnoxious

Rejoice in the Lord always. I will say it again: Rejoice!
Let your gentleness be evident to all. The Lord is near.
Do not be anxious about anything, but in every
situation, by prayer and petition, with thanksgiving,
present your requests to God.
Philippians 4:4-6, NIV

What do we do when we're anxious or stressed? We tense up, speed up, put up defences. Some of us get obnoxious.

What does Paul say here? "Let your gentleness be evident to all." Why? "Because the Lord is near."

God's got this. Whatever *this* is. And whatever happens, He'll be right there with us, able to work even in the worst messes.

Because God is near, Paul tells us to bring our concerns to Him.

We can be confident that He already knows what He wants to do in the situation. It may not be what *we* want, but if we truly believe Him to be wise, good, powerful, and loving, we can choose to trust Him.

It really comes down to a question of whether we trust God or not.

Holy and majestic God of the universe, it's scandalous to even suggest You're not trustworthy, yet You know my weakness and my doubts, and the fears that snare me. You know that sometimes I don't trust You. Or I don't act on the trust I think I have. Please forgive me and help my unbelief. Help me surrender the fight or flight reflex that can make me obnoxious. Teach me to rely on Your goodness and Your presence, so I can show others how good You are.

Responding to God

In view of all this, make every effort to respond to
God's promises.
2 Peter 1:5a, NLT

Peter's been talking about the abundance of what God has given to those who have received Him.

God's promises are "great and precious" and they're what enable us to draw nearer to Him and to escape the corruption around us (verse 4).

How do we respond to God's promises? And do we truly "make every effort"? Part of responding is discovering and relying on His promises. Believing them.

Relying on His love and promises, we'll grow and be productive and useful (verse 8). We won't forget what God has done for us (verse 9). We'll prove our faith is real, and staying focused will keep us from drifting from God (verse 10). There will be a reward (verse 11).

Growing deeper into the abundant life God gives will be reward enough.

God my Deliverer and Redeemer, on my own I can't stay spiritually focused to remember You and Your promises, but this is the sort of prayer I can be confident You want to answer: Give me the desire to grow in relationship with You, give me a heart willing to make every effort to respond to Your promises. Remind me when I forget, and help me begin again, as often as needed. Your patience is great, and Your mercies are new every morning.

Life and Death

Christ died for us so that, whether we are dead or alive
when he returns, we can live with him forever.
1 Thessalonians 5:10, NLT

The Apostle Paul said, "For to me, living means living for Christ, and dying is even better" (Philippians 1:21, NLT). He wasn't indulging in a self-absorbed death-wish. He was giving his all to his Lord each day, knowing there was a reward at the end of the race.

The assurance of eternity with Jesus means that whatever we're living now, there's something better coming. Pain will be wiped away. So, too, will our present treasures, so let's not hoard them.

Jesus is the only way to Heaven. We can't force others to choose Him, but we can pray persistently and we can surrender our lives fully to Him so that they'll see the difference He makes. We can obey when He tells us how to love them.

How do we practice now for eternity? Consciously spending time with God today — each day — will make all the difference.

Quiet moments in prayer, reading the Bible (His love letter to us), learning to rest in His presence while we work or play... it's not easy to retrain our spirits to check in with Him regularly, but it's a worthwhile goal. And it's the sort of prayer He'd love to answer.

God my Father, Jesus my Saviour, Holy Spirit my Sustainer, how can I thank You for saving me from eternal separation from Your love? Give me a healthy longing for Heaven, and give me a stronger longing for Your presence with me each moment of my days on earth. Work in me so that others will catch glimpses of You. Work through me to show mercy and compassion and to break chains and barriers.

Remembering Our Purpose

> I am writing to God's church in Corinth, to you who
> have been called by God to be his own holy people. He
> made you holy by means of Christ Jesus, just as he did
> for all people everywhere who call on the name of our
> Lord Jesus Christ, their Lord and ours.
> 1 Corinthians 1:2, NLT

Do we sometimes forget our purpose as Christ-followers?

God called us "to be His own holy people," and He made us holy through Jesus. He gave us "everything we need for living a godly life" (1 Peter 1:3, NLT). Paul said, "You have every spiritual gift you need as you eagerly wait for the return of our Lord Jesus Christ (1 Corinthians 1:7, NLT).

Too often it seems our focus and energies become tangled up in our own interests and goals, or in the behind-the-scenes struggles to keep our churches running smoothly. These and other short-term issues fill our sight until we forget it's all about God.

He called us to live for His glory. Not in flashy holiness, larger than life but surface-only. In true holiness, depending on Him, following His lead. Trusting Him, so that others can see the difference He makes in our lives.

Holy and so-merciful God, thank You for saving me from darkness and spiritual death. Remind me of my calling, and of who You are. Overwhelm me with a glimpse of Your presence. Give me perspective, and the joy of belonging to You, and help me to live for Your glory.

Keeping Our Focus

So you must live as God's obedient children. Don't slip
back into your old ways of living to satisfy your own
desires. You didn't know any better then.
1 Peter 1:14, NLT

It's so easy to get caught up in the cares of the day and to forget the big picture. Heads down, burdened, we're slogging through deep mud and our focus shrinks to taking the next step.

Can we keep Heaven in our hopes, and take that next, heavy step, trusting that Jesus is with us and that He will bring all those future promises to pass in His perfect time? Can we hold on, and trust that He's holding us? That by His grace, we will make it?

Peter tells his readers to "Think clearly and exercise self-control" (verse 13). This battle is won in the mind.

"Live as God's obedient children" (verse 14). Again, a deliberate choice. "Don't slip back into your old ways" (verse 14). Vigilance, and ongoing choice. This isn't just a warning to stay out of past overt sin like drunkenness, sexual promiscuity, theft, lies etc.

We need to be on guard against the small things, too. Attitudes, grumbling, petty thoughts… even daydreaming about perfectly good things at a time when we're supposed to be focusing on something else.

Keeping focus may seem impossible, but that doesn't mean that practice won't improve it with God's help. He wants us to draw nearer to Him, so we know He'll help.

In retraining our minds, we need to "take captive every thought to make it obedient to Christ" (2 Corinthians 10:5, NIV), remembering who He is and who we are in Him.

Father, forgive me for those times I've slipped back into my old ways, and those times I've stalled instead of growing. Give me a heart to know You better and to live to please You, and help me focus on living as Your obedient child, with Your help.

Choosing to Love

> You were cleansed from your sins when you obeyed
> the truth, so now you must show sincere love to each
> other as brothers and sisters. Love each other deeply
> with all your heart.
> 1 Peter 1:22, NLT

Sincere love. Deep, whole-hearted love. This isn't surface-friendly love. Nor it is always warm and fuzzy. This is love as a choice. An act of the will, a decision of the mind. If the heart is slow to catch up, it can't be allowed to affect the acting out of the love.

Let's be honest. The whole reason onlookers were surprised to see how the early church loved one another is that we're not a lovable bunch. We're real people, like everyone else, with hurts, hang-ups, and habits.

Our love for the God who loves us — that's the glue that binds us together. He loves us, and He says to love one another, so we do it for Him.

An important way to start is by asking God what He sees when He looks at each one. Not what dirt does He still see to clean up, but what potential? What did He design this person to become? What gifts has He given that He'd like to see developed and used? And what hurt does He see that He'd like to use you or me to help heal? What need, to help meet?

Then we need to pray for one another. Individually, by name, for God's best in the person's life. Sincere prayer grows love.

We'll likely also need to pray for ourselves. "Lord, change me" is a prayer God loves to answer. After all, we can't change others. As we let Him change us, though, that may inspire change around us.

Lord, change me... and thank You for Your patience and mercy in the changing. Grow Your church and help us to love one another as You love us, for the glory of Your Name. May others see enough of You in us to draw them to know You.

It Matters How We Live

But you are not like that, for you are a chosen people.
You are royal priests, a holy nation, God's very own
possession. As a result, you can show others the
goodness of God, for he called you out of the darkness
into his wonderful light.
1 Peter 2:9, NLT

"You are not like that..." Not like what? They're not like the people who are still stumbling "because they do not obey God's word" (1 Peter 2:8b).

Peter's been reminding his readers that they've *been* saved from an empty way of life and that they're *being* saved... growing and being built into God's glorious kingdom. And that they *will be* saved on the last day. It's a process, and they're living for God.

This isn't about coming to Jesus and then carrying on with life, theirs or ours. We belong to Him now, and our lives need to reflect that.

Can our neighbours or co-workers see the goodness of God in how we live? In our behaviour? In our words, not just about Him but about one another? Our developing peace, patience, etc. as we grow in Him?

If we're learning to bring our thoughts under His authority, that will affect our attitudes, our body language, and what comes out of our mouths.

It's not about being saved and then forgetting God in our busyness. It's about an ever-deepening relationship with Him, craving that "pure spiritual milk" (1 Peter 2:2, NLT), actively loving Him. Obeying Him.

If we don't let our faith affect us, we're missing a huge opportunity, and a huge blessing. And we're letting down both God and the people He's placed in our lives.

Father God, I have no words to thank You for saving me, for adopting me into Your Kingdom and giving me purpose. Forgive me for my distraction, and help me focus first on You. Change me, so that others will see Your goodness.

Our Desires, Or God's?

You won't spend the rest of your lives chasing your
own desires, but you will be anxious to do the will of
God.
1 Peter 4:2, NLT

Peter's talking to new Christians, who have made a radical lifestyle change and "no longer plunge into the flood of wild and destructive things" with their former friends (1 Peter 4:4, NLT). They've left the old life behind and are learning to live for — and with — God, and they're suffering for it.

That's the context, but those of us who've been Christians longer, or who didn't come out of such dramatically sinful backgrounds, can still take something from today's verse. We're growing in Him, and He's revealing areas in our lives where we need to let go of sin and hurt.

Are we continuing to chase our own desires? Self never goes away, and it finds new ways to rear up. Our own desires may even be good, at least on the surface. That's not the issue. Our reality check is this: are we chasing what *we* want, or what *God* wants?

It comes back to surrender, again and again. Putting God first, listening for His will *today*.

He may want to redeploy us, while we're fine-tuning the routine we've created for what He led us to do yesterday. Or He may want us in the same role, but we need to see that we've started owning it, when it's His. Or maybe we've become ruled by our lists, and He wants to remind us to be quiet with Him first and enjoy His presence.

However He has us serving today, and with every person we meet, let's cultivate a heart that's eager to hear His will for each moment.

God, You are my Shepherd and my Leader. Sometimes I get distracted chasing my own desires, like a dog with its tail, and I forget about being eager to do Your will. Slow me down, re-focus me on You. Quiet my heart, open my eyes and ears to Your leading. Help me put You first.

How Do You Handle Suffering?

So if you are suffering in a manner that pleases God,
keep on doing what is right, and trust your lives to the
God who created you, for he will never fail you.
1 Peter 4:19, NLT

Here in North America, the most "suffering" we do for our faith is putting up with snide comments, misunderstanding, and a culture bent on denying our God.

But we face other forms of suffering, too. Sickness, financial crises, broken relationships, worry... it's a long list.

How do we handle these things in a way that shows others who God is? Peter says we're to "keep on doing what is right, and trust your lives to the God who created you," confident that "He will never fail you."

That means we guard our words and our actions, and keep our attitudes pure before God, because we trust Him. Proverbs 15:1 says, "A gentle answer deflects anger, but harsh words make tempers flare" (NLT).

It means we repeatedly choose to trust God, instead of giving in to the fear and the pain. It means we make time to care for the person beside us in the hospital waiting room. It means that even when we "deserve" some self-pity, we need to ask God how He wants to use the situation.

And it means "if someone asks about your hope as a believer, always be ready to explain it" (1 Peter 3:15, NLT). Gently, not pushy. Tell the story of how He's made a difference and given strength to endure. It's all about Jesus, and we forget that in our daily routines.

Mighty and loving God, You saved me and called me to live for Your glory. Help me learn to walk with You each moment, living in response to You instead of reacting to my circumstances. Show me how to live in my relationships and responsibilities with my heart turned to You and my spirit depending on You. Give me faith to know that You will never fail me.

Want More Grace and Peace? Grow.

May God give you more and more grace and peace as
you grow in your knowledge of God and Jesus our
Lord.
2 Peter 1:2, NLT

Coming to Jesus is just the beginning — the rebirth. We're not to remain as spiritual babies, but to thrive and grow up into a vibrant Christian life. Peter tells us to grow in our knowledge of God and of Jesus our Lord. How do we learn more about the power and character of our God and Saviour?

We learn by reading the Bible, and through experience, as we trust Him and live for Him. We learn through other Christians, as we spend time with them in prayer and in working for the Kingdom. And we learn in private prayer, and in quiet times with God.

Peter says coming to know God means receiving "everything we need for living a godly life" (verse 3), and that we need to grow by responding to His promises (verse 5). Verses 5-7 give detailed advice on what to cultivate in our lives by the Spirit's help.

Growing will make us "productive and useful" (verse 8). It'll keep us from falling away. We need to remember what we've been taught about Jesus from His word, and to rely on it. To base our lives on it.

The better we know our God, the more we can rely on Him. The easier it is to trust and obey Him. And the more others will see and respond to the difference He makes in our lives.

God my Father, thank You for drawing me to Yourself to be spiritually born again. Thank You for Your promises and for all that You've given me. Help me receive and respond, for my own sake and for the sake of Your Kingdom.

Wholesome Thinking

This is my second letter to you, dear friends, and in
both of them I have tried to stimulate your wholesome
thinking and refresh your memory.
2 Peter 3:1, NLT

We're living in just as much a culture of ungodliness as the early church. The difference is, in North America people think they've "been there, heard that" and have no need of our truth. In Peter's day, it was new information, and some were eager to receive it.

"Wholesome" doesn't have to be "boring." Look back over Peter's letters. He's been calling us to a vibrant life of obedience, holiness, joy, love, and trust. And more. That's a challenge, and it'll take more than we can give on our own. We'll need the Lord's help.

Peter also calls us to "remember what the holy prophets said long ago and what our Lord and Savior commanded through your apostles" (2 Peter 3:2, NLT). Don't forget God's word and His ways. Don't accept the lie that because times have changed, so has God's definition of right and wrong.

We need to be vigilant, to guard our thoughts and behaviours. Love the people around us without being absorbed by popular culture. Show there's a more satisfying way, and that everyone is welcome to try it. Renew our minds (Romans 12:1-2). Live obedient to Him who saved us, so that others can see the difference He makes and can find Him too.

Holy, righteous, and merciful God, forgive me for allowing sin to so easily entangle me. Clean me again, and renew my commitment to You. Through Your Holy Spirit within me, enable and motivate me to live a clean life that pleases You. Help me love those around me who don't know You, without falling into their ways of living. Instead, shine through me to draw them to Yourself.

Living Worship

Work willingly at whatever you do, as though you
were working for the Lord rather than for people.
Colossians 3:23, NLT

A willing heart is key — not a grudging, grumbling, bitter one. It's not about what the management or that difficult co-worker "deserves." It's about what our God deserves.

What does God deserve? Worship.

Paul expands on this in his letter to the Romans when he urges them (and us) to "give your bodies to God because of all he has done for you. Let them be a living and holy sacrifice — the kind he will find acceptable. This is truly the way to worship him" (Romans 12:1b, NLT).

In all aspects of our lives, as employees, in relationships, volunteering, attending church meetings... in everything. We need to bring willing hearts, open ears, and eyes that are looking for what God might show us.

God isn't distant, watching and waiting to reward us in the future. He's present with us in each moment. Part of Brother Lawrence's way of practising God's presence was to do each task out of love for God and as an offering to Him. Could we learn to live like that? We have the rest of our lives to work at it.

Oh, God, You formed me for worship, and I'm only complete in You. Forgive and change my forgetful, self-indulgent ways, and draw me to live and serve out of love for You... because You loved me first and saved me. Soften my heart and help me lift it to You with each thing I do.

Peace With God

Therefore, since we have been made right in God's
sight by faith, we have peace with God because of what
Jesus Christ our Lord has done for us.
Romans 5:1, NLT

No wonder one of Jesus' names is Prince of Peace. What a gift!

Peace with God means we don't have to be afraid of God seeing us or discovering what we've done wrong.

We've been forgiven — and we can be forgiven again when we mess up. We can come to Him confidently with our needs and concerns... and mostly just come to be with Him. We can thrive and grow because we're no longer cut off from God. Now we *know* that God loves us.

Now the Holy Spirit lives in us, and will "fill our hearts with His love" (Romans 5:5, NLT). We have a better perspective on the present: our circumstances are opportunities for growth (Romans 5:2). We have confident hope of eternal life.

It means even more than that... why not take a few minutes to pray and ponder?

Holy and righteous God, I could never make peace with You on my own. I could never make myself right in Your eyes. I thank and praise You for giving me faith to believe in You and to receive the gift of salvation that Jesus bought for me. Help me mature in faith and live for Your glory.

The Reason for All the Seasons

Who will free me from this life that is dominated by
sin and death? Thank God! The answer is in Jesus
Christ our Lord.
Romans 7:24b-25a, NLT

This is why we celebrate Christmas, and Easter, and every other day of the year. We had an impossible need, and God, in His love, mercy, and grace, sent His own Son to meet it.

To walk among humans and reveal what the Father's heart and will looked like. To lay down His life to ransom and redeem us and to break sin's hold on us.

For this, we have Jesus, and a lifetime of thanks is not enough.

Let's walk with Him each day, hearts surrendered to His, in worship, obedience, and adoration.

God my Maker, Redeemer and Sustainer, without You I'd be lost and hopeless, marking time and deceiving myself. Thank You for setting me free — at such extreme cost. Help me receive Your gift of salvation and live it fully, so that others will see the difference You make.

God Stepped In

And I am convinced that nothing can ever separate us
from God's love. Neither death nor life, neither angels
nor demons, neither our fears for today nor our worries
about tomorrow — not even the powers of hell can
separate us from God's love.
Romans 8:38, NLT

Fear wants to tell us we're cut off from God, but fear lies.

Circumstances can be painful, overwhelming. But God is with us, and that is our hope. His love holds us, His grace sustains us, and He refuses to leave us to suffer alone.

We can get angry at Him for allowing our pain, but that doesn't help. All it does is reduce our capacity to experience His presence.

Or we can press into Him and pray to see Him at work in our trouble. And when we see evidence of His care, we can praise and thank Him.

Our faith will grow, and others will see that He makes a difference

Creator and Redeemer God, thank You for Your strong love that can never be broken. Teach me to rely on Your character and Your promises, and to anchor on the truth that You will never leave me.

God Came to Us

Instead, he gave up his divine privileges;
he took the humble position of a slave
and was born as a human being.
Philippians 2:7a, NLT

When disaster strikes a nation or community, the leaders make a point of visiting the area. To assess the situation first-hand, but also to encourage the survivors, who need every bit of hope they can possibly receive.

What did God do with our sin-damaged world? He promised from the beginning that He would provide disaster relief. His timing is longer-term than ours, but that's exactly what He did — and is doing.

He came. Into our disaster. Never mind we made the mess ourselves and then it multiplied out of control. Never mind it wouldn't have happened if Eve and Adam had followed His instructions in the first place.

He came. Jesus experienced birth, life, and death as a human being. He understands our circumstances. He showed us how to live for God in the midst of them. He paid the ultimate price to ransom us back to Himself. And He's coming back to take His rightful place as King.

How can we not love a God who would give everything for us? How could we not give ourselves back to Him in trust and gratitude?

God the Father, God the Son, God the Holy Spirit... You came into this world's need, You are with me now in my need, and You will come again to reign. Thank You. You've proven Your faithfulness, Your love, and Your care. Help me trust and obey You, honour You, and help me receive the full life You offer to Your children.

Light Inextinguishable

The Word gave life to everything that was created,
and his life brought light to everyone.
The light shines in the darkness,
and the darkness can never extinguish it.
John 1:4-5, NLT

This darkness is a spiritual, or perhaps moral, darkness. Not a physical lack of light. If it has the capacity to understand, it's a malevolent darkness (because it tries to extinguish the light).

We know this kind of darkness is in our world. We see it in global and local events. In the motivations of groups and individuals. We see it blinding friends and loved ones.

But don't you love this verse about the light that Jesus' life brought?

The light He gave can't be extinguished or overcome. Can't be smothered or snuffed out. Can't be swallowed or contained. And no, it can't be completely understood even by those who have eyes to see.

Who among us can know the unknowable, understand those things beyond our mental scope? But we who recognize — and love — the light's Source can live "in the light, as God is in the light" (1 John 1:7, NLT).

We can live to please Him, and we can live in confidence that no matter how dark the world gets, His light will endure. His light will have the victory.

God my Rescuer and Sustainer, Your promises are true and Your purposes are good. Grant me the faith to hold onto Your light in the darkness. Help me live faithful to You so Your light can shine through me to those whose eyes You are opening. Have mercy on this darkened world, Lord, and draw the lost to Yourself. May I never be a barrier to their search.

Praying Scripture

I pray that God, the source of hope, will fill you
completely with joy and peace because you trust in
him. Then you will overflow with confident hope
through the power of the Holy Spirit.
Romans 15:13, NLT

We have the privilege of eavesdropping on Paul's heart-felt prayers for the congregations he's writing to. Sure, parts of his letters are direct to the point of sounding harsh (although always with a motive of love), but in his prayers we see how deeply he cares.

We can borrow these prayers for those we love, or for ourselves. Take this one as an example. We can ask this for anyone who knows the Lord, no matter their circumstances.

We may not know how God plans to work out someone's particular struggles, but we know this is the sort of prayer that's always in line with His will.

To apply this verse for a non-believer, we could begin by asking God to reveal Himself as the Source of hope and to give the person faith to trust Him.

Take a second look at Paul's words. Who might God want you to pray them for?

Holy God, You alone are the Source of hope. Real hope, not wishing. You are the Source of joy and peace. And You are trustworthy. Forgive any doubts that taunt me. Help me trust You fully. Open me to receive the joy and peace You give. Fill me with the Holy Spirit and the confident hope He brings. Fill me to overflowing, and flow through me to reveal Yourself to those who don't yet know you, for their sakes and for the sake of Your Kingdom.

Renewing or Regressing?

For you are still controlled by your sinful nature. You
are jealous of one another and quarrel with each other.
Doesn't that prove you are controlled by your sinful
nature? Aren't you living like people of the world?
1 Corinthians 3:3, NLT

Is it any wonder Christians often find ourselves "living like people of the world"?

We live among people who give no allegiance to God. Some are our family, friends, co-workers. Others produce most of the current entertainment and music. And we still have the seeds of our former sin nature lurking within.

If we're not actively pursuing intimacy with God, it's easy to fall back into (or remain in) thought and behaviour patterns that are much less than He desires of us.

Paul says that, in this state, we're not ready for deeper teaching. We need spiritual "baby food" until we develop.

The Bible calls us to renew our minds (Romans 12:2). We have so far to grow in the faith, and so much to leave behind, that this needs to be an ongoing, daily practice. We don't dare settle for a half-grown Christian life, or we'll miss so much of what God has for us.

God my Good Father, grow me into an intimate relationship with You. Teach me Your ways, develop my trust in You, and bring me into the abundant life Jesus promised. Let others see through me the difference You want to make in each one.

Temples

Don't you realize that your body is the temple of the
Holy Spirit, who lives in you and was given to you by
God? You do not belong to yourself, for God bought
you with a high price. So you must honor God with
your body.
1 Corinthians 6:19-20, NLT

Think about the care that went into building the Israelites' temples in the Old Testament. God has put that same care into us (see Psalm 139:14).

The temple building was a place to meet with God, a place to bring sacrifices and find forgiveness. It was a sign to others of God's glory, and a sign of the Israel's unity and identity.

Because our bodies are now temples, we can meet with God throughout the day.

His Spirit dwells within us, so let's intentionally practice His presence. We've been cleansed and forgiven, based on one completed sacrifice; now we're to keep receiving cleansing and forgiveness as needed, so our lives can be signs to others of God's glory and goodness.

Corporately as well as individually, we need to find our identity in the Lord, and to show unity (not uniformity).

Since we represent God in the world, let's keep our "temple" clean, guarding against decay and defilement.

Majestic and holy God, it's beyond understanding that You would choose to show Yourself through me despite my weakness. Even more amazing is that You'd choose to dwell in me. Fill and change me, and lead me in Your ways.

Too High a Price

God paid a high price for you, so don't be enslaved by
the world.
1 Corinthians 7:23, NLT

How is it possible to forget the Cross... and the full cost of Jesus' sacrifice? Yet over time as believers, we get caught up in life and responsibilities, and it's not foremost in our minds.

If God had simply found us at the side of the road while He was out for a stroll, just handed us spare change for a coffee or enough cash for bus fare home, it wouldn't matter so much if we didn't reach our potential.

Instead, His investment was huge. He came looking for us, in the person of His Son. He gave up His life to pay our ransom and to erase our sins. That's much too high a price to squander.

But if we're not vigilant about our choices and attitudes, our focus can slip. We can find our lives diluted — even dominated — by things that don't have eternal value. Sometimes that's from buying into society's mindset, but sometimes it's from listening to our own selfish natures.

God has given us many blessings to enjoy, so let's enjoy them. But let's be careful to keep Him first in our hearts and to put His priorities above our own.

God my Rescuer and Redeemer, You know how often I need to be rescued again. Forgive my blindness, selfishness and inattention. Draw me closer to You, and teach me to delight in Your presence. Change and grow me, so I'll forget my wandering ways and thrive in Your kingdom.

Tempted

The temptations in your life are no different from
what others experience. And God is faithful. He will
not allow the temptation to be more than you can
stand. When you are tempted, he will show you a way
out so that you can endure.
1 Corinthians 10:13, NLT

What's your strategy against temptation? Common sense says to use willpower and avoidance. Sometimes that's enough, but the Bible promises that God Himself will show us a way out of it.

God saved us, cleaned us up, and wants us to live for Him. He's invested in our success, and He equips us with what we need. He's given His own Holy Spirit to live in us, to lead, and empower.

We still have a part to play. First, we need to be alert to recognize temptation. Not just the overt opportunities to sin, but the attitude triggers: things that spark complaining, resentment, bitterness, etc. The Lord wants to keep us clean on the inside as well as the outside.

Once we recognize the danger, we need to ask for God's way out. When He shows us, we need to seize it. No stopping to consider. Instant obedience.

It may be an obvious physical escape — leaving the scene. Or it may be re-setting our mind with a verse of truth that God causes us to remember. Whatever His way is, it'll work — if we obey Him.

Of course we mess up, over and over, in our human weakness, but growing in Christ is about learning to live in His strength. We're a work in progress, and He promises to forgive us when we ask Him.

Holy and righteous God, I'd have no chance of pleasing You without Your grace. You paid the price to reclaim me, You teach and equip me, You lead me. And You forgive me over and over again. Grow me in love and faithfulness, so my life will become more pleasing to You and so others will see the change You can make.

Called to Share

> But whatever I am now, it is all because God poured
> out his special favor on me — and not without results.
> For I have worked harder than any of the other
> apostles; yet it was not I but God who was working
> through me by his grace.
> 1 Corinthians 15:10, NLT

Paul began by persecuting the early Christians, but when Jesus got his attention, he surrendered and threw his whole heart into spreading the news that the promised Saviour had come.

Paul didn't dare let his past disqualify him — not when Jesus had personally commissioned him.

He didn't let the unusual circumstances of his calling inflate his opinion of himself, or of those who'd served the Lord from the beginning. Nor did he allow his "thorn in the flesh" hold him back — instead he learned to rely on God's strength (2 Corinthians 12:9).

He never claimed to have deserved God's special favour — anything but. Yet he seized what God gave him, and poured out his own life in service to his new Master.

If we look around us, we'll see many who appear better equipped to spread the good news about Jesus. But the God who called Paul, and whose grace was enough for him, wants to use us too. He seems to like to work through the unlikely... perhaps because we're more aware of how much we need to rely on Him.

God my Saviour... my King. Thank You for the privilege of belonging to You. Rekindle my wonder that You saved me, and open my eyes to see the opportunities You give to share You with others. Help me not to think less — or more — of myself than I should, but instead to think most about You. Show me how to live for You so others can come to know You as well.

Not Worthy, But Chosen

This letter is from Paul, chosen by the will of God to
be an apostle of Christ Jesus, and from our brother
Timothy.
2 Corinthians 1:1, NLT

Paul was "chosen by the will of God to be an apostle..." But he also wrote: "I am the least of all the apostles... not even worthy to be called an apostle after the way I persecuted God's church" (1 Corinthians 15:9, NLT). Don't you think the enemy of our souls tried to use Paul's past to sabotage his future?

The same with the unnamed weakness that Paul called his "thorn in the flesh" — in fact, he called it "a messenger from Satan" (2 Corinthians 12:7, NLT). Imagine if he'd listened to these taunts about his unworthiness and his weakness. If he'd accepted them and quit the ministry.

Today's verse shows us the secret of his victory.

He knew it wasn't about him — his worth or lack of it, his weakness or strength. It was about God. The God who saw Paul's offences, who allowed the weakness. The God who loved him and chose to save him and to call him as an apostle of Christ.

What about us? Paul wasn't an exception. We're all unworthy in one way or another. We all have weaknesses. What might God want to do through us?

Father God, You know my heart. You know my unworthiness and my weakness. You know I can't change on my own. Yet You love me. You saved me, and You're saving me still. Forgive me for the ways I've allowed my limitations to disqualify me from what You've set before me. Help me find my strength in the fact that it's You who called me to Yourself. Teach me to reject what would hold me back, and help me follow You.

What Qualifies Us?

*It is not that we think we are qualified to do anything
on our own. Our qualification comes from God.*
2 Corinthians 3:5, NLT

Paul has plenty of educational background and other accomplishments, which he elsewhere refers to as "worthless" in comparison to knowing the grace of God.

It's not that he's not qualified, but that any credentials, official or unofficial, would not be enough if he didn't also have the Lord's anointing on him to do the job.

He's writing here about his ministry, about sharing the good news of Jesus, and nurturing believers. This is serious Kingdom business.

What about you and me, in the daily details of our lives?

Who you are today, with the background and abilities you have... is there something you need to do that's generating anxiety? Something that's too hard, or it's a stretch, or messing it up could cause problems? Maybe it's major, like Paul's work, or maybe it's smaller. Nothing is too big or too small for God's notice.

What we need to cling to is this: it's God who makes the difference. And it's God who works with us when we've failed, too. He'll never leave us, and He can work good out of our messes. He never intended us to do life on our own.

God my Creator and my Equipper, help me repeatedly choose to rely on You. You promise to give wisdom when I ask, so help me to ask and to believe. Give me what I need to conduct myself in a manner worthy of Your Name, and to carry out my responsibilities competently. Help me to not allow fear to rob me of my peace and to distance me from You, because You are the Provider of all I need.

Ignoring the Gift

As God's partners, we beg you not to accept this
marvelous gift of God's kindness and then ignore it.
2 Corinthians 6:1, NLT

The gift Paul's speaking of is a new life in Christ, reconciled to God and freed from the penalty of sin and death (2 Corinthians 5:18).

In the same verse, Paul asks the Corinthian believers to reach out and be agents of reconciliation, bringing others to know this gift of life. He wants them to fully live — to demonstrate this gift, vibrantly, contagiously, so others will want in, too. The gift is for everyone who'll receive it.

There's another aspect of ignoring the gift, though: literally ignoring it. Not letting it change us at all. We've escaped a Christ-less eternity, but here and now, life goes on with no appreciable difference.

Jesus doesn't want to be just our Saviour, He wants to be our Lord. Not distant, issuing rules, but personal. Close. He wants our obedience, but also our loyalty. He wants our hearts more than He wants our outward obedience.

How can He have our hearts if we don't spend time with Him? And if He doesn't have our hearts, of course we won't change. Others won't see His goodness. We won't see it, either.

What if we took a few minutes, just five or ten, every day? Even twice a day? A little break for quiet with the Lord, to spend time in His presence. To reorient ourselves under His Lordship. To know Him more.

Father God, forgive me for the times I ignore Your gift. Draw me back to Yourself. Forgive those who've ignored the gift long enough that they don't even think of You now. Like the Roman soldiers, they don't know what they've done. In Your mercy, draw their hearts back to Yourself. Remind them of the gift, and help them to embrace it.

Trusting God's Timing

All those listed above include fourteen generations
from Abraham to David, fourteen from David to the
Babylonian exile, and fourteen from the Babylonian
exile to the Messiah.
Matthew 1:17, NLT

Matthew opens his account of the birth of the Messiah with a genealogy. Did you notice the pattern? Fourteen generations each time. If the priests and scribes had been aware of it and had been counting, they'd have known the timing of God's next big step.

But God prefers to work in surprising ways, ways we look back on and see clearly even though we didn't anticipate them.

The same with the "where" of Jesus' birth: One prophecy said Bethlehem (Matthew 2:5) but another said He'd be called out of Egypt (Matthew 2:15). Clues to keep the faithful anticipating, yet not to reveal the full picture. If we had sight, we wouldn't need faith.

God has a plan. *He* knows the various details and intricate inter-weavings that will bring it all together in His perfect time. *We* know His character, His power, and authority.

We can trust Him to look after all that, and we can be about the daily elements of our Father's business, loving our families, caring for our neighbours and co-workers, conducting ourselves as Christ-followers in a very confused world.

Author and the Finisher of my faith, help me trust You. Please keep me from discouragement when I don't see Your plans unfolding, and keep me equally from trying to "hurry" or "help" You. Keep me from fear when I look at the world around me. Reassure me of Your perfect wisdom, power, and timing. Help me live each day in confidence in You.

God Wants Us Back

The LORD gave [King Nebuchadnezzar] victory over
King Jehoiakim of Judah and permitted him to take
some of the sacred objects from the Temple of God. So
Nebuchadnezzar took them back to the land of
Babylonia and placed them in the treasure-house of his
god.
Daniel 1:2, NLT

And so began Israel's bleak captivity. Nebuchadnezzar credited his own god (or himself) for this triumph. After all, it was his army that achieved it. But did you notice the key words in the verse? "The Lord gave him victory... and permitted him to take some of the sacred objects..."

Not that God had abandoned His chosen people. This was part of His plan to draw them back to Himself after they'd repeatedly rejected Him. The prophets had warned them again and again, but they refused to listen.

It's sad how often our own blindness and self-will makes us insist on our way instead of following God's way. We think we can have both, but we can't.

What an amazing, loving God and Shepherd we have. Instead of immediately giving us over to the things we're so quick to chase, He continues to call us back to Himself.

The more we resist, the more painful the process may become. May we be quick to hear when we get off-track.

God of love and righteousness, grant me a heart that's quick to hear and to respond to Your leading — a heart that loves being in close relationship with You and that doesn't want to let anything come between us. Help me love You more than I love those things that would lead me away. Thank You that when I turn back to You, You forgive, restore, and embrace me.

Showing God's Glory

Now I, Nebuchadnezzar, praise and glorify and honor
the King of heaven. All his acts are just and true, and
he is able to humble the proud.
Daniel 4:37, NLT

The story of Nebuchadnezzar's madness and return to power in Daniel 4 not only shows God's power, it shows His mercy.

King Herod had a similar moment of self-exaltation, but he received only judgement and death (Acts 12:20-23). The difference may be that God saw in Nebuchadnezzar the potential to repent and be restored.

The taking down of the world's most powerful man at the time, and then his restoration, demonstrated God's power to grant authority and to take it away. Nebuchadnezzar told the world, once he was restored. Many of his subjects may not have believed him, but those with open ears heard. And he knew the truth.

The Bible shows that God works in our lives for our own good but also for His glory, that those watching can see His character and come to Him as well. He doesn't want anyone to go into eternity without Him.

May we who know Him keep close, so He doesn't need to do anything dramatic to bring us back. May we keep our spirits lined up with His, and be open to recognize — and to share — what He does in and around us, for the glory of His name and for the sake of those who need to hear.

God Most High, You are worthy of all praise, for Your power, Your mercy, and for all that You are. Help me remember Your character and live in confidence in Your care. Help me trust You even when all I see in the world is trouble and disaster. You are supreme, and Your Kingdom will come.

Darkness has Limits

Then I heard two holy ones talking to each other. One
of them asked, "How long will the events of this vision
last? How long will the rebellion that causes
desecration stop the daily sacrifices? How long will the
Temple and heaven's army be trampled on?"
Daniel 8:13, NLT

This is from one of Daniel's visions, and in it, everything looked disastrous. Verse 12 says "The army of heaven was restrained from responding to this rebellion."

Daniel saw evil winning — permitted to win — but even then the heavenly beings knew this was only for a time. God had allowed it for a purpose.

When things seem out of control, when God seems absent or not working, He still has the ultimate authority and He will work even this into His redemptive plan.

There are things God allows as a consequence of our sin-soaked world, things that should never happen and that we wouldn't allow if we had His power. The people living in these circumstances are suffering greatly.

Knowing His goodness and the other aspects of His character helps us choose to trust Him even in the worst of times.

At the Lord Jesus' return, when everything is made new, when His glory is fully revealed and all tears cease, somehow He will make everything right.

God my Creator and my Saviour, Your ways are beyond my understanding, and You are good. Help me trust You when I can't see. Strengthen my faith to hold onto You. And thank You that You will work everything out according to Your plan, and that it is a good plan, involving our salvation and our rescue. Thank You that Your glory will ultimately be revealed and Your people comforted, and that the enemy of our souls will be forever overcome.

In Awe of God's Goodness

But afterward the people will return and devote
themselves to the LORD their God and to David's
descendant, their king. In the last days, they will
tremble in awe of the LORD and of his goodness.
Hosea 3:5, NLT

We're a pretty unfaithful bunch, aren't we, as humans? It's worth noting that the people whose return to the Lord is anticipated in this verse only come back after a serious intervention on God's part. Their choices lead to consequences.

The Book of Hosea is a beautiful picture of how much God loves His people and desires a relationship with us — and how easily we'll turn away from Him.

Even those of us who know and love Him need to be careful not to drift away. Those who don't know Him yet don't want to get closer in the first place.

But God...

Read Hosea and see God's love, mercy and grace — and the impact of human unfaithfulness. See how God takes it upon Himself to bring us back, because He knows we won't come on our own.

And see the promise of how it will be when we "finally know Him as the LORD" (Hosea 2:20, NLT).

God my determined and loving Rescuer, thank You. Help me to devote myself to You. Overwhelm me with Your goodness. Keep me close. Please draw those who don't yet know You. Open their eyes and hearts to who You are, so that they will tremble in awe of Your goodness.

Coming (Back) to the Lord

So now, come back to your God.
Act with love and justice,
and always depend on him.
Hosea 12:6, NLT

In the middle of declaring His chosen people's unfaithfulness to Him and of pronouncing the consequences, God adds this invitation.

It's followed by "But no..." (verse 7). Realistically, the people are fully intent on going their own way. They don't see the need to return to God — yet.

In praying for our world today, we see the same thing. Most people aren't ready to turn to God. And as trouble comes, instead of making them re-think, it seems to harden them in their desired independence from God.

Meanwhile, we who know Him wait sadly, knowing He loves them too much to leave them that way, and that to get their attention, things will likely grow worse instead of better.

Some are finding Him, though. And each one is cause for rejoicing.

My God and Redeemer, I praise You for Your love and mercy that keeps reaching out to the lost and wayward. Open their hearts to respond to Your call. Move my heart to echo Yours in prayer for them. What can I say but thank You?

To Depend on God

So now, come back to your God.
Act with love and justice,
and always depend on him.
Hosea 12:6, NLT

Depending on God is an active reliance. We depend on His strength in us to equip us to serve. We depend on His Spirit in us to replace our natural reactions with the "love, joy, peace, patience, kindness, goodness, faithfulness, gentleness, and self-control" that He wants us to display (Galatians 5:22-23, NLT).

When we're mistreated, instead of taking revenge, we depend on "Him who judges justly" (1 Peter 2:23, NIV), and we dare by His Spirit to forgive the offender and to pray that instead of staying hard and receiving what he or she deserves, that person will surrender to God and receive mercy.

We read the Bible and learn about God's character, His ways, and His will. And about His promises. We choose to depend on who He is and what He says, not on what we feel and see. We learn to recognize how He speaks to us as individuals, and we step out in faith to obey Him.

We overcome our fears by choosing to depend on God's care and His power — and on the assurance that His presence will be with us, no matter what.

God of Abraham, of Isaac, of me: because You don't change, I can know and depend on You. Draw me nearer to Your heart, and grow me in my faith. Draw those who don't yet know You. Help them see their need of You, and how ignoring and defying You diminishes their lives. Because of Your great mercy, don't give up on them.

Whose Kingdom?

So when the apostles were with Jesus, they kept asking
him, "Lord, has the time come for you to free Israel
and restore our kingdom?"
Acts 1:6, NLT

The resurrected Jesus had been appearing to the disciples, proving He was alive, and continuing to speak of the Kingdom of God (Acts 1:3).

The disciples were still looking for the restoration of *their* kingdom: for the nation of Israel to be powerful again as it had been in the past.

God had much bigger — and longer-term — plans.

What are we asking Him for that's too small, even if it seems huge to us? What are we asking for that's a return to what was, instead of an expansion to what He promises?

As we pray and listen to God, as He reveals glimpses of His purposes, let's resist the tendency to fit them into our own understanding and experience. Into the framework of the past.

Holy and omnipotent God, Your ways and plans are much bigger than I can grasp. I praise You for what You will do, and for how You will reveal Your glory. In this as in the rest of my life, help me trust You wholeheartedly and not to cling to my own understanding. Lead, guide, and direct me, and make me useful for Your Kingdom.

Finding Courage in God

And David was greatly distressed; for the people spoke
of stoning him, because all the people were bitter in
soul, each for his sons and daughters. But David
strengthened himself in the LORD his God.
1 Samuel 30:6, RSV

While David (not yet crowned king) and his men were away on a mission, enemies had sacked their town and taken captive all the women and children. No wonder he was "distressed."

But he found courage — and strength — in the Lord his God.

How can we do that?

Stop: instead of jumping into action or into despair.

Look: at who God is. At what He says. And at what He has done in the past.

Listen: to what He says. Then, by faith, we can choose to obey Him, whether that's in action or in waiting.

God my Refuge and my Strong Tower, help me trust You even when everything has gone wrong. Help me rely on You as my source of courage, strength, and hope. Quiet me to know Your presence. Work in my circumstances and in my heart, to Your glory.

Little Idols

In the book of the prophets it is written,
"Was it to me you were bringing sacrifices and offerings
during those forty years in the wilderness, Israel?"
Acts 7:42b, NLT

You'd think faith would have been easier for the Israelites during their wilderness wanderings. They ate the manna: daily evidence of God's care. Their shoes and clothing didn't wear out. They were led by God's pillar of fire and cloud. They carried with them the Tabernacle where their leader, Moses, talked to God directly.

Yet Acts 7:43 says they carried their pagan gods and idols with them, too. They were following God's leading, but worshipping whatever they chose.

So although God brought them into the Promised Land, it was temporary. Exile was in their future, because they wouldn't change and devote themselves completely to Him despite all the wonders they saw Him do for them.

These verses call us to search ourselves now, even as believers in Jesus Christ.

What are we holding onto that's dividing our loyalty and diluting our worship? What does God see in our hearts that's crowding in on His space?

God sees these things, and they offend Him. But Scripture tells us He longs to draw us nearer, not push us away. He will point out the trouble, if we'll only ask.

God my Creator and my Saviour, You alone are worthy of our worship and devotion. Open my eyes to those things I've allowed to have too much importance in my life. Forgive me, cleanse and restore me to full fellowship with You, and grow me in the life everlasting.

Opportunity and Adventure

As for Philip, an angel of the Lord said to him, "Go
south down the desert road that runs from Jerusalem to
Gaza."
Acts 8:26, NLT

The Book of Acts reads like a series of adventures. Here, Philip had been preaching in Samaria (Acts 8:5-25).

Many people had come to know the Lord, so Peter and John came from Jerusalem to see what was happening. Their involvement continued God's work, and that seems to be the end of Philip's role there, although looking on, we could assume there was plenty more for him to do.

Instead, the angel gave him a new assignment. Philip obeyed, and found a new opportunity prepared by God.

It's not easy to be redirected when we're in the middle of something, especially in ministry or service. Our focus is engaged. We want to finish the task, whatever it is.

Sometimes, we also want a bit of down time before taking on the next thing. A chance to relax, to feel "off duty."

What if we could be open to see each new thing from God as an adventure? An opportunity to watch Him work in and through us? What might He do with enthusiastic workers instead of weary ones?

God my Shepherd and my Leader, You are always at work, and Your plans are always good. Forgive me for those times I allow myself to grow weary in Your service and lose the wonder of the privilege of serving You. Please give me open eyes, an eager heart, and a willingness to work for Your Kingdom.

An Encourager

Then Barnabas went on to Tarsus to look for Saul.
Acts 11:25, NLT

Gentiles were coming to faith in Antioch, and the leaders in Jerusalem sent Barnabas to visit. He was excited to see what God was doing, and some time after arriving, he left to get Saul. When they returned to Antioch, they stayed a whole year. Clearly, there was a lot to be done.

Paul had been sent away from Jerusalem for his own safety, because his preaching about Jesus was so powerful it made him a target. Perhaps Barnabas thought bringing him in to speak to Gentiles instead of Jews would be safer.

The New Testament shows Barnabas as an encourager, one who believed in people, saw their abilities, and who spoke up for them when needed. He also brought them alongside to work with him.

He saw an opportunity in Antioch, or perhaps a need, and rather than trying to do it all himself or even just recruit the locals to help, he went for Saul. Did he have to go personally because he thought he'd need to convince Saul?

Sometimes it's easier to keep slogging by ourselves, especially if we have a certain way we like things done. Barnabas reminds us to be open to God's leading about partnerships and about encouragement.

God who gives each one different gifts and abilities, please help me to discern the abilities in the people around me, and give me a willing heart to involve them in my life and my work. Help me affirm in others what You have placed there, for the overall increase of Your Kingdom.

Closer to God

When he [Barnabas] arrived and saw this evidence of
God's blessing, he was filled with joy, and he
encouraged the believers to stay true to the Lord.

Many Jews and devout converts to Judaism followed
Paul and Barnabas, and the two men urged them to
continue to rely on the grace of God.
Acts 11:23; 13:43, NLT

How do we stay true to the Lord and continue to rely on His grace?

It takes ongoing, persistent behavioural patterns, of prayer and praying Scripture, practicing His presence, reading — and thinking about — the Bible, and talking, praying, and studying with other believers.

It means serving where He leads, relying on His strength in service and in all areas of our daily lives, getting to know His character through life and His Word, and noticing and keeping a record of where we see God at work in our lives. It means telling our stories of faith, and listening to others.

In these ways and more, may we let God deeper into our lives.

God my Sustainer and my Source of life and hope, just like John the Baptist, I need to decrease so that You can increase. Thank You for giving the Holy Spirit to indwell me. Please help me give Him full access to my heart, so that You can grow me in faith. Help me stay true to You and rely on Your grace every day.

God Hasn't Moved

"Sir," Gideon replied, "if the LORD is with us, why has
all this happened to us? And where are all the miracles
our ancestors told us about? Didn't they say, 'The
LORD brought us up out of Egypt'? But now the LORD
has abandoned us and handed us over to the
Midianites."
Judges 6:13, NLT

God had already sent a prophet to explain why Israel experiencing this oppression. Perhaps Gideon didn't hear that message, but now he was talking with the Angel of the Lord.

Gideon's own father had an altar to idols. Did Gideon realize this was wrong before God told him to destroy it? He knew about God from history and tradition, but perhaps he thought, as many do today, that those days were gone, that God had changed or maybe faded.

It sounds like he blamed God for the trouble and didn't see it was sin that had caused the separation. God hadn't moved. The people had.

We see the same tendency today, sometimes in ourselves, and often in the world around us. There's no easy answer about why God allows pain, and suffering is not always a consequence of our sin. Sometimes it's because of someone else's sinful choices, and sometimes it's just life with no apparent reason.

Whatever the cause, when we're hurting, we can trust the God who promised to never leave us. We can press into Him, asking Him to reveal anything that we may have allowed to come between us and to restore us to Himself. We can trust Him to forgive us if needed, and to carry and sustain us. He loves us and will be with us.

Father, forgive me when I doubt Your goodness, and when I blame You for any distance I've allowed to grow between us. Whatever trouble comes my way, let it motivate me to rely more on You. Help me cling to the truth of Your promise to never leave me, and help me not give any foothold to the enemy of my soul. I belong to You, and You will not abandon me. Help me stand on Your truth.

Testing Our Thoughts

For God has not given us a spirit of fear and timidity,
but of power, love, and self-discipline.
2 Timothy 1:7, NLT

Paul is writing to Timothy, a young leader in need of encouragement. This verse offers that, and more. It's also a partial description of our two natures: the natural self and the Holy Spirit-led self.

With that perspective, the verse can be used to test our responses. Are we feeling fearful, timid, anxious?

That's our old nature, not God. We don't have to accept, obey, or believe it. We can ask the Holy Spirit to be power, love, and self-discipline in us.

Then, of course, we have to choose to accept, obey, and believe what He gives. Building up the spiritual muscles of our new nature takes consistent effort, and testing our responses is a learned skill.

We can never quote this verse blindly and forge ahead over our fears into obvious trouble. Instead of fear, though, or timidity or anxiety, God's way of reining us in is more like a check in our spirit, or a knowing. It's constructive, not like the nameless dread that clouds an anxious heart.

Because of what Paul's trying to say to Timothy, the verse focuses on what this anxious young man needed.

In facing different areas of weakness, we can use the verse as a template. Just fill in the specific weakness in the "not" category, and in the Bible, find the Spirit's corresponding strengths for the "yes" side.

Mighty God, thank You that You have given Your Holy Spirit to live in me and guide and grow me. Help me learn to distinguish between my old ways and Your ways, and align me with Your Spirit so I can become all You have for me to be.

The Right Kind of Open-Mindedness

And the people of Berea were more open-minded than
those in Thessalonica, and they listened eagerly to
Paul's message. They searched the Scriptures day after
day to see if Paul and Silas were teaching the truth.
Acts 17:11, NLT

In Berea (after being run out of Thessalonica) Paul and Silas found open-minded hearers. The people were eager to learn more about God, but they were careful to test this new teaching against the truth of Scripture. They were ready to learn, but guarding themselves against deception and false teaching.

Later, in Athens, Paul found a different sort of open-mindedness: "... all the Athenians as well as the foreigners in Athens seemed to spend all their time discussing the latest ideas" (Acts 17:21, NLT).

These people were open to ideas too, but only for discussion, not for application or for allowing what they heard to change them. It sounds like they viewed all ideas as equal, without investigating for truth.

That likely made it easier to get along with everyone else, and it's what we need to do in many matters, but when it comes to what's true or false, we need to be like the Bereans in discernment — and like Paul and Silas in teaching the truth in a way that doesn't attack those who don't believe it.

Creator God, All-Wise and True, open my heart and mind to long for a closer relationship with You, and grow me in Your truth. Protect me from ideas that would divert me from intimacy with You or lead me in wrong paths. Give me a burden to share Jesus with those around me in love and respect, and give them a desire to seek You and to know You.

Healthy Repentance

I have had one message for Jews and Greeks alike —
the necessity of repenting from sin and turning to God,
and of having faith in our Lord Jesus.
Acts 20:21, NLT

These days, if people say "that's a sin," they either mean "what a shame; that's unfortunate" or they mean "you're disqualified; that's offensive."

But it makes sense that in the eyes of a holy God, we often do, think, or say things that fall short of His perfect standards. All of us do it, so there's no ground for pointing fingers. We *do* sin. Sometimes even on purpose. It's natural, but that doesn't make it right.

For a healthy spiritual life, we have to repent of our sin. We acknowledge it as wrong and choose to change. We turn to God.

Anywhere but *to* God is pointing away from Him. We can only grow in wholeness if we're moving in the right direction.

Faith in Jesus is essential for receiving salvation in the first place, so we can be cleansed from what's offensive and damaged.

We also need it in our daily life, for ongoing salvation and cleansing, and to receive leading, power, growth, comfort, wisdom, courage, and more. And we need it for the future: He is our hope of heaven.

God my Father, thank You for sending Your Son to be my Saviour. Thank You this gift is for everyone who will accept it. Thank You for the faith to believe. Please help me grow in You, and help me share Your message with those who still need to hear.

Remember Our Hope

I asked you to come here today so we could get
acquainted and so I could explain to you that I am
bound with this chain because I believe that the hope of
Israel — the Messiah — has already come.
Acts 28:20, NLT

For years, the Jews had been waiting for the Promised One. They expected Him to rescue their nation from Gentile domination and restore it as a powerful kingdom.

The Kingdom Jesus said had come, and the liberation He brought, didn't match their understanding. And of course some of the prophecies are waiting even now to be fulfilled at His return.

Think about what it means, though, to believe the Messiah has already come.

Yes, we're waiting for Him to come back — which means living in a way that will meet with His approval no matter when He does — but how does it change our outlook?

The Kingdom of God has come, even though it hasn't yet been outwardly manifested. The Holy Spirit rules in our hearts, and He can work in and through us. We are under the authority of the King, not of a decaying world system.

We have been and are being liberated from the hold of darkness. Our spirits have been brought out into the Light. We have hope. Peace. A Source of joy. God has ransomed, redeemed, and restored us, and has adopted us as His own children — every Jew and Gentile who believes.

He *has* come. We are free. What difference will this reminder make in our days?

My God and King, teach me afresh the wonder of Messiah's coming, and help me live fully in Your hope, as an ambassador of Your Kingdom and anticipating its fullness.

Confident in God

Let us then approach God's throne of grace with
confidence, so that we may receive mercy and find
grace to help us in our time of need.
Hebrews 4:16, NIV

We're encouraged to approach God's very throne. With confidence.

In what circumstances? When we're at the peak of our success and have it all together?

No. Believers in Christ are to come to the All-Powerful Ruler of all creation when we most need grace and mercy. To come with confidence, at our lowest point.

Not with a brash, in-your-face boldness that thinks He's somehow obligated to us, but with a confidence based on God's character and on His promises.

He has committed to receive us, because of His goodness and Jesus' finished work on the Cross. It has nothing to do with our merit.

Because we know who He is, we know we'll find the mercy and grace we need.

Thinking in these terms, the confidence we express is faith. We're choosing to believe Him and to stake our needs on Him.

God my King, awesome in majesty and holiness, I am perpetually in need of Your grace and mercy. Thank You for making a way for me to receive what I could never earn or supply on my own. Even faith is a gift from You, so please give me the faith — the confidence in You — that will bring me into Your presence to receive what You long to give. Thank You for loving me enough for this.

Remember and Rejoice

So now we can rejoice in our wonderful new
relationship with God because our Lord Jesus Christ
has made us friends of God.
Romans 5:11, NLT

New Christians are so vibrant and full of joy. Whatever our spiritual "age," let's think about what relationship with God means.

There need be no dread, or fear of punishment, no hopelessness about our lives. We have confidence to approach God with our needs. We have peace in our spirits, forgiveness, and cleansing from our sins.

He is changing our character and behaviour. We have the hope of Heaven, the Holy Spirit's presence with us each moment, and ongoing access to God's wisdom.

He has given us spiritual eyes that are learning to see what He sees, and healing for our hurts. We are growing in usefulness to the Master.

And more...

Some of these things are still developing. We haven't fully arrived, but it's so good to be on the path with Him.

More than any of these things, relationship with God means we have Him, and He has us. Let's take time today to rejoice in this wonderful relationship.

God my Maker and Redeemer, it's beyond wonderful that You have brought Your children back into relationship with You through Jesus' life, death, and resurrection. Forgive me for getting used to this great gift and not seeing the wonder of it. Teach me to rejoice in You, and make me contagious, so that others will want to know You too.

Taught by Trouble

We can rejoice, too, when we run into problems and
trials, for we know that they help us develop
endurance.
Romans 5:3, NLT

When trouble comes, or something goes wrong, how often do we respond this way? Or do we react, taking it personally, like it's one more thing to fight?

Paul writes these words in the midst of teaching about the right relationship and peace with God that we've received, the "undeserved privilege" (verse 2) we've been given through Christ. He highlights God's great love for us, and our hope of salvation.

In this context, it's easier to see that he's not asking us to somehow celebrate hardship. He's giving us a different perspective on what's happening, and showing a healthier response than our natural one.

If salvation life is all about relationship with God, then problems and trials are opportunities to practice depending on Him. They keep us from drifting back to trusting our own strength. They develop our faith by letting us prove His faithfulness and power.

They may be meant for harm, but God can use them for good.

God my Rock and my Refuge, grant me spiritual sight to recognize the deeper realities in the trials and difficulties that You allow. Help me choose to rely on You, so that You can grow my endurance, character, and hope. Draw me deeper into relationship with You, for my joy and for Your glory.

It's All About Him

For everything comes from him and exists by his
power and is intended for his glory. All glory to him
forever! Amen.
Romans 11:36, NLT

Our minds process, evaluate, react, and scheme, as we try to make the best lives we can for ourselves and for those in our care.

That doesn't mean we're selfish, although sometimes we are. Each of us is the point of view character in our own story, and it's easy to slide from there into thinking that it's all about us.

Paul reminds us of the truth. It's all about God.

He didn't make us for *us*. We were made for relationship with Him, designed to only be complete in Him.

He intends us for His glory. What does that mean?

Just like "the heavens declare the glory of God" (Psalm 19:1, NIV), our lives, lived in loving submission to God and in reliance on His power, demonstrate that there is a Good Shepherd.

There is hope, forgiveness, healing. There is an ultimate authority who defines good and bad, who can rescue and rebuke... and who would rather restore than condemn.

God my Creator and Sustainer, You alone are worthy of all honour and glory. Forgive me for those times my perspective revolves around myself. Help me remember I'm to live for Your glory. Shine through me to bring glory to Your name.

Highly Valued

So guard yourselves and God's people. Feed and
shepherd God's flock — his church, purchased with his
own blood — over which the Holy Spirit has appointed
you as leaders.
Acts 20:28, NLT

Let's face it, church is a collection of sinners saved by Jesus' blood, plus those still fumbling toward saving faith. Some are easy to love, but most of us have sharp edges, abrasive surfaces, or other sources of irritation.

We're in the process of spiritual growth, and what God sees in us is not always visible to those looking through human eyes. But He's building us into the Body of Christ, and into His Temple. He sees value in us. Enough that Jesus died to redeem us.

He commands us to love one another (John 13:34-35). He's not asking us to do anything He hasn't done first, and He offers the Holy Spirit within us to produce that love for one another. We just need to choose to obey, even when it's hard.

What if there's someone in our church who's impossible to love? We can pray for him or her. Regularly. If we ask God to grow His love in us — and persistently choose to cooperate with Him — He'll surprise us.

Most times it's not that extreme, but may we remember to ask what He sees, instead of focusing on what we see. May we remember the high value He sets on us, as individuals and as His flock.

God my Shepherd and my Saviour, I dare not dismiss any soul You love. Please help me see what You see, and grow Your love in my heart for each member of Your Body. Show me what You see in me, too, and help me surrender fully to Your cleansing and growth.

Set Apart

And now I entrust you to God and the message of his
grace that is able to build you up and give you an
inheritance with all those he has set apart for himself.
Acts 20:32, NLT

God has set us apart for Himself. Not because of anything we've done to earn it, but because of His great mercy and grace.

We're set apart for His glory, in our conduct and in the transformation others will see in us.

We're set apart for His service, as and where He leads and empowers, and for personal relationship with Him, because He has adopted us.

He has set us apart for our rescue and resuscitation, to build us up, and to give us an inheritance in eternity.

He chose us, while we were still dead in our sins (Romans 5:8).

God my Rescuer and Redeemer, You have given me new life and hope, not just for myself but that I may live set apart for You. Help me fully embrace Your rule in my life, so I can be filled with Your Holy Spirit and live a life that pleases You. Shine through me to draw others who are still in the darkness.

Tested Trust

I pray that God, the source of hope, will fill you
completely with joy and peace because you trust in
him. Then you will overflow with confident hope
through the power of the Holy Spirit.
Romans 15:13, NLT

This level of trust isn't a casual belief, nor is it taking something for granted. It's an active, deliberate choice to trust God, regardless of the circumstances — or the consequences.

Trust like this seems risky at first, like sitting in a chair that looks rickety. You might lower yourself gingerly onto the seat, listening for creaks, leg muscles tensed to spring up if the chair collapses. Gradually, you relax and let the chair take your full weight. It holds you well.

The next time you may still be cautious, but not as much so. Each time you experience the chair's solidity increases your ability to trust it. The chair has been strong — trustworthy — all along.

With God, we have many proofs of His faithfulness, from His Word and from experience, both others' and our own. It's still up to us to choose to place our trust in Him in each situation.

That choice locks out the enemy's mind games and focuses us on our true Help. It's a choice that sometimes we'll need to make minute by minute.

The more we rely on God, and the more fully we do that instead of keeping our options open, the more we will prove His faithfulness. This is when we discover the hope and confidence He gives.

God my Rock and my Salvation, my Help and my Sustainer, be my Source of hope. Give me the faith to actively trust You so I'll be open to your infilling of joy, peace, and confident hope — for my own sake, but also for the sake of those who need to see that You're real.

God First

They sweep past like the wind
and are gone.
But they are deeply guilty,
for their own strength is their god.
Habakkuk 1:11, NLT

This prophecy describes the Babylonians, whom God says He will "raise up" (verse 6) to conquer everything in sight.

He calls them "a cruel and violent people" (verse 6), yet it seems their worse offence isn't wicked behaviour — it's the attitude of their hearts. It's what they worship.

Today's verse reminds us that, as important as our conduct is, of greater importance is the orientation of our hearts. Even outward righteousness wouldn't be acceptable to God if it came from a wrongly-focused heart.

God requires our obedience, but even deeper, He requires our worship. Not because His ego needs it, but because we were designed to worship Him.

We are only complete when our spirits are lined up with His. When He is our Source, our focus. Our God.

Holy and all-powerful God, You alone are worthy of worship. If I fixate on anything else, I'm missing the fullness of life that You have for me — and I'm offending You by exalting something of lesser value above You. Forgive me for how easily I get distracted. Capture my heart with Your goodness, and draw me to worship You alone. Only You are worthy, and only in You do I find life.

To Hear and Obey

*... and the whole remnant of God's people began to
obey the message from the LORD their God. When
they heard the words of the prophet Haggai, whom the
LORD their God had sent, the people feared the LORD.*
Haggai 1:12b, NLT

What was the Lord's message that the people obeyed?

A remnant of Israel had returned to Jerusalem, but in the busyness of rebuilding the city and their homes, they'd neglected to finish rebuilding the Temple.

God asked, "Why are you living in luxurious houses while my house lies in ruins?" (Haggai 1:4, NLT), and He said that was why the people were working so hard for meagre results. They weren't honouring Him.

Prophetic messages were often rejected, but not this time. These people listened. They chose to obey.

We can be like them, getting off-track or drifting away from what the Lord would have us do.

He may let us wander for a while and miss the best He wants to give us, but isn't it wonderful that He will call us back?

Let's be quick to listen and to respond.

Good and merciful God, You know I'm prone to distraction. Please guard and direct me, and make me responsive to Your correction. Give me ears, heart, and spirit attuned to You, for Your glory and my own wellbeing.

Worship is for God

Say to all your people and your priests, "During these
seventy years of exile, when you fasted and mourned
in the summer and in early autumn, was it really for
me that you were fasting? And even now in your holy
festivals, aren't you eating and drinking just to please
yourselves?"
Zechariah 7:5b-6, NLT

True worship is a heart-and-spirit response to the Living God.

Sadly, we can lose focus and make our Christian gatherings about us instead. Congregations can take sides over music styles, service format, formality of prayers, etc.

It becomes all about us — what pleases us, what we deem the best way to express ourselves. It becomes *our* activity — the routine we follow for personal satisfaction.

But God wants first place in our hearts. When the structure or control of the event means more than the One we gather to honour, we have a problem. When we fight among ourselves over it, we have a problem. When we're there for what we get instead of the God we worship, we have a problem.

We need to worship God privately and corporately. Different people will bring different styles and ways of expression. Our focus must always be on God, not on personal gratification or on how well we've "done the job."

It's the pure hearts He's looking for, not the people who are trying to make it all about themselves.

God who is King over all, help me not seek to worship for the experience, although may I experience You. Gathering with other believers, help me not to insist on my preferences in song and structure at the expense of others who know a different way. Join our hearts to desire and to bless You, and unite us in worship that is pleasing to Your heart.

Rest from the Ordinary

You have six days each week for your ordinary work,
but the seventh day is a Sabbath day of rest dedicated
to the LORD your God.
Deuteronomy 5:13-14a, NLT

Rest. God insists on it. He rested on the seventh day of creation, not because He needed it, but because we would need it. Because otherwise we'd find ways to go nonstop in the pursuit of our "ordinary" work.

Stopping becomes an act of faith as well as obedience. It's a sign to us, and to others, of God's trustworthiness and His care for us. It means we trust Him to help us accomplish the "ordinary" work He has for us in the other six days.

Truly resting and trusting means not just stopping the work for a day. It means stopping *thinking about* the work for the day. Otherwise our minds keep working, and we miss the point.

Choosing rest makes us see where our worship and affection really lie. It may reveal a few things that need trimming from our schedules. It also recharges us to return to work with new energy and stamina.

Worship is a key part of soul-rest and restoration. Other aspects of a day of rest dedicated to God may mean different things to different people.

Without legalism, and with daily resting in His presence as well, how might we expand our understanding of a designated day of rest?

God my Creator and my Shepherd, You know I need rest of body, mind, and spirit, and that I can turn my own agenda into a mini-god if I'm not reminded of my true allegiance. Thank You that You desire relationship with me: my love, not just my labour. Teach me what it means to rest, including how to carve out a day of rest in this fast-paced world. May my obedience be a sign for me and for others of Your goodness.

Our Victory Comes from God

I wait quietly before God,
for my victory comes from him.
Psalm 62:1, NLT

Where do you need victory today? In an external conflict? A health issue? Inside your own thoughts or fears?

The victory David expected is the same one we need today. With God as his — and our — fortress, we have the security and salvation we need. By faith we can keep our eyes on the Lord and declare with David, "I will not be shaken" (verse 6).

We can't even quiet our souls without God, but that's a prayer He will love to answer.

David's method was to concentrate on God's might and character until he had a true perspective of where the real power lay, and then he could trust in God's care. We can learn to do the same.

Here's where we can discover the assurance of victory. Whatever happens, Jesus will be with us. He will sustain us. He will be enough. If we choose, by His strength, to quiet ourselves before Him and trust His deliverance, others will see His goodness.

We may or may not see the external victory we long for, but we can experience daily victory over our thoughts, attitudes, and fears by choosing to dwell each moment in God's fortress.

Father, fear shouts so loudly that victory seems impossible. Have mercy on Your fragile child and give me the faith and strength to choose Your security. Quiet my flailing spirit so I can rest in You. Give me confidence in Your care, because You are indeed good.

Lifestyle and Hope

And we are instructed to turn from godless living and
sinful pleasures. We should live in this evil world with
wisdom, righteousness, and devotion to God, while we
look forward with hope to that wonderful day when
the glory of our great God and Savior, Jesus Christ,
will be revealed.
Titus 2:12-13, NLT

Paul has been coaching Titus in how best to teach and shepherd the Christians in his care, for their personal growth, but also so that people around them will see God's goodness. Their — and our — lives as Christians are to be positive reflections of God's character and grace.

Because salvation is meant for everyone (verse 11), Christian conduct should show that Jesus is the way to salvation, freedom, and abundant life.

In this context, it's clear that Paul doesn't call this world evil in the sense of judging and condemning the people still living without God. Paul wants his hearers to be beacons to attract those who still need rescue.

He wants us to live as lights for good, not with negative attitudes toward the not-yet-saved, but neither with lifestyles that suggest "godless living and sinful pleasures" are okay.

Paul's letters are filled with practical instruction on the sorts of attitudes and behaviours to embrace and to avoid, and he sums it up in today's verses.

He's calling us to holy living, and not with sour faces or legalism. No, looking forward in anticipation of Jesus' return.

God my Saviour and my righteousness, forgive me for blending in with the world's ungodly behaviour patterns. Show me where I need to change, and give me the courage to do so. You've promised to give me wisdom and to be my righteousness. Help me to receive and rely on Your provision. Draw me into a lifestyle of devotion to You and of hope in Your Son's return. Thank You for being my light.

Eagerly Waiting

Now you have every spiritual gift you need as you
eagerly wait for the return of our Lord Jesus Christ.
1 Corinthians 1:7, NLT

Waiting for Jesus' return is an active waiting. The only way it could be passive would be if we'd already finished everything He left us to do, so we'll be working until He comes. Working, and waiting expectantly.

Eager waiting feeds our hope, and reminds us not to invest too permanently in this life. No matter how good (or bad) today is, there are better days coming.

This attitude of eager waiting encourages us in hard times, and gives perspective when our faith leads to trouble in the here and now.

It calls us to keep active in sharing the gospel and in encouraging one another. There will be a day when it'll be too late.

Gracious God and King, thank You for giving me the spiritual gifts I need to serve in the ways You have prepared for me. Please help me serve in an attitude of willing worship, and help me eagerly wait for Jesus' return. Thank You that Your timing is perfect and that You always keep Your promises.

Noticing. And Remembering.

O LORD my God, you have performed many wonders
for us.
Your plans for us are too numerous to list.
You have no equal.
If I tried to recite all your wonderful deeds,
I would never come to the end of them.
Psalm 40:5, NLT

We recognize the truth in verses like these. And yet we forget. We forget who God is — how strong, how full of love and mercy, how trustworthy.

We see the troubles and stresses in our lives and in the world around us, the looming danger and darkness, and we lose sight of the truth that God is bigger.

Remembering what God has done helps us keep perspective. Look at what He's done in the Bible and in the lives of Christians around the world. Think back on how He's moved in your life, the lives of friends, in your church.

For every big thing God does, how many small ones might we overlook? A parking spot when it's needed most, a lost item found, a phone call at just the right time?

To "know and rely on" His love (1 John 4:16, NIV), we need to notice and remember the evidence.

O Lord my God, Your power and goodness are beyond human understanding, and truly I could never list all that You have done. Teach me to remember, and open my eyes to see what You're still doing. No matter what the day brings, help me to be secure in trusting You.

Rest for Our Souls

Then Jesus said, "Come to me, all of you who are
weary and carry heavy burdens, and I will give you
rest. Take my yoke upon you. Let me teach you,
because I am humble and gentle at heart, and you will
find rest for your souls.
Matthew 11:28-29, NLT

This much-loved and often-quoted passage brings comfort and hope. Most times we focus on words like "rest, teach, humble, gentle," and again, "rest." We skip over the "yoke" part.

It's often said that the yoke is for two oxen, and that a new, untrained animal would be paired with an experienced one to learn how to pull the plow. Jesus, the thought goes, is the experienced teacher, and we, learning to work alongside Him, are the novices.

That makes good sense, but let's look at the yoke for a minute. Jesus says it's His. He may or not mean He's wearing it, since He did indeed come to serve by showing us how to live for God. It's His because the Teacher, Shepherd, Suffering Servant is also the Master.

On our own, we get frazzled, weary, and definitely overburdened. The soul-rest Jesus offers isn't about collapsing under a shade tree for a nap, though. It's about dropping the loads we were never designed to carry, and taking up the load He has for us.

There's still work involved, but now we're working under the direction of a Master who loves us, a God whose compassion sent Him to die to rescue us. He knows our weakness, and His Spirit gives us strength.

Sovereign Lord God, You are my rightful ruler and King. Forgive me for the times I try to live under my own leadership, and for the stresses and messes I get into. Help me to surrender to Your authority, and open my spirit to Your Spirit's direction and strength. Thank You that the path of serving You is a path of fulfillment and soul-rest.

Embracing Weakness

Each time he [the Lord] said, "My grace is all you
need. My power works best in weakness." So now I am
glad to boast about my weaknesses, so that the power
of Christ can work through me.
2 Corinthians 12:9, NLT

Wouldn't the Apostle Paul have been more effective for the Lord without his limiting "thorn"? He might have been more successful in the short term, reaching more people, covering more territory, but might people have been distracted from Christ by the brilliance of the messenger? Or would pride have ruined him?

God gave Paul what He knew was necessary, even though it hurt. His goodness helped Paul wrestle through it to understand its purpose. By the time he wrote today's verse, Paul saw its value. He had pleaded three times for release. Did God tell him to stop asking, or was that when he received perspective?

What do you see as a limitation? A liability or weakness that holds you back? "If it wasn't for _____, I'd be so much more useful to God." God crafted each of us the way we are, and He has plans for us. Even if we've taken a detour and feel that our "thorn" is self-inflicted, God can use us as — and where — we are.

Just as Paul learned to embrace the things that kept him weak, knowing they kept him dependent on God's power, we can do the same, as God helps us to do so. It won't be easy, but even here His grace is enough. Instead of "doing things for God," we'll be positioned for God to work through us. After all, it's not about stroking our pride. It's about showing the world who He is.

Holy, powerful, and sovereign God, You have chosen to work through the weak, to show what only You can do. Sometimes this hurts, but please help me entrust myself to You. In my weakness and in my apparent strength, protect me from the snare of pride and from self-reliance. Help me find my sufficiency and my value in You, surrendered to Your purposes and living for Your glory.

Fear and Worship

The disciples were absolutely terrified. "Who is this
man?" they asked each other. "Even the wind and
waves obey him!"
Mark 4:41, NLT

The disciples had been afraid of drowning in the storm, but now they were terrified by the power Jesus displayed. Following Jesus, they'd seen Him heal people, but somehow this authority over the elements was even more awe-inspiring to them.

When they reached the shore, Jesus freed a demon-possessed man and sent the demons into a herd of pigs, which then dashed into the lake and drowned. The townspeople also responded with fear, but of a different kind. They pleaded with Jesus to leave them.

Peter had once begged Jesus to leave him, because he knew his sinful nature and feared to be in the presence of one so great. Instead, Jesus called him as a disciple. Here, the people asked Him to go and He went.

It's not about the "please leave," it's about the heart-reason behind it.

Peter and the other disciples were afraid with a holy fear of God. They worshipped, but knew their unworthiness. These town-folk were afraid of a power that shook things up and threatened their way of life. They didn't recognize it as from God, and they just wanted it gone.

God who speaks to sickness, storms, and sinners, please open my eyes to recognize Your holy power. Plant in me a holy fear of You, an awe and wonder that leads me to worship You. Let me never fear You in the way that would make me hide from You. Instead, draw me ever nearer like a moth to Your flame. Thank You for Your grace that saves us and takes away our fear of judgment, and that welcomes us into Your presence.

Love Obeys God

I reflect at night on who you are, O LORD;
therefore, I obey your instructions.
Psalm 119:55, NLT

We can't read Psalm 119 without sensing the devotion the psalmist has for God's instructions. It's not a dry list of rules that he loves, but the precepts and teaching of how God says he — and we — should live.

These regulations are so important because they teach us the way of true, abundant life. They keep us from straying away from God, or allowing sin or self to distance us from Him.

The Pharisees claimed to love God's laws too, and the negative examples of their behaviour toward Jesus and the common people may taint our view of this beautiful psalm.

The difference is, they were following their own understanding of the laws, while missing the heart of God. They saw the rules as the goal, not as the way to live with Him.

Today's verse gives us the key: it's knowing God's character and His ways, responding to His love and mercy, that motivates us to obey Him.

The more we discover of who He is and of how much we need Him, the more we'll value the instructions and principles by which He calls us to live.

Whole-hearted obedience is a love response. Not an attempt to earn points or avoid punishment.

Holy and loving God, in wisdom You have set boundaries for me, and in great mercy You have sent Your Son to ransom me from the power of sin and death. You are faithful to forgive when I ask, and to teach me Your ways. The instructions You give are for my good and for Your glory. You alone are worthy of worship and adoration. Please draw me to know You better, and teach me to rely on Your Spirit's power at work in me.

Reconciliation, not Rejection

Now repent of your sins and turn to God, so that your
sins may be wiped away.
Acts 3:19, NLT

Peter's not being judgmental here, not waving a big stick or speaking condemnation. If we could hear his tone, we'd hear urgency. Longing.

In the Temple, he's speaking to a crowd about Jesus. He has just put it to them plainly: Jesus is the Messiah from God, whom they and their leaders have rejected and killed.

He's also declared that they didn't know the full story, and their choices were part of God working out His plan (Acts 3:17-18).

Now that he has laid out the truth, he's calling for a response. He's inviting them into forgiveness. Into the Kingdom, where they belong.

This is Peter, who denied his Lord three times. He can't even claim ignorance for that. Only fear. But Peter knows from personal experience about the forgiveness and grace of God, about the love that longs to restore and reinstate and re-purpose.

We know that love, too, so as we encounter people who don't know Jesus, if the Spirit leads us to address some form of sin that's holding them back, let's remember that the goal is reconciliation, not rejection.

Addressing sin isn't about "look what you did." It's about "this is serious, but don't let it keep you from God's love." And instead of pointing fingers, we can speak from a place of experience: "God does forgive, because He's forgiven me."

Oh Holy God, You alone are Judge, and You are also Saviour. Give me compassion for those still trapped in sin, and speak through me to offer reconciliation. This is a hard topic, and many will take offence at the truth, but help me to speak it in love and to entrust the results to You.

Residual Strongholds

When Simon saw that the Spirit was given when the
apostles laid their hands on people, he offered them
money to buy this power.
Acts 8:18, NLT

Simon had been a magician and a man of great influence before Philip showed up and began teaching about Jesus and doing miracles. Along with many others, "Simon himself believed and was baptized" (Acts 8:13, NLT).

Old ways of life die hard, and his request here shows that he still doesn't understand the power of God.

Peter's stern response points out that Simon's motives aren't right, either. He's not wanting to be able to do this for God's glory. Peter sees evil thoughts, bitter jealousy, and captivity to sin (Acts 9:22, 23).

Simon had been using evil power before his conversion. Naturally there would be residual strongholds to tear down.

Whatever our backgrounds, the world around us and our own selfish sin-nature have formed mindsets, attitudes, habits we likely don't even notice, that keep us from all God has for us.

But God is committed to completing His work in us. When He brings one of these hidden issues to light, it's never to condemn us or to somehow revoke our salvation. It's to call us to repentance and into cooperation with Him in changing us to be more like His Son.

Merciful, gracious God, thank You for Your gift of salvation. You give me spiritual rebirth, and You grow me in maturity as Your child. Give me sensitivity to Your work in my heart, and help me work with You in clearing out the garbage so Your good can replace it.

BONUS DEVOTIONAL

Praise the Lord

Praise the Lord.
How good it is to sing praises to our God,
how pleasant and fitting to praise him!
... Extol the LORD, Jerusalem;
praise your God, Zion.
Psalm 147:1, 12 NIV

Our God is worthy of praise. Something within us needs to praise Him — was *made* to praise Him.

We need to praise Him privately, adoring Him and growing our trust and confidence in Him, and we also need to praise Him publicly.

Christians praising God together encourage one another's faith by sharing their stories. These stories also show His reality to those who don't yet believe, and may draw them nearer to His Kingdom.

Lord, I need to praise You more, to build my trust and confidence in You by thinking and talking about what You do. Help me see Your hand at work around me, and help me share it with others. I'm not the only silent one. Please wake Your body and loosen our tongues to declare Your glory.

Author's Note

Thank you for taking this journey through the Scriptures with me, and I pray the Lord has used this time to bless you.

You might also appreciate my 31-day devotional for the month of December, *Tenacity at Christmas.*

If you've found this book helpful, please share it with your friends, and consider leaving a review at Goodreads.com and/or at your favourite online store.

I'm predominantly a fiction writer, but these devotionals have been a labour of love on my blog, *Tenacity*, for many years. If you enjoy Christian fiction, I invite you to check out my novels, listed on the next page.

Special thanks to my sharp-eyed early readers, Ruth Ann Adams, Janice Dick, Russell Sketchley, and Beverlee Wamboldt. Any mistakes are my own, likely introduced while correcting other issues they found for me.

Blessings,
Janet

PS: I hope the contrast between American spelling in the Scripture quotes and Canadian in the devotional text wasn't too jarring. Bible publishers don't make Canadian versions, for some reason, and I feel strongly about not giving up my native spelling.

~~~

Author Janet Sketchley crafts clean, faith-filled mysteries and suspense with characters who feel like friends. She's also the author of two books of daily devotionals for Christian women, and the creator of a journal to track your next 100 reads. Janet writes in Atlantic Canada, where many of her books are set.

You can find Janet online at janetsketchley.ca, and you're invited to subscribe to her newsletter at janetsketchley.ca/subscribe or follow her on BookBub.

ALSO BY JANET SKETCHLEY

The Green Dory Inn Mystery Series:
(available in ebook and print)

Unknown Enemy
Hidden Secrets
Bitter Truth
Deadly Burden

The Redemption's Edge Christian Suspense Series:
(available in ebook and print)

Heaven's Prey
Secrets and Lies
Without Proof

Daily Devotions:

A Year of Tenacity
365 Daily Devotions to Warm Your Spirit and Encourage Your Heart

Tenacity at Christmas
31 Daily Devotions for December

Readers' Journals (print only):

Reads to Remember: A book-lover's journal to track your next 100 reads

www.ingramcontent.com/pod-product-compliance
Lightning Source LLC
Chambersburg PA
CBHW032146080426
42735CB00008B/604